# Love, SEX, DEATH & THE MEANING OF LIFE

## By *Foster Hirsch*

Elizabeth Taylor

George Kelly

Edward G. Robinson

The Hollywood Epic

Joseph Losey

A Portrait of the Artist: The Plays of
Tennessee Williams

Laurence Olivier On Screen

Who's Afraid of Edward Albee?

The Dark Side of the Screen: Film *Noir*

Love, Sex, Death & the Meaning of Life:
The Films of Woody Allen

Eugene O'Neill: Life, Work, and Criticism

A Method to Their Madness: The History of
the Actors Studio

Harold Prince and the American Musical Theatre

Acting Hollywood Style

The Boys from Syracuse: The Shuberts'
Theatrical Empire

Detours and Lost Highways: A Map of Neo-*Noir*

Kurt Weill On Stage: From Berlin to Broadway

# Love, SEX, DEATH & THE MEANING OF LIFE

---

## *The Films of Woody Allen*

---

## Foster Hirsch

**DA CAPO PRESS**

Cataloging-in-Publication data for this book is available from
the Library of Congress.

First Da Capo Press edition 2001
Reprinted by arrangement with the author.
ISBN 0–306–81017–4

Published by Da Capo Press
A Member of the Perseus Books Group
http://www.dacapopress.com

Da Capo Press books are available at special discounts for bulk
purchases in the U.S. by corporations, institutions, and other
organizations. For more information, please contact the Special
Markets Department at the Perseus Books Group, 11
Cambridge Center, Cambridge, MA 02142, or call (617) 252-
5298.

1 2 3 4 5 6 7 8 9—05 04 03 02 01

# Acknowledgments

Irene Cohen; Lillian Friedman; Joanne Dolinar; Barbara Bauer; Nancy Steffen; Michael Kerbel; Ted Sennett; the staff of the Motion Picture Section of the Library of Congress; the staff of the Library of Performing Arts, the New York Public Library at Lincoln Center; the Museum of Broadcasting; Dee Burton; Robert F. Moss; Mel Zerman and Roxanna Font at Limelight Editions; Ruth Nathan; Andrea Schulz and Jane Snyder at Da Capo Press; Howard Mandelbaum, Derek Davidson, and Robert Milite at Photofest. Photos courtesy of Photofest.

# Contents

# Introduction to the 2001 Edition

**W**HAT, again?" a friend asked when I mentioned that I would be updating my book on Woody Allen for a second time. "Why do you want to write about that pathetic creep?" another friend wailed. A third person, exasperated, made an unprintable comment. All three were women. "Women can't forgive him, guys can," a male friend generalized, trying to put the matter into gendered perspective. Clearly, writing about Woody Allen is to be plunged into a kind of ideological quicksand: If I am still interested in the films, does that mean I sanction or am somehow complicit with the sensational circumstances of Allen's 1992 "divorce" from Mia Farrow? Apparently, my choice of subject reveals as much about me as Allen's topics have always exposed about him. And indeed, critics, like creative artists, are always in one sense writing about themselves. Readers are therefore invited to read between and beneath the lines of my work in the same way, especially in the new chapter dealing with the work of the nineties, the work saturated by the scandal, as I attempt to deconstruct the film maker.

For any number of reasons, I cannot claim "Woody Allen, *c'est moi*," but on two counts—being Jewish and living in and loving Manhattan—I have a strong sense of identification with him. And it is on these common grounds that I continue to admire his wit and wisdom. As I have (tactlessly) argued before, to get the full flavor of Woody Allen, to appreciate just how good he is, despite lapses, you really have to be a Jewish New Yorker. I am aware, however, that using these similarities as a critical route into the work might place me in the same category as the Mira Sorvino character in *Mighty Aphrodite*, the would-be actress who chooses to work on a scene from *The Philadelphia Story* (for which she is wildly inappropriate) because, after all, she is from Philadelphia.

The original edition of this book, published in 1981, consisted of the first seven chapters. The two additional chapters, covering the work of the last two decades, were written at ten-year intervals. Although I hope readers will feel that they are being led by a single critical sensibility, a project separated by such lengthy sabbaticals is bound to have a less-than-perfect join. And shouldn't it? "Change is death," Woody Allen's character, Gabe Roth, a professor of writing, tells his wife Judy (Mia Farrow) in *Husbands and Wives*. "That's a bullshit line you tell your students," Judy answers. I trust that my work on Allen over the past twenty years is closer to Judy's point of view than to Gabe's, that between the original text and each new edition, there are fresh differences in tone, use of language, and methods of organization. There are also, perhaps inevitably, repetitions and contradictions that I have chosen not to edit out. I have updated but not revised my study of Allen's films.

I wanted to return to Woody Allen for another, more personal reason. When it first appeared, this book got me into trouble on the job. "Don't include this in your promotion dossier," my chair warned. "Just let the committee see the work that has footnotes." Disregarding the advice, I included *Love, Sex, Death & the Meaning of Life* in my packet, and was turned down. A classics professor who chaired the committee was offended because I discussed comedy without having cited the genre's roots in Horace and Juvenal. "And Professor Hirsch does not write with the objectivity and detachment of a scholar," he added in a final disapproving flourish. So here, once again, without "objectivity or detachment," is a critic from Manhattan writing on Manhattan's poet laureate.

*Foster Hirsch*

# 1

# The Last Laugh

FIRST, the face. It's a God-given clown's mask. You look at it, and your immediate reaction is to laugh. The thin lips, the slanted, jagged nose, the sallow complexion dotted with freckles and framed by the stringy red hair, and the eyes, nature's crowning touch to this great cartoon of a mug—staring, glassy, stunned, bemused, knowing, and accented by the arching eyebrows and the black, willfully old-fashioned horn-rimmed glasses: Woody Allen's face is his fortune. And he never lets us forget it as he shrewdly exploits the kinds of looks that mold destinies.

Woody's owlish, lopsided face creates an immediate comic aura. It taps our goodwill, our sympathy, our latent cruelty, and our laughter before he even says a word. A face to launch a thousand quips, it positively invites wit and insult, it requires a response, a rejoinder or comment, providing a field day for bullies and punsters. "He looks like a harassed sparrow"; "he's a goggle-eyed halfpint of neuroses"; "he's a waif in schnook's clothing"; "he's the

urban boychick as social misfit"; "he's a little mole, the
Samson of the sad sacks"; "he's thinner than a starved
elf": so wrote journalists after they had first seen Woody,
evidently delighted by and talking back to the comedian's
appearance.

"I'm really a typical Jewish intellectual with all that
that implies," Woody has said. Indeed, in looks, he is the
essence of a neurotic, brainy New York Jew, resembling
thousands of others who roam the city's streets. New
Yorkers especially can spot Woody's skewed assemblage
of features as those of a specific, familiar type. And yet
Woody is triumphantly himself, and no other: the one and
only, a great comic archetype.

With its reminders of Buster Keaton's stoniness,
Harry Langdon's childlikeness, Harold Lloyd's earnest
boyishness, and Chaplin's sweetness, Allen's face, like
those of the great silent comics, issues a fixed statement to
the world. Like Keaton, he uses the stubborn, immobile
set of his features as a defense against misfortune. "Keep
away!" the deadpan mask announces. But Allen is less
successful than Keaton in draining his face of observable
feeling—there's a constant struggle going on, among his
irregular features, between the attemptedly cool, blank,
impregnable pose and the perceivable underlying panic.
Allen's classic *punim* is a battleground between the
unruffled, keep-away image he wants to project and the
frightened boy a-twitch with neuroses who keeps breaking
through. Far from being the unchanging mask it aspires to
be, Allen's face is a mirror of conflicts, a reluctantly
revealing barometer of the turbulent, shifting weather
within. What a challenging face it is to read, this open
book that insists on its secrets and its privacy. Welcoming
and resisting, inviting us in and pushing us out, Allen
engages in an ongoing tug-of-war with his audience. The

fear of people that shadows the friendliness and genuine
kindliness that Allen projects is recorded in the thin,
spinsterish lips and the wary eyes that both beckon and
repel our identification and complicity.
"Here I am!" the Woody mask announces. "Enjoy me,
laugh at me, see yourself in me, but keep your distance."
Some faces point upward, with high sharp planes;
Allen's droops. "I have, by nature, an enormously sad
face," Allen has said. "I'm not a smiler. If you didn't
know I was a comic, I would be a study in sadness."
Except (there is always, with Allen, a "but," an "on
the other hand") the sadness comes with a kind of
sparkle—those baggy, forlorn eyes that register anxiety
are also bemused and quizzical, and the downturned
mouth seems poised to make a joke, ready to meet panic
and depression with a wisecrack. Allen's face "tells" us
that wit issues from sadness, that humor is a response to
being morose, that making jokes about yourself comes
from feeling bad about yourself. The essential, infectious
comedy of Woody's face flirts then with pathos and
tragedy: the comic's fabled anxiety is stamped on his
features, but the resilience and wisdom, the triumph of his
humor, are written there as well. Like circus clowns,
Woody advertises his unhappiness.

Both funny and sad, both open and closed, Woody's
face is a maze of conflicting signals. A barrier against the
world, this great stone mask yet contains a reservoir of
feeling. And on this resistant tablet are engraved the
anxieties and insecurities of modern urban man.

But the greatest paradox of all is that ugly Woody,
with his crooked face that only a Jewish mother could
love, is deeply sexual, and decidedly cute. When they
voted him one of the ten sexiest men in the country, the
editors of *Playgirl* magazine claimed that he has done

more than anyone else to sexualize neuroticism. At times, of course, from certain angles, and with unflattering lighting that broadcasts his sea of freckles, the man is almost breathtakingly homely—you gasp at the unkindness of nature. But there are other times, when he shoots a puckish glance, or when he looks like a pert little boy lost, or when he plays at being a suave lover, that his sad sack face is actually handsome.

Allen's voice and body are notably well matched to his face. Thin, with an ever-present trace of a whine, Woody's voice is deeply Brooklynese. It is not an impressive voice, not, heaven knows, a trained actor's instrument. It has little color or variety, and no melody. But how droll and knowing it is. Unlike many comics, Woody does not have an aggressive delivery. Rather than being on the attack, his tone is dry, quiet, a little bookish; he sounds like a nice Jewish boy gasping for air.

Like his face, his cracked, imperfect voice is double-edged, for tartness underlies the gentle delivery, conviction and assurance lurk beneath the general air of puzzlement. For him, as for all talking clowns, his voice is a weapon. Though soft and seemingly unassertive, it can be devastating as it levels those who have done him wrong, like ex-wives, parents, teachers, and rabbis. In affable tones, chuckling all the while, Woody lays waste his enemies. Comics like Groucho Marx and W. C. Fields sound nasty, with their staccato rhythm and stabbing tone. They are obvious con artists who defy you to call their bluff. Woody harbors hostilities no less pointed than theirs, but his method of attack is slyer. In a voice coated with apologies, he seizes command of his environment; his disarming manner rumbles with aggressive undertones, and his mockery is just as often directed at others as at himself.

Woody is a stammerer whose sentences unfurl in fits and starts. Performing verbal arabesques with his battery of pauses, repetitions, and backtrackings, his hesitations and circumlocutions, he often sounds as if he doesn't know where he's going. This show of being inarticulate is really a clever disguise intended to throw us off the track: that he seems to be floundering, groping for the next word or the next thought, only reinforces the impact of the punch line toward which he has been slyly doodling. Like all good stand-up comics, he is a master of timing. His face and his voice belie his true strength, then, his actual control of himself and of circumstances. Woody the comic loser, unlucky in love, pummeled from one erotic misadventure to another, is at heart the sneakiest of con artists.

As a performer,   Allen has never claimed his body the way he has taken charge of his face and voice. His is a talking comedy, a comedy of patter and word play. His humor depends on verbal surprises and often springs from the clash between what he says and how he looks. Though Woody often makes fun of his scrawny physique, exploiting his smallness in his jokes of sexual bravado, he is in fact rather well put together. In school, he was an athlete, and a good one, and his trim, compact body is reasonably muscled: only his size has comic possibilities, not his proportions. If he had a different face to go with his body, no one would laugh. But   Allen doesn't use his body the way a skilled physical comedian would. In some curious way, he is detached from it. His movements are often stiff, recalling the strangulated quality of his speech; but where the awkward verbal patterns are deliberate comic elements, his body often remains separated from the comedy. There are physical gags throughout his films, to be sure, but these aren't the parts that people remember in delighted recollection. And they're often handled perfunctorily, as if he feels obligated to pay homage to an earlier tradition, a body comedy, but one which remains at a distance from the real source of his own comic impulses.

Unlike Chaplin or Keaton or Lloyd, Allen is not an acrobat, a dancer or mime. Lacking the physical freedom and grace of the silent clowns, he can't lay claim to their visual eloquence. His energy is expressed verbally, not physically; he talks his comedy rather than acting it out. A curiously inert appendage, his body often seems to run interference with his verbal—and facial—wit. Chaplin and Keaton are wedded to their bodies, and their comic routines as a result usually depend on seeing them in long shot, as whole beings; Allen's by comparison is a comedy of close-ups: we don't often need to see all of him to savor the humor.

"The World's No. 1 Worst-Dressed Man" (according to Earl Wilson), Woody dresses with a plainness that strives for invisibility. The baggy sports jacket, the open, nondescript sports shirt, the loose pants: Woody chooses clothes to hide in. Offstage, he wears a large floppy hat which (naively) he hopes will conceal who he is. He dresses then like an unassuming boy-next-door who feels guilty about his body and as a result often walks around as if he doesn't have one. And yet, of course, much of Allen's comedy is about his body, as it craves sex and as its seeming frailty provokes bullies.

"His one regret in life is that he is not someone else": so ends the "about the author" identification for *Getting Even*, Allen's first collection of comic essays. As it happens, though, Woody Allen *is* someone else. He is a

comic fabrication, as much a result of conscious artisan-
ship as Chaplin's tramp.

Drawing on his own experiences, anxieties, beliefs,
and aspirations, and exploiting his own natural endow-
ments and shortcomings, Brooklyn-born Allen Stewart
Konigsberg created someone else, or to use one of
Woody's favorite words, someone "other": "Woody
Allen," a comic mask that hides as much as it reveals
about his real-life counterpart. Allen Konigsberg is
playing a shrewd burlesque version of himself, a made-up
character that exaggerates and distorts reality. "Woody
Allen" is therefore a pose, a masquerade, so cleverly
engineered that he—or someone else with the same
name—has become America's undisputed clown prince.

Who is "Woody Allen" and what is he really like? If
Allen Konigsberg has anything to say about it, we will
never know. "Woody Allen is the son of a Latvian
prince," reads his bio in the playbill for *Play It Again,
Sam,* which is as much as to tell us to mind our own
business. "He studied acting at The Neighborhood School
for Bit Players. Theatergoers may remember him as Lady
Windermere's Fan in the play of the same name. He also
played Willy Loman in *Mr. Roberts,* to the consternation
of many around him. . . . He is currently appearing on
TV in *Mother Wiltwick's Porridge,* a psychological musical spoofing the evils of diabetes. He is the father of two
children, although he denies it."

Sly Woody teases us into thinking that he is simply
playing himself, and that there is no separation between
who he really is and the role that he performs on stage. "I
expected Allen to be offscreen exactly as he is on screen,"
wrote Vivian Gornick (in 1976), expressing a common
erroneous assumption. "He is in fact—and of course—at

an unimaginable distance from that vision. He is . . . much better-looking offscreen than on screen, in analyzed command of a personality that is direct, extremely sweet, and altogether kindly."

While Gornick was relieved that Woody off was different from Woody on, Janet Maslin (in 1973) was disappointed—by Allen's soberness, by the general absence of the wit and sparkle that she expected from America's premier comedian. "I was surprised to find him so solemn, so adult, so composed, so controlled, so unneurotic," Maslin writes. " 'Oh, I'm very neurotic,' he said, 'but I'm so defensive and clever I don't give anything away.' " When Maslin accused him of being uncommunicative, he asked, with an imploring, quizzical tremor, "I've answered all your questions, haven't I?" as he confronted, along with his interviewer, the gap that separates Allen Konigsberg from Woody Allen.

Fans who go to see him play the clarinet with a New Orleans–style jazz band on Monday nights at Michael's Pub in Manhattan are similarly let down. That looks like Woody Allen on stage, but there's no sparkle or friendliness, and absolutely no contact with the audience. In over twenty years of jazz performing, Allen has never uttered one word to the audience. Intent on the music and clearly uninterested in playing "Woody Allen," he looks somber and humorless. His movements brisk and almost mechanical, his face relieved of expression, he masterfully repels any contact with the crowd.

As his fame has escalated, so has his skill in hiding behind it. Michael's Pub is a small room, with no more than a few feet separating the band from the front tables, but Allen erects an invisible barricade behind which he remains in inviolate seclusion. His one concession is to sign autographs. Beyond that, his aloof, uninviting manner, which shrewdly plays on the awe and fear of the fans, ensures his privacy.

Offstage, then, the real Woody Allen is sober, low-key, intensely private, polite but distant. "I am real sour," he has said. "I don't know why I am sour. I just am." Except for his small circle of terrifically loyal friends, he wants, like another screen legend, to be left alone. Reserved, possessed of an innate dignity and sense of self despite his famous neuroses, he is anything but a buffoon. He lives and writes in an elegant penthouse overlooking Fifth Avenue and Central Park. With its landscaped terrace and its sweeping views of his beloved Manhattan, Allen's   apartment is the home of a man who has his life in order. "The environment in the home is highly controlled yet appears unstudied, a reflection of its owner," writes Olga San Giuliano, in an aritcle in the November–December 1972 issue of *Architectural Digest* that celebrates the comedian's taste in interior design.

Traveling with chauffeurs, limousines, a protective entourage, escorting Mrs. Lyndon B. Johnson to a dance program, throwing a monumental New Year's Eve party — Allen  is embraced by all the tokens and perquisites of phenomenal success. On screen, he may act like a schlemiel, but in real life he is firmly in command—a man of destiny. "I don't consider myself a nebbish," Woody told interviewers early in his career, "but everyone else does."   Allen, and not everyone else, was of course right.

In his first movies, *What's New, Pussycat?* and *Casino Royale,* he was a mere hired hand, a position he detested. "I never bothered to see *Casino Royale,*" he said. "I knew it would be a horrible film. The set was a chaotic madhouse. I knew then that the only way to make a film is to control it completely." When he began to make films of his own, he demanded—and received—total artistic independence. Writing, starring in, and directing his own projects, he has almost never had to take orders. He works only for Jack Rollins and Charles Joffe, his producers and managers, who shield him, humor him, and seemingly obey him and worship him. The Rollins-Joffe unit casts a net between Woody and the studio brass, between Woody and the press, and between Woody and the public. No one except a few carefully chosen intimates can penetrate the palace guard, with the result that Allen has always been given the privilege of working in isolated splendor, answerable to no one but himself. Protected by his loyal producers from the byzantine bureaucracy of film making, Allen has claimed a degree of power over his projects that is virtually unprecedented.

Thus Woody Allen, professional schlemiel, has a passion for order and control. As Pauline Kael pointed out, "Free and messy people don't play the clarinet."

His ordering nature and his insistence on control over his environment are revealed in the way he casts his movies. He uses people he knows and trusts and can mold: friends, actors who are not stars, wives, girl friends, ex-wives, and ex-girl friends. Look at the supporting casts of his films and it appears that he's afraid of competition. It isn't that his films aren't well acted; it's that Allen is careful to reserve the spotlight for himself, using other actors mostly as foils and reflectors. He hired "name" actors only for cameo roles in *Everything You Always Wanted To Know About Sex* and *Annie Hall,* and for *Interiors,* in which he does not appear and which was, at any rate, an attempt to try something different.

Employing actors he's sure of and feels secure with, he has built up what amounts to his own repertory company. He and Diane Keaton, his preeminent co-star, play beautifully together, with a pleasurable sense of give-and-take that draws on their close offscreen relationship. A natural and charming actress, Keaton is a good team worker who knows her place. Woody made her a star, and she has continued to be dependent on him, professionally, adapting herself to his preconceived plans for her.

Imagine Woody starring opposite someone like Barbra Streisand, who is as egocentric and controlling as he is. The clash of these two strong personalities would be resounding. On screen, Woody can be generous only to those whom he has at a disadvantage—to Mariel Hemingway in *Manhattan,* for example, because, though wise, she is only a kid in a grown-ups' world; and again and again, to blustering, inarticulate, needy Diane Keaton.

A Woody Allen set is a closed shop. No press, no interviews. Before and during production, Woody's movies are shrouded in secrecy, as if they were vital government documents. The hush-hush atmosphere is underlined by the fact that the films often don't have a title and are referred to by the studios and by the snooping, irritated, barred press as the Woody Allen (Fall, Winter, etcetera) Project. Protected from the prying outside world by his band of fiercely devoted retainers—his producers, his staff, his handpicked co-stars—Woody works in a cocoon.

Woody is also the boss on how his movies are to be advertised. He favors simple lettering—black on white, or white on black—and no pictures. The way Woody announces his work, you would think he is an American Ingmar Bergman turning out austere chamber dramas. His genteel advertising campaigns, and his spare title designs, suggest remoteness and a longing, however muted, for WASP respectability.

Orderly and intensely disciplined, "crazy" Woody doesn't drink, or smoke, or experiment with drugs. He works. Compulsively. Tirelessly. And he doesn't seem to enjoy himself—to *be* himself or to *lose* himself—except when he is working. Woody says he suffers from anhedonia: the inability to have a good time, the state of being chronically depressed or melancholy. He takes no pleasure in his achievements because he is always dissatisfied. "I am surprised at the amount of people that go and see my movies," he has said. "All my films have been personal failures. This is not to say that an audience, not knowing the grandiose plans I had in mind when I undertook the project, can't go and find something to enjoy. I can't get to the point where they're a kick for me."

On the night of his Hollywood triumph, in 1978, when he won two Academy Awards, for the screenplay and direction of *Annie Hall,* and when the film and Diane Keaton also won statuettes, Woody was three thousand miles away, going through his usual Monday evening paces playing with his band at Michael's Pub. Disdaining applause or acknowledgment, he acted as if this night were like any other. And next morning, refusing interviews and seemingly unable to luxuriate in his success, he was at work on his next project.

Forever disappointed, he continues trying for the perfect comic premise. You can see the man's restlessness in his work, in the way one movie answers and attempts to correct an earlier one: his canon is really one lengthy ongoing text riddled with cross-references, echoes, internal responses. His attitude toward work is almost like a parody of the neurotic Jewish overachiever who's been made to feel guilty and unworthy and who tries to make up for the sin of being alive by always having to prove that he does in fact exist, that he is after all worth something. Like most zealots, Allen stands self-accused, and self-convicted. Nothing he's done, he feels, is big enough, or important enough. And even on its own terms, nothing has been just so. A quest of this magnitude leads, of course, straight to the analyst's couch, where Allen has been, sometimes as often as five sessions a week, for the past quarter of a century. "You go to analysis to relieve a pressing sense of fear and anxiety and guilt—which I still have," he said in 1965. In 1978, he said he couldn't conceive of "living without analysis, but it hasn't helped me as much as I'd hoped. . . . I feel the same anxieties everywhere I go. It's a general sense of suspicion, paranoia, and fear. . . . I think I'm being followed. I don't know who is after me."

Allen has made a fortune advertising his nuttiness to the world. Telling jokes on himself is therapeutic, a way of releasing his anxieties and obsessions. Like therapy, creating comedy alleviates the pressures of being neurotic. His nightclub routines, his comic essays, his plays, and his movies are a catalogue of his own personal maladjustments, grievances, humiliations, fantasies of sex and power; his work is his life story adjusted to and transformed by the demands of the comic muse.

And it's as much as we're ever going to know about the man behind the mask. These are the salient facts about Allen Stewart Konigsberg, as revealed through the comedy of Woody Allen. He was born (in 1935) in the Flatbush section of Brooklyn, to a family whose values, he tells us, are God and carpeting, and who wanted their only son to go into some safe profession like pharmacy. At age seven, seated with his mother in the ornate Loew's Kings on Flatbush Avenue watching *The Road to Morocco* starring Bob Hope and Bing Crosby, he realized he wanted to dedicate his life to comedy. He flunked out of New York University and City College in record time and has never quite recovered from his brush with the academic mind. He had a rocky first marriage (in one of their typical arguments, his wife Harlene Rosen tried to prove to him that he didn't exist). His second marriage, to Louise Lasser, also ended in divorce, and since then he has free-lanced, most publicly with Diane Keaton.

His major interests are women and philosophy. He's mad about women. He chases them, objectifies them, fears and worships them, wants desperately to succeed with them, has wild fantasies about them. Philosophy intrigues, amuses, and antagonizes him. Obsessed with the idea of death, he lives his life feeling judged by the eye of eternity.

His looks, his family, his intellect, his sexuality, his neuroses—Woody has fashioned his comedy from these autobiographical fragments. As a public personality, he seems refreshingly open and self-revealing, positively confessional, while offstage he is studiously remote, in hiding from his audience. He seems, the public Woody Allen, so warm and accessible, while his private life is exactly that, conducted behind the closed doors of a palatial, fortresslike penthouse.

A sad comic, a seeming nut who has an iron discipline and self-control, a self-deprecator and a braggart, a meek nice guy and a sharp-tongued wiseacre, friendly and Olympian, Woody Allen is a quicksilver compound of contradictions and paradoxes, a fascinating enigma who is determined that we see him only through the inevitably transfiguring lens of his comedy. "Life is difficult for Woody," Louise Lasser told Jack Kroll in a *Newsweek* cover story in 1978. "He's one of the unfortunate tormented people. His mind is working all the time."

In the same article, Diane Keaton proclaimed Allen's "great capacity for joy." "Like many great comics," Kroll concluded, "Woody is a saintly schizophrenic, a man at odds with himself." Allen's comic mask may well be his ultimate defense against being found out. But will the real Allen ever want to escape from the fabricated Woody only to discover that his audience won't accept him as anybody else? Is he at some point going to feel imprisoned by his created persona? Nonetheless, even if one day he may want to break free of him, "Woody Allen" has been astonishingly good to Allen Konigsberg. Playing the sexual loser who is really a winner, the clever schlemiel, the crackpot who is saner than anyone else, the goony-looking Jewish outsider who speaks in a voice of Jewish comic complaint while peering at the dominant goy culture with a mixture of longing and sarcasm, Allen has created a character who expresses the frustrations of millions. Basing his comedy on his own hang-ups, Woody is a shrewd showman with his ear to cultural currents. His persona's loneliness, uncertainties, dissatisfactions, his problems in finding a lasting relationship, his sexual traumas, his trips to the analyst, his breakups and reunions, his gripes, his mockery of bureaucrats and academics, of people out of touch with life and rendered mechanical by their rigidity and fanaticism, his catalogue of irritations, in short, with the assorted madnesses of the American moment—all these connect him to a large popular audience. His privately focused comedy, of anxiety and outsiderdom, is actually a celebration of community rather than a retreat from the group. His work lines up the world into two camps—outsiders versus insiders, symbolically Jew versus gentile—with those on Woody's team people of feeling and common sense amazed by the rigid establishment types who are really far wackier than Woody could ever hope to be.

Laughter both at Woody and at Woody's targets is, then, an invitation to join a club, to shed something of our own feelings of being an outsider, and to give up some of our own guilt and fear and alienation in a threatening, illogical world. The lesson, and the appeal, of Woody's comedy, is that he is *just like us*—only more crazy, more insecure, more unhandsome, more unlikely.

"Woody Allen, *c'est moi*," wrote Richard Schickel in a *New York Times Magazine* article in 1973. "All of us, no matter what our sizes or shapes, harbor a Woody Allen inside ourselves just waiting to jump forth." "The tension between his insecurity and his wit makes us empathize with him; we, too, are scared to show how smart we are," suggests Pauline Kael. "For me and my friends," writes Vivian Gornick, "he was—in a word—*us* . . . his humor was everything we had come out of, everything we were at that moment . . . growing up smart and anxious, huddled on the edge of a world we could see but not touch . . . transforming our worst fears about ourselves into an act of recognition through the radiant anxiety of his wit . . . we drank in his anxiety like adrenalin."

Dee Burton, a New York psychiatrist, discovered that so many people have unconscious fixations on Woody that she decided to write a book, *I Dream of Woody*, which "presents and interprets the Woody Allen dreams of over one hundred individuals living in New York and Los Angeles." In these dreams, Woody emerges as a larger-than-life hero, a savior. Dispensing benedictions, the dream Woody is noble, sensitive, kind, romantic. He helps the dreamer to better himself. He bestows calm and even a sense of completion and fulfillment. Some of the male dreamers want to *be* Woody Allen; many of the women want to be *with* him.

Woody is truly a hero for the age of anxiety, whose extraordinary success is based on how well he communicates his battery of neurotic symptoms. Claiming to speak only for himself, he has become the neurotic's Everyman, the comic repository of contemporary malaise. Playing the loser, the yo-yo, the shnook, Woody skillfully manipulates and even to some extent absolves our own worst fears about ourselves. Complaining about his love life, he has triggered the romantic fantasies of millions of men and women. "Is he . . . a forerunner of Western Woman's ideal Western Male," asks Joseph Gelmis, "antiheroic, cuddly, passive, sex-obsessed, bully-able?"

Allen's genuine folk-hero status—the degree to which he has penetrated popular consciousness—was certified when he became the subject, in 1977, of a syndicated comic strip, "Inside Woody Allen," a hit in over sixty foreign countries as well as throughout the United States. In 1978 Random House published selections from the strip (which is drawn by Stuart Hample), giving it an Allenesque title, *Non-Being and Somethingness,* and dividing the cartoons into six distinctly Woodyish subheadings: philosophy, psychiatry, relationships with women, family history and early childhood, artist/ celebrity, and forces of evil. ( Allen oversees the strip, but does not write most of the gags.) The cartoons are really a parody of Woody's shtick; the jokes depend on audience familiarity with Woody's phobias and gripes, his enemies list, and his complaint, by now, fabled as Portnoy's.

"Hey! Woody Allen! I want to thank you for giving me lots of laughs!" a groovy-looking girl says to Woody in the first panel of one of the jokes, in the artist/celebrity category. "You see my movies?" Cartoon Woody says, in the second, looking delighted and sheepish. "No," says the girl, moving out of the frame. "I have the window opposite your bedroom." Leaving behind one crestfallen comic. In Private Journal Entry No. 2,377 Woody writes: "There are only two things in life that are important. One is sex. And (as he sits staring at the wall) the other's not that important." Private Journal Entry No. 2,965: "Politics is the art of the possible," Woody jots down, "psychoanalysis, the art of the impossible." "Tell the lighting man to cut the overheads. They emphasize my nose," nervous Woody says, preparing the stage for a comedy performance. "The spotlights make my glasses gleam. Kill 'em. Good. But the wing lights make me look skinny." When the stage is pitch black, Woody announces, "Perfect. Now I feel I look my best."

"Laugh if you like," Woody told interviewers in 1964, "but I consider myself attractive, virile, literate, a scholar, an acid wit—all in all, a sort of intellectual Cary Grant." Beneath the self-mocking pose and the invitation to laughter, he wasn't fooling. Orderly, sober, controlled and controlling, rich and powerful, the real Woody Allen is no comic bumbler, and he's no likable schlemiel either. Difficult, stubborn, deeply private, he's the ruler of the roost. On film, he's constantly bedeviled by a comic fate; shoved and poked, badgered and beaten, he's the fall guy of the universe, kicked about by a fickle, sadistic destiny. But as himself he has been divinely lucky. *He* may wish he was born someone else; but who in his right mind wouldn't want to change places with him?

# 2

## The Comedian's Progress: The Sixties

W OODY was a hit right from the start. As gag writer, stand-up comic, essayist, television personality, playwright, actor, screenwriter, and director, he has enjoyed uninterrupted success. No doubt the critical and popular approval has encouraged him to move ahead, to shift from one medium to another, to exchange pen and paper for greasepaint, and to switch from appearing in front of a camera to directing the show from behind it. With the help of the steadfast Rollins-Joffe team, Woody has orchestrated his career with a cunning that immediately gives the lie to the loser image. Far from being victimized by his environment, frail-looking Woody has conquered the Hobbesian world of show business: David has subdued Goliath.

Whether he's doing stand-up comedy or writing a screenplay or a comic piece for *The New Yorker,* Woody aims for the wisecrack, the gag, the one-liner, the punch line that punctures our expectations. He's a verbal smart aleck working in a distinctly American tradition. Unlike

the comedians of an earlier generation, trained in vaudeville, Allen's alma mater is the nightclub. And the
patter, the impeccable timing, and the sly manipulation of
the audience that are the stock-in-trade of the stand-up
comic underlie all of his comedy.

The job of the stand-up comic is intimidating. Alone,
in the glare of a spotlight, with only a microphone for
company, he must entertain a roomful of strangers; by his
wit and the sparkle of his personality, he must coax
laughter from the dark. He is on his own, naked before an
audience demanding to be amused. For someone as
withdrawn as Woody, the prospect of confronting, and
then controlling, a roomful of drinkers must have been
terrifying. He used to become visibly ill before going
onstage. "He approached the microphone as though he
were afraid it would bite him," wrote Arthur Gelb, an
early Woody-spotter, in 1962.

Allen began to perform, with great reluctance
(Rollins and Joffe had to shove him, kicking and screaming, into the spotlight), after an apprenticeship as a gag
writer. A teen-ager from Flatbush with his eye on the
Great White Way, Allen began to send jokes to
columnists like Earl Wilson, who then placed the one-
liners, wisecracks, and puns into the mouths of reigning
celebrities. Allen's quotable quips proved so consistent-
ly bright that he soon got a job writing material for
television stars like Sid Caesar. Which meant that he was
no longer in business for himself but was part of a team of
writers who would have prolonged sessions in which they
would throw out ideas. Any premise, no matter how
farfetched, was tested for its comic potential. For an
irrepressible cutup, a comic wild man like Mel Brooks,
these brainstorming sessions were a pleasure. Brooks
carried on like a banshee, tossing in a welter of gags

seemingly dredged up from his unconscious. But for a loner and disciplinarian like Woody, being part of a comic think tank probably was uncomfortable. At temperamental odds with Brooks's antic disposition,    Allen chafed under the atmosphere of inspired spontaneity. And despite his shyness and his real fear of presenting himself before an audience, he knew that he could never be satisfied as an anonymous jokesmith working to make other people seem witty. Though daunting, the notion of delivering his own material in public, as himself or as a character audiences would assume was himself, was also tempting.

Allen made his club debut in June 1962 at the Duplex in New York. He caught on immediately with an urban, sophisticated crowd, and he was soon appearing in other smart rooms like the Blue Angel, the Bitter End, and the Hungry i in San Francisco.

A nightclub atmosphere seems to call for a lusty, sozzled kind of humor, rapped out in a staccato, upbeat style. Yet here was a quiet-spoken, decidedly bookish-looking young man, who really had little in common with the traditional stand-up comic except his litany of complaints and the fact that he was Jewish. Incorporating his nervousness into his act, Woody was no brash Borscht-belt heckler flinging assaults at his audience. In place of the aggressive vulgarity of a Milton Berle or Henny Youngman or Alan King he substituted a droll, quizzical wit. Looking chaste, he seemed out of place in a roomful of drinkers—a few blasts in the face from the audience and he looked as if he would topple over.

In a wispy, thickly accented voice, he talked about himself, concentrating mostly on familial, romantic, and academic misadventures. "I'll tell you about my private life," he often began his sets, "and then we'll have a question-and-answer session." What emerged from the anecdotes and sketches was a portrait of the artist as a good-natured schlemiel, a man who seemed to attract misfortune. The comic hero of Woody's routines suffered a traumatic childhood. He was breast-fed from falsies, and his parents bronzed his baby shoes with his feet still in them. His family was so poor (one of his father's jobs was as a caddie at a miniature golf course) that they took him to a store for damaged pets where the choice included a bent pussycat and a straight camel. The young Woody selected a dog that stuttered: "He barked 'b-b-b-bow-wow' and then blushed." (In another version, he came home with an ant called Spot.)

A funny-looking four eyes, he was bullied by neighborhood kids like Guy de Maupassant Rabinowitz and Sheldon Finkelstein. Sent to an interfaith camp, he was beaten up by children of all races. His one childhood triumph, at age five, was his acclaimed performance as Stanley Kowalski.

He had no better luck at school, flunking out of New York University for cheating—on one occasion, with the dean's wife; on another, on a metaphysics final, when he was caught looking into the soul of the boy next to him.

By a fluke, of the sort he is prone to, he spent nine weeks in the canine corps, where he was bullied by a large Mexican hairless.

Dating, like school and the army, produced another series of mishaps. Once, on a blind date, his girl was arrested for being an Israeli agent. Another time, he picked up a girl at a crap table (he's very sexy, shooting crap, he would tell us) and took her up to his room. They undressed, taking off one piece of clothing at a time, until he realized he was looking into a mirror. For weeks afterward, he removed pieces of glass from his leg. To prolong sex, he confided, he often thought of baseball plays; once he got so involved in the game he was unaware that the girl had been in the shower for ten minutes. When Peter O'Toole aced him out of a date with a hot-looking girl in boots, Woody asked her to bring along a sister. She did. Sister Maria Terese. They talked about the New Testament and how well adjusted He was for an only child.

With a track record like this, he of course married a lemon. "My first wife, Quasimodo, was not officially animal. She was officially reptile. She's one of the few White Muslims in New York." He should have known something was wrong right away, because his parents liked her. He and Quasimodo were married by a reformed rabbi. Very reformed. He was a Nazi. Cursed from the start, the short-lived marriage didn't have a happy moment. "She was very immature, my first wife. Once while I was taking a bath, she came in and sank my boats." Finally, they had to make a choice: two weeks in Bermuda or a divorce. They got the divorce, because a vacation is soon over, whereas "a divorce is something you always have." "I saw my ex-wife the other day. I almost didn't recognize her, because I'd never before seen her with her wrists closed."

Luckless Woody fared no better with objects than with people. A sun lamp rained on him. A talking elevator, who spoke more clearly than he did, passed an anti-Semitic remark. His tape recorder said, "I know, I know." He held a conference with his appliances, calling for reasonableness and respect.

The city ganged up on him too. He moved from a brownstone, where he was regularly beaten and robbed, to a swanky building on Park Avenue, where, wouldn't you know it, he was mugged by his doorman. Cornered one night in his lobby by a Neanderthal, he tried the old Navaho trick of screaming and pleading.

With all this *tsuris,* is it any wonder he was neurotic? But he took advantage of being nuts. "I'm captain of the latent paranoid softball team," he boasted. And he participated in a neurotic exchange program: when he was in Italy making a movie, he went to an Italian analyst, while an Italian in America went to his.

Woody played Falstaff as well as Harlequin, and occasional blasts of braggadocio intercepted the ongoing self-mockery. His wife interrupted their wedding night, he told us, in order to give him a standing ovation. And he has successfully played God in a play called *Gideon.* To get in the mood, he acted the part offstage as well, tipping big "because He would have"; when someone hit his fender, he issued a lordly pronouncement: "Be fruitful and multiply. But not in those words."

Whether deriding himself or boasting, Woody's cabaret humor was compulsively self-centered. Unlike a Lenny Bruce, he paid almost no attention to politics, to the state of society or the world. One of his few topical quips was the passing comment that he was at work on a nonfiction version of the Warren Report. Neither global nor reformist, this comedy was deliberately small-scale, personal, made up of everyday problems exaggerated and multiplied for comic effect. As in his movies, comic reality was invaded by surreal details as his characters said and did unexpected, far-out things. He told his mother he flunked out of college, and she took an overdose of Mah-Jongg tiles. He told his parents he was getting a divorce, and his mother, who had been knitting a chicken, got up from her chair, went over to the stove, and got in. Woody's skits were filled with absurdist inversions of reality: a rabbi with his eyes on show business who could name the Seven Dwarfs but not the Ten Commandments; a defrocked Mother Superior who ran a floating nunnery; a man who was half-Mexican, half-nonfat milk; a girl who became a streetwalker in Venice, and drowned; a disco populated with topless rabbis (they didn't wear yarmulkes); a Jewish American Princess who got her nose lifted by a golf club; a Village club called the Integration Bagel and Yoga where an Eskimo sang "Night and Day" for six months at a time.

Sometimes not only passing details but entire stories were delirious. For these explosions of nonsense, which regularly intersected the sketches about daily life—the world of marriage and the family—Woody changed his pace and the pitch of his voice, chanting in a falsetto that had a surprising singsong intonation, as if to signal us that he was sailing off into the comic wild blue yonder. The sheer, liberating silliness of these comic episodes—their bizarre combinations of reality and fantasy, their wacky, jolting juxtapositions—released gales of helpless laughter, as audiences gave in to the comic's utterly mad, unmoored imagination. In one such bit of Allenesque zaniness, his kidnappers were apprehended by police who, instead of using tear gas, captured their quarry by enacting the final scene from Camille. The culprits were sentenced to fifteen years, twelve of which they escaped by passing by the guards disguised as an enormous chain bracelet.

"I shot a moose," began Woody's most famous cabaret anecdote. "It was still alive. There is a law in New York State against driving with a live moose on your fender, on Tuesday, Thursday, or Saturday." He took the moose to a costume party, introducing it as the Solomons.

The moose mingled. Scored. At the party, dressed as a moose, were the Berkowitzes. Who won first prize in the costume contest. The moose, placing second, was furious. Woody took the moose back to the country. But it was the Berkowitzes. And there's a law in New York State against riding with Jews on your fender, on Tuesday, Thursday, and especially Saturday. Mr. Berkowitz got shot and stuffed, and was hung up at the New York Athletic Club. "The joke's on them, because the place is restricted."

The story is a model of Woody's orchestration, as a series of reversals and deflations, and a hallucinatory yoking of realism and absurdity, lead to a startling punch line, Woody all the while narrating in a bland, droll tone, as if he were reporting utterly commonplace events.

Telling jokes mostly at his own expense, Woody chuckled right along with his audience. Curling himself around the microphone and peering into the darkness, waiting for answering laughter, and speaking with an assortment of verbal tics, a medley of stammer and hesitation, he was clearly not a slick, big-time comic, ramming his jokes home in a raucous style, but a timorous gentleman with a bemused slant on reality, a man of logic and common sense buffeted on all sides by absurdity. Typically, Woody started a set slowly. He seemed almost to be stalling, marking time. He was feeling his way, checking out the room. He couldn't have been more modest as he stood before the darkened room, wondering aloud about what he was going to tell about himself. He skittered from one subject to another, a performer seemingly in search of a theme, and you wondered, in flashes of sympathetic panic, how this affable goon was ever going to be able to hold your attention for the next twelve or fifteen minutes. But your concern soon disappeared; the stumbling and hesitation, the apparent absence of direction, had been a shrewd act. Sliding from quips to anecdotes in an unstoppable flow of comic invention, the comedian steadily picked up his pace as the room rippled with eddies of laughter. "I'm basically a stud," he announced, a gleam in his voice; a woman shrieked in laughter that bordered on hysteria. The room erupted; the comic stood there, enjoying the acknowledgment and joining tentatively in the laughter. Silence. Pause. A renewed whoop from the woman at the back. "She wants me," Woody improvised. Another volcano of laughs. Woody surveyed the room in mastery.

Pretending not to be cool created a smoke screen behind which Allen worked the house. Seemingly casual and unstructured, his sets were scrupulously timed, with cunning pauses at exactly the same point night after night. Allen's quiet delivery was another kind of masquerade, for beneath the genial veneer, the sheer politeness of his manner, lay a series of vitriolic detonations—against his parents, his first wife, the women who had done him wrong, the academic sensibility that he has never stopped making fun of. Like most comics, Allen uses his wit as a lethal weapon, a way of getting even; and his attacks are the more potent for being filtered through his charming, boyish façade. Woody's bite is worse than his bark.

The intimate rooms of places like the Blue Angel and the Hungry i enabled Allen to develop the low-key, conversational style that became his trademark. He wasn't, after all, playing the Palace, and so he didn't have to pitch his delivery to the balcony. He could play it small, close to the chest, in an understated way that was exactly right for his wry humor. Working in these small clubs proved good training for acting in movies. Unlike stage performers, who must subdue their style when facing movie cameras, Allen didn't have to make any major adjustments in the volume or scale of his delivery: he could talk to his audience through the camera as quietly, and with as much of an illusion of intimacy, as he had in the clubs.

Indeed, echoes of his stand-up comedy technique reverberate throughout his films. Like the comic monologist, Woody often narrates his jokes rather than acting them out, and his screenplays are pitted with tricks of the trade like one-liners, running gags, jokes with quick payoffs, vignettes, and blackout sketches—with, in short, a verbal humor that does not require any visual support. Early work of his, like *Take the Money and Run*, doesn't have to been seen to be laughed at; most of the gags would be just as funny heard in a club or on record. "For a while, Virgil Starkwell earns a meagre living selling meagres," the narrator tells us. One of Virgil's colleagues is arrested for assault, armed robbery, and dancing with a mailman. Another is booked for marrying a horse; a third for dancing naked in front of his in-laws. In the later *Love and Death* many of the best lines are again narrated, though there is a greater interplay between verbal and visual gags. "My father owned a piece of land," says Boris, the hero, as we see his father holding up a small piece of earth. "My brothers played games, but I had a completely different concept of myself," he announces, as we see the young Boris hanging on a cross.

In *Annie Hall* Woody plays a stand-up comic, claiming on film the same kind of control over and intimacy with his audience that he enjoyed during his cabaret period. He begins with two comic anecdotes, looking directly into the camera and thereby establishing himself as the master of ceremonies, the man who will summon the characters and arrange the order and duration of the scenes. *Manhattan* opens with a more disguised version of the controlling comic monologue as Woody recites (in voice-over) different versions of the first paragraph of his character's work in progress, a novel about the city. The opening alerts us to the fact that what we are about to see is Woody Allen's Manhattan, and no other.

One of the amused listeners at the Blue Angel one night in 1964 was a Hollywood producer named Charles K. Feldman who (the comic later told his audiences) thought Wood· was sexy. "Feldman's a short guy with glasses and red hair," Woody said. Feldman liked Allen's humor, which he called "way out swinger's comedy," and hired him to write the screenplay of *What's New, Pussycat?*, which was to become one of the most financially successful of all movie comedies.

It was his experience writing and acting in this film, and then co-starring in Feldman's *Casino Royale (1967)*, that made Allen realize that he could only work in movies if he had complete control. Both films were big-budget, all-star extravaganzas superintended by the gruff, cigar-chomping Feldman. On both projects, Allen took the money and ran; but in both you can see his efforts to protect the persona that he had created in his cabaret act.

It's even possible to see why Feldman thought Allen would be the appropriate writer for *What's New, Pussycat?*, which is about a subject dear to Woody's comic heart: sex. Like the characters in his comic monologues, those in the film are bewitched, obsessed, and paralyzed by sex. Oversexed or frigid, hot or cold, they are all full-fledged sexual neurotics who love to talk about their problems and who go to therapy to air their fantasies and tame their libidos.

The film's fantasy premise is: What would life be like

for a handsome editor of a high-fashion magazine, a man
women find irresistible? And the conflict is: What happens when this man with a fantastic scoring record and a
roving eye is about to get married?

Allen's script compares this charmed character to
two sexual outsiders, a quite mad psychiatrist who drools
over women, is married to a Hun, and would love to
change places with his suave patient, and a New York
schlemiel (played by guess who) adrift in Paris who pays
for working as a dresser in a striptease joint. If the men in
this low sex fantasy are pegged as sexual winners or losers,
the women are categorized as the marrying kind; they're
the ones who want to relate, to settle down, to have
enduring monogamous relationships. Aside from this,
they're regarded by the men as objects to be admired,
lusted after, run from; they're dewy-eyed, lascivious,
frigid, divine, castrating, unknowable. You can tell that
the mind who created these female archetypes is both
enchanted by and fearful of women. Like all of his work,
then, even this novice, interfered-with script reveals
aspects of the comic's psyche.

*What's New, Pussycat?* is an adolescent fantasy
—Woody being sleazy—blown up to stupendous proportions. The preoccupation with sexual image, the stereotyped sexual labeling of both male and female characters,
the obvious envy with which the slick stud hero is
regarded—these are to be staples of Allen's later work.
When he had the freedom to make the kind of comedy he
wanted, he turned out movies that are thematically
similar to *Pussycat.* Allen's comedies are better, but
they're not fundamentally different.

Woody plays most of his scenes with Romy Schneider
and Peter Sellers. He's appealing opposite Schneider,
who's no comedienne, but curiously stiff with Sellers,

who, in a fright wig and Little Lord Fauntleroy outfit, camps it up as the dotty psychiatrist. Sellers's strutting, vaudevillian performance pushes Woody off the screen, whereas he skillfully plays off Schneider's comic ineptitude.

"Left to my own instincts," Woody later said, "I could have made the film twice as funny and half as successful." Critically dismissed as a prolonged dirty joke, and attacked for its juvenile humor, its slapdash structure (part old-fashioned French farce, part *nouvelle vague* sex comedy), its mélange of acting styles, its strained attempts to be hip and daring, the film, unaccountably, was a smash hit. "No one in his right mind could have written this excuse for a script," Bosley Crowther sniffed in *The New York Times*. "The idea is neurotic and unwholesome . . . as though the characters were all disturbed children engaged in violent, sex-tinged water-play."

But this bloated, mostly witless farce lifted Woody from a cult favorite in the supper-club circuit to national and even international prominence. The film was released in the summer of 1965, and from that moment on, Woody was a celebrity. Between 1965 and 1969, when *Take the Money and Run*, the first film which he wrote, starred in, and directed, was released, he appeared in *Casino Royale;* he concocted *What's Up, Tiger Lily?*; he continued to appear in nightclubs; he wrote two Broadway plays (*Don't Drink the Water,* in 1966, and *Play It Again, Sam,* in 1968); he began to contribute comic pieces to *The New Yorker;* he turned up on television as a frequent guest on talk shows, as a pinch-hit host for Johnny Carson, as a guest on a Gene Kelly special, and as the host of two comedy specials of his own. And he appeared with statuesque Monique Van Vooren in a series of ads for Smirnoff vodka which contrast her elegance and sexual poise with Woody's disheveled little-boy puzzlement. Allen straddles a wooden rocking horse, in a pose that highlights the kind of leering adolescent sexuality that has always been a part of his image. What the ads signal, perhaps more than anything else, is that Allen, a self-proclaimed outsider, has begun to make an impact on the Establishment: here he is, after all, a funny-looking fellow, featured in a slick ad with a svelte woman of the world. This unholy alliance between Madison Avenue know-how and Allen's idiosyncratic individuality has been a continuing factor in his career.

So by the time his own first full-fledged film was released in 1969, Allen was a master of all the media, his record of achievement in so short a time testifying to his compulsive work habits.

Except for his *New Yorker* pieces, which were brilliant from the start, this early period does not represent Allen at his best. He's warming up. But it's possible to trace his development and growth within each medium, spotting the way one project suggests another, the way one premise generates further ideas. *What's Up, Tiger Lily?*, like *What's New, Pussycat?*, asks a silly question with sexual overtones. Both *Tiger Lily* and *Casino Royale* send up the James Bond thrillers by treating their ingredients—a suave sexy hero; luscious available women; gadgets; exotic locations; complicated plots, with an epidemic of double- and triple-crosses—as the stuff of farce and burlesque.

In *Pussycat,* Allen played essentially the same character he had created for his comic monologues; in *Casino Royale,* in what is to become a standard ploy in his own films, he is cast extravagantly against type—as studlike super-spy Jimmy Bond. Thrown into alien territory, he is stranded in a delirious Bondian fantasy, cavorting with Daliah Lavi (another international beauty with no sense of humor) in abstract white backgrounds and dressed nattily in a vanilla summer suit. Most of his scenes are solo turns, with Allen delivering monologues to the camera and, in point of fact, ad-libbing many of his lines. Holding court over the big white room where Jimmy Bond is held captive, and cut off from the rest of the film, Allen in effect does a cabaret set, playing variations on his cowardly, lecherous image in a verbal cartoon that mixes low-key self-mockery with surreal flights of fancy.

Writing themselves into a corner, the team of harried screenwriters end the movie by blowing it up. They bring on the entire cast, as well as cowboys and Indians and Keystone Kops, for a climactic free-for-all. Off to the side, watching the mayhem with owlish bemusement, is Woody Bond, himself soon to become as familiar a movie icon as the genre types that tumble onto the set. As always, Allen has the last laugh, since he explodes the whole show when an atom-bomb time capsule he has swallowed goes off.

In *What's Up, Tiger Lily?* Allen supplies a new sound track to a made-in-Japan James Bond rip-off. Adding a chorus of New York voices, and a dotty plot, he treats the action-packed, oversexed spy thriller as a kind of found object, a piece of putty to be molded and twisted out of shape. "Making it up as we went along," Woody and a group of friends, including Louise Lasser, improvise a series of verbal riffs around a basic storyline, a hunt for the recipe for the world's best egg salad, an egg salad so good it could make you *plotz*. Like much of Allen's comedy, the dialogue is laced with wild incongruities. "Bring the dynamite," one of the spies calls out, in a climactic moment, "and a coffee and toasted muffin."

Wing Fat, the bad guy, threatens chief spy Phil Moskowitz: "You and each of your partners will be put in an
empty drum which will be filled with fat Lithuanian
midgets." "I'm dying, call my rabbi," cries another evil
Oriental, Shepherd Wong. The heroine wants to know
who planned her escape from prison: "I had an idea it was
the Mormon Tabernacle Choir, but they had no motive."
"Would you like a drink?" Phil Moskowitz asks her. "Or
another bath? Or to see my display of Italian off-color
hand gestures? Or naked pictures of Hugh Hefner?" In
the middle of a fight, one man hurls insults: "Take that,
Saracen dog! And this, Spanish fly!"

"Two Wongs don't make a white," a spy says to Wing
Fat, apropos of nothing. "For that joke you should only
drop dead," Wing Fat says in thick Brooklynese. "We've
found the recipe," Phil Moskowitz announces, "and now
I'd like to take the opportunity of doing my movie
imitations . . . Mr. Jimmy Cagney." "Will the owner of
rickshaw 406 remove it at once. Your coolie has a hernia,"
an announcer interrupts the action, from out of the blue.

The story, such as it is, is drenched with non-sequi-
turs, puns, deflations, asides, and wisecracks, in a display
of silliness that is sometimes inspired and always good-
natured.

"They came to me to supervise this definitive spy
story," Woody announces in a mock interview that opens
the film, "because if you know me you know that death is
my bread, danger my butter. . . . No, death is my butter,
danger my bread." Giving up his attempt to be pithy, he
throws in the towel: "Death and danger are my various
breads and butters." To round off the "authorship"
framework, Woody—the New Hollywood's answer to
he-men directors like Howard Hawks and Raoul Walsh—
appears again at the end, now reclining on a couch eating

an apple as a beautiful Oriental strips for him. "I promised her I'd put her in the film, somewhere," Woody the blasé stud tells us. As the girl disrobes, subtitles explain that the characters and events depicted in the film were fictitious—"and if you've been reading this, go to a psychiatrist or a good eye doctor."

*Tiger Lily* gave Allen the chance to try out his verbal humor in a movie without actually having to make a movie. Rearranging existing footage and experimenting with clashes between word and image, he clearly has a good time with this spoof. Outlandish and fitfully hilarious, Allen's verbal collage shows comic nerve and a winning, playful spirit.

The film had a limited but genuine success which led to Allen signing for his first *real* movie, *Take the Money and Run.* But before his premiere as a full-fledged film writer-actor-director, he scored success after success on stage and television and in *The New Yorker.* While he was working on *Casino Royale,* he wrote the first draft of a play that was to become *Don't Drink the Water,* which opened on Broadway in the fall of 1966.

Allen set out with the express purpose of concocting a commercial Broadway comedy. Typical of his work, the humor springs from a wild disparity between the characters and the setting, as a deeply bourgeois caterer from Newark and his equally conventional wife and daughter are besieged in the American Embassy of a politically unstable Eastern European country. "I was writing my family," Allen said at the time. "I wanted to show what they would do if they were caught in a country behind the Iron Curtain. . . . I put in what they would say, the normal hostile things people say to one another and still love each other." Complaining, bickering, and spraying the air with a steady flow of wisecracks, the Hollanders

are less reflections of Woody's family—of *any* real-life
family—than they are stock theatrical and ethnic types;
they are collections of gags rather than freshly observed
comic characters. Perhaps because he didn't write a part
for himself in it, *Don't Drink the Water* is Allen's most
impersonal and mechanical comedy; sizing them up for
the number of laughs he can squeeze out of them and
their predicament, he looks at his characters with utter
detachment.

Papa Hollander is a domestic bully and full-time
worrier. Prone to aggravation and griping, he is a stock
Jewish paterfamilias. Mother Hollander is a whiner, a
gabber, a compulsive housecleaner (you can be sure that
her livingroom furniture is covered with plastic), and, as
her husband cracks, "a professional Mah-Jongg hustler
who carries her own tiles." Daughter Hollander is a simp
who has a dull boyfriend back home, a lawyer with
asthma, and who falls for Axel Magee, the closest counterpart in the play to the patented Woody persona, the
well-meaning, blissfully incompetent son of the absent
American ambassador. "I'm a big Jackson Pollack man,"
he says. "His drippings best express my mental state."

Though Allen usually has trouble telling a full-
length story, *Don't Drink the Water* is surprisingly well-
made, in the slick Broadway comic tradition which it
imitates. Its three short acts proceed smoothly from
exposition to complication to denouement as Allen sets
up a comic dilemma—how will this batty family ever
manage to escape?—then rings a number of increasingly
frantic variations on it, and then at last provides a frankly
contrived finale. Within its modest framework, the play is
an efficient formulaic entertainment, a Neil Simon–like
machine-made comedy guaranteed, with the right cast, to
produce if not a laff-a-minute at least a chuckle or titter

once every three or four minutes, a guffaw or two, and a full belly laugh once or twice in each act. Woody said his model was George S. Kaufman, and indeed the comedy is filled with Kaufmanite wisecracks and rigorously timed repartee. The Hollanders are always ready with a smart answer, meeting every emergency with a sense of humor that is pure Borscht belt. "We're Americans! I swear!" Walter Hollander blurts out, as he makes his first entrance. "Willy Mays! Hershey Bars! Kate Smith! I pledge allegiance to the flag!" "And to the republic for which it stands!" Marion Hollander, Walter's straight man, chimes in. "All of a sudden I'm a spy," Walter sighs, and then, as always, completes his thought with a gag: "I'll go on 'What's My Line?'—they'll never guess." "I'm a caterer," he tries to explain to his Communist accusers. "Creative catering—our specialty. We were the first to make bridegrooms out of potato salad." "I will not sleep on a cot," he growls. "I am a dignified man with a hernia."

"I hope I can write as well as Kaufman did and be as entertaining to people who buy tickets," Woody said at the time. "I want to write show shows . . . a show that is really a show. No messages, no undercurrents, no blasphemies, no dirty language, no people in ashcans." At this level, of artificial, gag-ridden domestic comedy, his play succeeds. It is an agreeable enough fabrication which would have disappeared if it didn't have Woody's name attached to it; but because he "signed" it, it has become a little theater staple, and it was made into a movie, a perfectly awful one that Woody had nothing to do with. Instead of emphasizing the vein of Jewish humor that runs through the material, giving it what flavor it has, the film was oddly de-ethnicized, the Hollanders cast not with echt-Jewish performers like Sam Levene and Molly Picon, but with quintessential goyim, Jackie Gleason and Estelle Parsons, who deflate the lilting Yiddish rhythms and intonations of much of the dialogue.

But more damaging than this, more harmful even than the sledgehammer delivery and the flatfooted direction of Howard Morris (an alumnus of "Your Show of Shows," who should have known better), more crippling than the inappropriately gaudy setting, is the unmistakable stagebound aura of the material. *Don't Drink the Water* can come alive only in the proscenium frame for which it had been conscientiously tailored. On screen it is airless and cramped, and its theatrical stitching shows. The more frantic the performance becomes—the more the director tries to disguise the stage origins of the material by adding exterior locations and moving the action among a number of settings—the more it proclaims its stubborn, unalterably theatrical essence.

Although he had a popular if not critical success with the play, Woody of course was dissatisfied. He must have been aware that it didn't have the stamp of his own particular wit (almost anyone with an ear for a gag, and sense of comic timing, could have assembled it), and so, the following year, 1967, he wrote another play, one this time that cut closer to the bone, a comedy not about his family but one that is all about Woody, in which his interest in sex is mixed with his love of movies. In *Play It Again, Sam,* Allan Felix (the character Woody created for himself) is a recently divorced film critic with sexual problems whose idol and romantic adviser is Humphrey Bogart. Allan has trouble with women because, among other things, he's afraid to be himself. He is always playing a part—and he is a bad actor. On the make, he fails; when he relaxes, as he does with the wife of his best friend, he's appealing and sexy, he's all the things he wants to be and thinks he isn't. For film critic Allan, life imitates art, as he plays out the Bogey role in *Casablanca*, giving up his newly won woman because he sees that she is really in love with her husband.

A comedy with some real affection for its characters, *Play It Again, Sam* is a fresher, more authentic piece than *Don't Drink the Water*. It is filled with the wise sense of people that is always a part of Allen's best work. A forerunner of *Annie Hall* and *Manhattan*, it is a wry comedy of manners, or as Allen suggested in a piece in *The New York Times* the Sunday before the play opened, "a droll spoof aimed more at the heart than the head, a puckish satire of contemporary mores based on the conquering of chapped lips by two British scientists in 1860."

Although the dialogue is less mechanical than in the earlier play, the characters still speak in a style of self-conscious witticism that is the continuing legacy of Allen's nightclub origins. The play is splattered with one-liners, with clever turns of phrase, plays on words, smart-aleck asides, and many of the best jokes occur in monologues, with Woody alone on stage mumbling to himself and in effect doing stand-up comedy. "If only I knew where my damn analyst was vacationing. Where do they go every August? They leave the city. Every summer New York is full of people who are crazy till Labor Day. . . . I'm a normal decent-looking guy . . . maybe slightly below normal. . . . I hate to be there on a blind date when the girl sets eyes on me. What if she looks at me and laughs or screams. . . . Has a girl ever once reacted by laughing or screaming? Once. That little coed from Brooklyn College came to the door, saw me, and passed out . . . but she was weak from dieting."

Audiences loved Woody and the play, but the critics

weren't as pleased. "It's a series of night club monologues pretending to be a play," complained Martin Gottfried. "It is stringed with jokes, some hilarious, but it is not a play," agreed Walter Kerr. "He's still out front, *telling* us about this funny thing that is rumored to have happened to him. It's all hearsay, never the happening itself." And *Variety* griped that "if Woody Allen were only a better performer, he'd have a whopping big hit . . . he is all too obviously a TV and cabaret comic who's never learned to vary his emphasis, pace, or voice."

Containing none of the anarchic or surreal humor that appears in most of his early work, *Play It Again, Sam* presents Woody in a purely charming, romantic guise. By design it is a comedy with broad appeal. The film version (with  Allen starring, Herbert Ross directing) was released after *Take the Money and Run* and *Bananas* had established Woody as a comic wild man, and  Allen hoped this accessible, conformist comedy would earn him a wider audience than his two earlier movies. "I think it has a chance of being one of those Radio City pictures. Clean and funny. It would be a big help to me in getting customers for my own movies." Genial and modest, *Play It Again, Sam* is "soft" comedy—comedy with no real teeth in it.

Since he starred on Broadway in *Sam,*  Allen has written and published, though not yet produced, three one-acts, on subjects that are recurrent, indeed obsessive references in his comedy: God and death. These three short pieces have the imaginative daring and flair that the safe, Broadway-bound full-length plays carefully avoided. In these manic, and wildly flawed, dramas,  Allen's comedy goes cosmic. *God, Death,* and *Death Knocks* are Kafkaesque vaudeville in which  Allen attacks big themes like faith versus skepticism, art versus life, the relationship of the artist to his art, free will versus determinism, and God's silence. Casting aside all the restraint of his Broadway comedies, Woody cuts up in an extravagant, bravura style, lacing his shows with highbrow references and surreal juxtapositions.

Set in ancient Greece, *God* is a play within a play. A dramatist, Hepatitis, talking to his leading actor, Diabetes, bemoans the fact that his new piece lacks a satisfactory ending. Arriving flushed from a meeting with Socrates, who proved he didn't exist, Trichinosis says he has just the thing for the ending, a new machine, with God in it, which descends from the rafters to resolve the action. "Wait'll you see this thing in action." Trichinosis toots his own horn. "It flies Zeus in. I'm going to make a fortune with this invention. Sophocles put a deposit on one. Euripides wants two." Hepatitis is skeptical. "If God saves everything, man is not responsible for his actions. . . . I'm a free man. I don't need God flying in to save my play." But he agrees to try out the machine.

An announcer in modern dress introduces the show: "Good evening and welcome to the Athenian Drama Festival. We got a great show for you tonight. A new play by Hepatitis of Rhodes, entitled *The Slave*. Starring Diabetes as the slave, with Bursitis as Zeus, Blanche du Bois, and Doris Levine from Great Neck. The show is brought to you by Gregory Londos' Lamb Restaurant, just opposite the Parthenon. . . . Remember, Homer liked it . . . and he was blind." In the play within the play, the Fates (Bob and Wendy Fate, *naarish* American tourists) dispatch the slave to take an urgent message to the king. The message: Yes. The question: Is there a God? For the King, it's bad news, for he reasons that "if there is a god, then man is not responsible and I will surely be judged for my sins." As Diabetes is about to be killed for being the bearer of gloomy tidings, enters Zeus, strangled by the wire of his machine. So God is dead. And Diabetes and Hepatitis end up where they began, pondering an ending. "The trick is to start at the ending when you write a play," Diabetes says. "Get a good, strong ending, then write backwards." "I've tried that," Hepatitis answers. "I got a play with no beginning." "That's absurd," Diabetes says. "Absurd? What's absurd?" Hepatitis questions, as, quickly, there is a blackout.

*God* reads like *Hellzapoppin,* the Marx Brothers, and the Living Theater crossed with Ingmar Bergman, Samuel Beckett, and Kafka. It is continually under invasion—by characters from different time periods, by wild anachronisms in language and sensibility, by at one point, Woody himself, who makes an offstage voice-over cameo appearance, and by the audience, who talk back to the play, questioning motive and intent, demanding their money back, or, like Doris Levine from Great Neck, becoming involved in the action. A play of literary echoes, it evokes, along its bumpy path, the shades of ancient tragedy as well as avant-garde absurdism. Anarchic, free-form, vaudevillian, it flirts with philosophical "issues": "So often people think they grasp reality when what they're really responding to is 'fakeositude' "; "the basic philosophical question is: If a tree falls in the forest and no one is around to hear it—how do we know it makes a noise?"

Beneath the gabble, the play does address, in its own wacky way, a *genuine* issue: the godlike powers of the artist, who creates and controls the reality of his own fictional worlds. It's a concept that Woody uses several times (most prominently in *Annie Hall*) and that reveals his own powerful drives for control over his work and environment. Woody is the true God of the play, the offstage voice whose vision these characters are enacting. At one point, Blanche du Bois runs across the stage, trying to escape the dreadful fate to which her creator, Tennessee Williams, has assigned her; and the relation of this rebellious fictive character to *her* author echoes not only the embattled relations in *God* between the characters in the play within the play and the playwright Hepatitis, between Hepatitis and Woody Allen, his creator, and between the play and the restive audience, but on a grander scale, the conflict between man and *his* Creator, who may not even exist. It's a heady scheme, with manifold layers, as in a play by Pirandello, as life and theater, reality and illusion, engage in resounding counterpoint.

Having behaved himself with *Don't Drink the Water* and *Play It Again, Sam,*   Allen clearly felt free to cut loose with a play that is both structurally and thematically experimental. Winging it, he throws out cultural debris culled from his omnivorous reading. Citing major influences on his work, from vaudeville to the Marx Brothers and Beckett to the kind of philosophical inquiry he is drawn to, as much as anything, for the sheer sound of its inflated windy rhetoric, *God* reads like an introduction to the writer's unconscious, Woody Allen raving in public. Self-indulgent and reckless, the play nonetheless has terrific energy, and real intellectual daring, containing Allen's   deepest treatment yet of the abstract, ultimate questions that have cast their enchantment over him. *God* is an enticing preview of the more polished, philosophically witty and probing play that   Allen may one day write, on a sabbatical from films.

Less cosmic, *Death* and *Death Knocks* also enact weighty themes in a knockabout burlesque style. *Death Knocks* is a parody of Bergman's *The Seventh Seal* in which the two antagonists are stand-up comics with Yiddish intonations, two *hondelers* doing some quick bargaining. Woody's Death (unlike Bergman's majestic figure) is a schmo, entering the play breathless after climbing up a drainpipe and panting for a glass of water or a Fresca. His victim is Nat Ackerman, a dress manufacturer from Queens who has just merged with Modiste Originals and who has a wife at the Eden Roc ("fifty dollars a day because she wants to be near her sister"). Nat challenges Death to gin rummy, and wins. Death owes him twenty-eight dollars and trips going down the stairs; he will give Nat one more day, waiting it out over coffee at Bickford's. Nat calls his friend Moe Lefkowitz: "Listen, I don't know if somebody's playing a joke, or what, but Death was just here. . . . In person. . . . But, Moe, he's such a schlepp!"

In *Death* another of Allen's bourgeois yokels (Kleinman=little man) is invaded, in the middle of the night, by the knock of destiny. He's inducted into a vigilante group intent on capturing an elusive killer and then abandoned, in the nighttime middle of nowhere, to do battle with the Enemy. With his luck he ends up accused of being the killer and is about to be executed when the real killer is spotted and the bloodthirsty mob stalks off in pursuit. *Death* is second-rate theater of the absurd—Ionesco splashed with Kafka; the dialogue is uncharacteristically long-winded, the paranoia theme naked and obsessive. In this one Woody is having his nightmares in public.

These three genuinely experimental plays present Allen  in his most abrasive posture, as the puckish, brilliant, childlike clown taking on death and God with his wit and deflating irony. All three pieces don't really fill out their ambitious themes as  Allen whistles in the dark, flailing audaciously in the face of concepts that mean something to him but that, to varying degrees, have escaped his comic net. The knottiness and lack of control, however, the very absence of perfect pitch of these would-be metaphysical comedies, are a measure of their ambition. These short, imperfect plays are something of a self-reprimand for the bland containment of his two Broadway hits.

As a playwright, then, Allen wears two hats. He can be the disciplined comic artificer of *Don't Drink the Water* and *Play It Again, Sam* as well as the misbehaving perpetrator of *God* and *Death.* His stage comedy can be tame as well as subversive, traditional as well as modernist, though so far Allen hasn't scored a major achievement at either end of the spectrum.

Allen's last play to date, *The Floating Light Bulb,* which opened in 1981 at the Vivian Beaumont Theater in Lincoln Center is minor Broadway realism a domestic comedy-drama which recalls *The Glass Menagerie.*

Allen began publishing comic pieces, mostly in *The New Yorker,* in 1966. Like his one-act plays, his essays provide a release for the extremist outer edge of his humor, though unlike the plays, the essays present his zany, wild man streak in firm control. They're the jewels in his clown-prince crown.

He probably has continued to write them to free his imagination and to work out ideas which might later be used in his movies. In them he can experiment with a manic, high-pitched comedy that he can't use anyplace else. He can make esoteric references, without fear of losing his audience; he can invent supernatural comic events—tables can fly, grown men can cry through their ears—without wondering about how he is going to film or stage them. His language can be richer, more thickly textured, because it can be savored at the reader's leisure: it is language to be read rather than heard. And yet Woody's origins as a gag writer and nightclub comic are everywhere apparent in the essays: in the stabbing one-liners, the punch lines, the cracks that deflate and surprise, and in the way gags pile on gags as the comedy escalates to the heights of inspired lunacy. But the essays, unlike some of the club sketches, go deeper than their best laugh lines. At their peak, they are trenchant satires of language and culture.

Released from the need to make his writing "popular," freed from the restrictive demands of the Broadway marketplace, the rules of nightclub comedy, and the high finance of moviemaking, Allen can let go in these verbal cartoons with a brand of humor that is epically surreal and antic. You can picture him with a wicked gleam in his eye as he concocts these comic zingers.

As a performer, Allen has never been a good mimic; he simply plays the one persona he has created for himself. But as a comic essayist, he has chameleonlike skills. Because "Woody Allen" rarely appears in the essays, they do not constitute further chapters in the comic misadventures of a character familiar from his club work and his movies; rather they are parodies, mostly, in which Allen undermines the work of other writers. In *Getting Even,* his first collections of essays, published in 1971, Woody takes on Dostoevsky, hard-boiled private-eye fiction, Hemingway, the Dracula legend, political memoirs, scholarly exegesis, Hasidic tales, epistolary communication, and course descriptions in college bulletins.

In his mock Hemingway piece, "A Twenties Memoir," he catches the simple sentence structure and the clipped, taut rhythm of the master himself.

I first came to Chicago in the twenties, and that was to see a fight. Ernest Hemingway was with me and we both stayed at Jack Dempsey's training camp. Hemingway had just finished two short stories about prize fighting, and while Gertrude Stein and I both thought they were decent, we agreed they still needed much work. I kidded Hemingway about his forthcoming novel and we laughed a lot and had fun and then we put on some boxing gloves and he broke my nose.

In "Mr. Big," he tackles the he-man style of the boys in the back room (as Edmund Wilson called them) like Dashiell Hammett, Raymond Chandler, and James M. Cain:

I was sitting in my office, cleaning the debris out of my thirty-eight and wondering where my next case was coming from. I like being a private eye, and even though once in a while I've had my gums massaged with an automobile jack, the sweet smell of greenbacks makes it all worth it. Not to mention the dames, which are a minor preoccupation of mine that I rank just ahead of breathing. That's why, when the door to my office swung open and a long-haired blonde named Heather Butkiss came striding in and told me she was a nudie model and needed my help, my salivary glands shifted into third. She wore a short skirt and a tight sweater and her figure described a set of parabolas that could cause cardiac arrest in a yak.

In "The Metterling Lists" he writes like a humorless academic, turning molehills of information about the august Metterling's laundry into mountains of metaphysical and symbolic hogwash:

Metterling's dislike of starch is typical of the period, and when this particular bundle came back too stiff Metterling became moody and depressed. His landlady, Frau Weiser, reported to friends that "Herr Metterling keeps to his room for

days, weeping over the fact that they have starched his shorts."
Of course, Breuer has already pointed out the relation between
stiff underwear and Metterling's constant feeling that he was
being whispered about by men with jowls. (*Metterling:
Paranoid-Depressive Psychosis and the Early Lists,* Zeiss
Press). This theme of a failure to follow instructions appears in
Metterling's only play, *Asthma,* when Needleman brings the
cursed tennis ball to Valhalla by mistake.

In each of these three representative pieces,    Allen
expertly mimics the technique as well as the rhythm of his
models (the strained similes in "Mr. Big," the repetition
in "A Twenties Memoir," the use of the colon in the
pompous title of the book published by the Zeiss Press,
referring to another academic—Breuer—by his last name
only, in "The Metterling Lists"), and then proceeds to do
them in by going too far, undercutting their style and
beyond that, their world view, by emphasizing their
insularity and single-mindedness. Satirizing clichés of
language and thought, he can make any literary style
seem ridiculous. No writer, from the author of a course
description to Dostoevsky, is safe from his reductive
touch.

In addition to writers and critics,    Allen takes swipes
at organized crime, Freud, Nazis, politicians, philosophers, rabbis, and educators, In all his comic pieces, his
standard technique is reversal, treating trivia as an
occasion for mock high seriousness, and writing of crucial
concerns in a tone of deadpan silliness. He discusses the
invention of the sandwich and the discovery and use of the
fake ink blot in swelling, orotund cadences, while God,
death, and the meaning of life are reduced to absurdist
doodlings: "It is impossible to experience one's own death
objectively and still carry a tune."

In *Without Feathers,* his second collection (1976), he

revisits his abiding concerns—love, sex, death, etcetera—in an even more absurdist vein. Reversals, distortions, inflations, and deflations become increasingly surreal. His humor grows more fabulous and otherworldly, taking off into a cloud cuckoo land of supernatural flights of fancy. "Hot, salty tears pent up for ages rushed out in an unabashed wave of emotion. The problem was they were coming out of his ears." "Whosoever shall not fall by the sword or by famine, shall fall by pestilence, so why bother shaving?" "Dr. Joshua Fleagle, of Harvard, attended a séance in which a table not only rose but excused itself and went upstairs to sleep."

Again, as in *Getting Even,* he dismantles the pomposities of academic criticism, as in "Lovborg's Women Considered," a parody of Strindberg and Strindberg scholars. He mocks various literary forms, burlesquing popular legends in his mad "Fabulous Tales and Mythical Beasts," taking off on biblical texts (and scholarly interpretation thereof) in "The Scrolls." He slices into official culture, as in "A Guide to Some of the Lesser Ballets" and in his dotty supposition "If the Impressionists Had Been Dentists." He makes fun of the Mind in "Examining Psychic Phenomena" ("There is no question that there is an unseen world. The problem is, how far is it from midtown and how late is it open?") and of the Body in "The Whore of Mensa." In this widely admired piece, an Allenesque private eye, Kaiser Lupowitz, is hired to break up a circle of blackmailing prostitutes. The catch is that the whores sell not their bodies but their brains. The more high-priced they are, the more substantial their intellectual credentials. Littered with names from the academic pantheon—Kant, Blake, *Commentary,* Tanglewood, Dwight Macdonald—the story substitutes intellectual for sexual hunger, and in inverting the values—

treating intellect as pornographic—makes telling points about prevalent attitudes toward both sex and intellect. Woody exposes faddishness as a habit of mind, as he presents characters who want instant intellectual gratification: culture without commitment.

Through a glass, crazily, he offers fragments of his own philosophy in the mock formally titled "Selections from the Allen Notebooks" and "The Early Essays."

Do I believe in God? I did until Mother's accident. She fell on some meat loaf, and it penetrated her spleen. She lay in a coma for months, unable to do anything but sing "Granada" to an imaginary herring. Why was this woman in the prime of life so afflicted—because in her youth she dared to defy convention and got married with a brown paper bag on her head? And how can I believe in God when just last week I got my tongue caught in the roller of an electric typewriter? I am plagued by doubts. What if everything is an illusion and nothing exists? In that case, I definitely overpaid for my carpet. If only God would give me some clear sign! Like making a large deposit in my name at a Swiss bank.

While taking my noon walk today, I had more morbid thoughts. What is it about death that bothers me so much? Probably the hours. Melnick says the soul is immortal and lives on after the body drops away, but if my soul exists without my body I am convinced all my clothes will be loose-fitting.

Today I saw a red-and-yellow sunset and thought, How insignificant I am! Of course, I thought that yesterday, too, and it rained. I was overcome with self-loathing and contemplated suicide again—this time by inhaling next to an insurance salesman.

And running through all the essays is Woody's interest in the way we use and abuse language, pumping it up to swell our own importance, manhandling it so as to maintain noncommunication.

Attacking logic, convention, and propriety, making

hay out of language and reason, the essays are a feast of inspired nonsense. And as always, there's method to Allen's madness, for the cracked mirror of his surreal comedy reflects the assorted idiocies and pretensions of the moment.

Allen has continued to publish comic pieces because they're good for business. They stimulate his wit and allow him to play with words and intellect. On the other hand, he abruptly ended his association with television because, after his two specials and his scattered appearances on talk shows, he felt he had exhausted its possiblities. "Television is a medium run by cretins to pander to the lowest taste of the American public," he said in 1969. He used television, in the late sixties, when he was consciously broadening his national base, and then, having achieved greater visibility, he abandoned it.

Looking at two of his television appearances, you can see why. His guest shot on a Gene Kelly special is especially revealing. The program is a salute to New York; and despite the location photography, it manages to make the great teeming city look as bland and well-scrubbed as Disneyland. This is New York packaged for the boondocks. Affable Gene Kelly and his chorus line drop by the Bitter End to catch Allen in his club act: Woody is thus cast as a Village weirdo being introduced to Middle America. "I don't know what it is about me that women find so attractive," says Woody, launching into his show on familiar territory. "They sense I'm willing to be violent, and it excites them." He then switches to a zany history of the Allen family, offering what is in retrospect a parody of *Roots* over five years before *Roots* was published. "The first comedian in history was an Allen," Woody explains, with pseudo-professorial seriousness. "We were orgy caterers in ancient Rome. In 1500 the

Allen family lived in England because they couldn't get
hotel accommodations in Italy for the Renaissance. A
General Allen introduced cowardice to this country."
After he crashes through world history, flinging far-out
anachronisms along the way, he lands with a winsome
"Anyhow, that's my family." He says thank you, nods,
and looks apologetic, even crestfallen, as if to say, I'm
sorry, but that's the best I can do under the circumstances.

Timed down to the second, his own specials have a
prepackaged, airless quality, although the better of
his two programs has many promising moments. In its
most disappointing segment, Woody Allen, Super Jew,
squares off against the Reverend Billy Graham, Super
Christian, in amiable debate, in an improvised question-
and-answer session. "God is perfect," Graham says. "Oh
yeah?" Woody says. "When I look in the mirror in the
morning it's hard for me to believe that." "What is your
favorite commandment?" he asks his guest. "If you have
faith in me, I will lead you," Woody says impishly (playing
God again). Graham says he hopes he can at least convert
Woody to agnosticism. "What is your worst sin?"
someone in the audience asks Woody. "I had impure
thoughts about Art Linkletter," he fires back. By simply
appearing together on the same stage, the irreverent
Jewish comic who has boasted of his infidelity and the
Christian orator who has become the Lord's chief salesman generate a certain amount of tension. But there are
no real sparks in their encounter. Woody is polite and
charming but he's so tense that he's even more tongue-
tied and flabbergasted, more of a stammerer, than usual,
and this time it isn't a pose. Graham is surprisingly
good-natured, and quick-witted too: he answers Woody
tit for tat and racks up more points than his host in the

verbal jousting. But the debate—between skepticism and faith, between Jew and Christian—is sanitized for television viewers.

The comic skits—a rehearsal for an avant-garde play in which the actors are to appear nude, a parody of a silent movie comedy, and a vignette about a matchmaker who trains a dumb girl to appear smart by rattling off cultural code words—are on themes close to Woody's heart. The rehearsal skit plays on his self-consciousness about his body, and his adolescent prurience. "The country is not ready for my body," he boasts. "Black students will revolt." He convinces his co-star Candice Bergen to disrobe (head shots only, of course). "My goodness," she gasps. "Is that your chest?" "Yes, technically, it is. I'm sorry."

In the silent movie routine Woody plays a garbage collector who falls for a rich girl who loves him when she is suffering from amnesia and doesn't recognize him when she remembers who she is. The schizophrenic motif recalls Chaplin's *City Lights,* one of Woody's favorite movies, in which a rich man, when drunk, befriends the tramp and, when sober, throws him out of his house. In the final sketch, billed as an original folk tale, a Jewish man with a stupid daughter takes her to a tutor (Woody, in rabbinical getup). "Three months under my tutoring and she'll be a leading pseudo-intellectual," he promises. He instructs her in all the current cultural passwords and then unveils her at a Norman Mailer party, where she proves an expert name-dropper and therefore a smash hit. Because she knows the right words, it doesn't matter that she gets everything scrambled: "Dostoevsky if he could sing would sound like Ray Charles" is an example of what she has learned from Rabbi Woody.

Silent comedy, Jewish folkways, sex, and God

— Allen treads on familiar ground, managing to smuggle some bright comic ideas onto national television. The show is several cuts above the norm for specials, despite the slick packaging ( Allen is forced to interrupt the comedy to introduce the Fifth Dimension, a vacuous singing group who provide chewing gum for the ear) and the pressures of time.

Although he usually avoids topical or political humor, in 1970 Allen made fun of Kissinger and Nixon in a program he wrote for public television. When the network canceled the show, he promptly ended his dubious alliance with the medium in order to concentrate on writing, directing, and starring in a series of films which ensured his position as America's best-loved and most respected comic. Since 1970 he has taken time out from films only for his elegantly written and hilarious essays. For Allen himself, the nightclub years, the television exposure, the dabbling in theater, the appearances as an actor in other people's movies, were only warm-ups to his true calling—Woody Allen, film maker.

# 3

## The Comedian's Progress: The Seventies

IN a ten-year period, from *Take the Money and Run* in
1969 to *Manhattan* in 1979, Allen has displayed an increasingly passionate involvement with making movies. At
first he was both skeptical and bemused. "I never had a
burning desire to direct," he told an interviewer in 1968.
He claimed that his goal was a really quite modest one: to
be funny.

*What's Up, Tiger Lily?* had given him a taste of the
medium's possibilities but it had been, after all, a gag, a
burlesque of moviemaking before he knew what making a
movie was all about. Creating a new sound track for a
Japanese imitation of a James Bond thriller, he discovered
that movies consist of disparate sounds and images that
can be deconstructed and reassembled in a flash of the
editor's scissors. After his disillusioning experience with
*What's New, Pussycat?* and *Casino Royale,* and after
shredding the Japanese junk movie, he approached film
making with a healthy irreverence. When he got the

chance to make *Take the Money and Run,* he had no expectation of becoming an internationally celebrated director.

Showing an immense improvement over *Take the Money and Run* a decade earlier, *Manhattan* is clearly a film signed by a master. Photographed in black and white, and mixing comedy with pathos to achieve a rare bittersweet blend, *Manhattan* has a silken elegance. It opens, spectacularly, with a montage of cityscapes cut to the swelling rhythms of Gershwin's "Rhapsody in Blue." East Side chic and West Side casualness; crowded streets simmering under a summer sun and deserted, snow-covered canyons; Delancey Street overflowing at high noon, Park Avenue in dignified repose at dawn; haughty high-rises and humble tenements; slim glass boxes and squat Belle Epoque curiosities; Broadway with its nervous blinking lights, Wall Street at dusk, crouched in silence; fireworks over Central Park, piercing the hushed night sky with bursts of light—the opening kaleidoscope is a tribute to the city's vitality and diversity, a visual bouquet to Woody's beloved hometown. And a gorgeous piece of film making, the crowning touch to his first decade as a director.

At the risk of subjecting   Allen to the kind of academic pigeonholing he loves to mock, let us chop up his first ten years as a film maker into three separate but contingent phases. The first period—Woody's apprenticeship—includes, along with *Take the Money and Run,* *Bananas* (in 1971) and *Everything You Always Wanted To Know About Sex\** *(\*but were afraid to ask)* (in 1972). *Sleeper* (1973) and *Love and Death* (1975) form a second grouping, while *Annie Hall* (1977), *Interiors* (1978), and *Manhattan* (1979) make up a third.

Allen   also starred in two films he did not direct
—*Play It Again, Sam,* the 1972 adaptation of his 1968
play, directed by Herbert Ross, and *The Front* (1976),
directed by Martin Ritt, with a screenplay by Walter
Bernstein. Without too much strain, these two films can
be placed in the third phase of Allen's  film career, the
*Annie Hall–Interiors–Manhattan* sequence.

For all their genuine shifts in style and sensibility,
however, the ten movies are more alike than they are
different. They are all vehicles for Woody, and we go to
see them because we like him and want to see more of
him. The films are continuing chapters in the comic's
autobiography, providing frameworks in which Woody
the professional neurotic, the noted, admired *meeskeit,*
can cut up. With an egocentricity that is monumental,
Woody has used his movies as a showcase for his
self-infatuation. In contexts both bizarre and down-to-
earth, both fantastic and real, the movies offer a catalogue of Woody's psychological and sexual *tsuris*; regard-
less of the visual embroidery, of where his comedies of
sexual fact and fancy are set, the central concern is the
same: Woody wants to get laid.

What vanity, what self-absorption, what *chutzpa,*
these movies reveal. And yet we continue to support this
most self-centered of performers, and those of us who like
him like him inordinately, because  Allen  has succeeded
not only in coating his egomania with enormous charm
but also in getting us to identify with it, making us catch
an image of ourselves in his own parochial obsessions.
Loyally, therefore, and with continuing payoffs, we go to
his movies because  Allen's  fantasies about himself
stimulate our own self-analysis; the daffy, bemused,
ironic, unhappy, intelligent, single-minded, self-mocking,

preening character he has created welcomes us, and enfolds us. Watching him, we feel like one of the family.

Allen's first three comedies are filled with far-out verbal and visual gags. Going after laughs with a wild abandon and thrown together like a series of vaudeville routines (or closer to home, like the riffs of a stand-up comic), they aim to please. Some of the jokes work; some die. Some sound like material left over from Allen's cabaret act; others have been shrewdly adapted to the movie framework.

*Everything You Always Wanted To Know About Sex* is a series of blackout dirty jokes, while *Take the Money and Run* and *Bananas* try (feebly) for narrative continuity; but all three films are a pastiche of comic styles and ideas given a semblance of unity by the presence of their goofy star-author-director. *Take the Money and Run* and *Bananas* are both variations on an outrageous comic premise: Woody as a bank robber and Woody as the leader of a revolution in a South American country. With *Everything You Wanted To Know About Sex* Allen released himself from the chore of constructing a full-length comedy by making a movie of separate sketches, each of which is a burlesque of Dr. Reuben's foolish question-and-answer sexual digest. Each skit takes off on a particular kink: a middle-aged man is a transvestite, a doctor falls in love with a sheep, a woman can have sex with her husband only in public places. Once each idea is milked of its comic potential, Allen is free to go on to the next "turn." *Sex* represents the culmination of his early fragmented, revue-humor movie style.

Anecdotal, frazzled, disjointed, and exuberant, these first three films represent the rag heap and junk shop of

Allen's zany comic heart. Their humor is cocky and extroverted and juvenile. All three films are bananas—a surreal jumble of characters and settings and incidents carried by their wild man's energy. At their best the films bombard us with jokes, establishing a dizzying comic rhythm and creating a world which defies reason and for which the only response is tonic, bracing laughter. Without any reputation to lean on or the mantle of Noted Director to weigh him down, Woody works in these early pieces with a kind of slapdash improvisatory freedom; and the comedy brims over with an essential goodwill. When he's on, the results are joyous, and audiences erupt in full-throated laughter.

These are comedies of mayhem and chaos in the tradition of the Marx Brothers. But Allen's verbal farces, unlike those of the Marxes, are not visually flat. From the beginning, almost in spite of himself, Allen had an eye for a pretty picture.

"I think I would have made the kind of criminal you see in *Take the Money and Run*," Allen said before the film was released. As in all of his later movies, Allen here casts himself in a role based on a private fantasy of his, and the comedy springs from the inappropriateness of the fantasy image: the mousy, bespectacled, prone-to-humiliation Woody persona as Little Caesar, or Clyde Barrow! The narrator informs us that Virgil Starkwell (the name of Woody's character) "takes to crime at an early age, and is an immediate failure." The compleat buffoon, Virgil can't do anything right. As a child thief, he gets his hand stuck in a bubble-gum machine that he tries to steal. He commits petty crimes in order to pay for cello lessons. "His cello playing was just plain terrible," his teacher says. "He had no conception of the instrument. He was blowing into it." By dint of hard work he improves to the point where he's good enough to play the cello in a marching band.

As an adult criminal he has one bad break after another. When he tries to rob a bank vault, he finds a family of gypsies living in it. When he tries to rob a pet shop, he's chased out by a gorilla. Sticking up a bank, he misspells the holdup note, writing "gub" for "gun" and "abt" for "act," thereby provoking the teller into a discussion of his penmanship. On another fouled caper, he and his gang try for a robbery at the same time as another gang. "We'll take a vote," Virgil says. "How many people would like to be held up by our group?" When a scheduled prison break is called off, Virgil is the only one who isn't told and he ends up alone in the middle of the yard. For another attempted escape, he carves a gun out of a bar of soap, hoping to bluff his way past the guards. It rains. His gun melts.

He meets a girl. "I knew I was in love. I was feeling nauseous. I was either in love or I had smallpox." After sprucing up for his first date, he looks at himself admiringly in the mirror and then walks out the door, without his pants on.

"To think that idiot was a criminal," Louise Lasser, as a former neighbor of Virgil's, says in an interview near the end. "You'd never believe it. It was the best cover-up job you've ever seen . . . that there was a mind in there that could rob banks. He was the biggest schlemiel and nothing you ever saw."

But like most schlemiels, Virgil survives by his wit. His goofiness gives him an edge over straight society, and protected by his fool's disguise, he delights in scrambling reality. "I think crime pays," he tells a bland interviewer. "The hours are good, you travel a lot." What happened to his old gang? he's asked. "A great many have become homosexuals," he answers, not missing a beat, "others entered into politics and sports." Any questions? a grizzled gang warden asks the men under his charge. "Do you think a girl should pet on the first date?" Virgil pipes up, confounding his boss. At a job interview Virgil gives his name as John Q. Public. What kind of office did he work at before? the unfazed interviewer inquires. "Rectangular." What kind of work did he do? "I used to manufacture escalator shoes for people who were nauseous in elevator shoes." This seeming nincompoop, shrewdly concealing his basic common sense beneath a smoke screen of lunacy, wins the Gangster of the Year Award and is asked to speak at luncheons.

In *Take the Money and Run* Woody's inept gangster is a parody of Horatio Alger, that clean-cut, hard-working fellow who makes good against all the odds. But despite its satire of the American Dream, this is not primarily a public-spirited comedy. It's more a showcase for Woody than it is a social statement; it provides a comic frame for Allen's puckish, witty, appealing loser-as-winner more than it sends up American infatuation with Making It, no matter how. As Woody said at the time, "It's a comedy done for laughs, not for satire."

"I have to regard this film strictly as a learning process," Allen said before he began to direct. "I think there will be 100 percent improvement in the second." His statement reveals a becoming modesty; and indeed the film's very lack of self-importance gives it the fresh, winsome quality that audiences responded to. "It asks only that we like Woody Allen," noted Richard Schickel.

Clearly a novice work, the film has many problems. It's too long. The jokes aren't spaced out evenly over the course of the action. The story meanders. Many of the comic targets—gangster movies, *cinéma vérité*, "March of Time" newsreels—border on the esoteric. And the basic comic premise—Woody as gangster—is a little private, Woody having a joke on himself; it misses the larger reverberations of Woody's later appearances in incongruous roles. Although there are sight gags throughout the movie (Virgil fires a gun, it's a cigarette lighter; Virgil's parents wear Groucho Marx masks; frisked by a burly prison guard, Virgil proves ticklish, and collapses in giggles; two dummies are placed in the background when his girl friend visits him in prison), most of the jokes are narrated rather than acted out. The film presents the life story of noted criminal Virgil Starkwell in a documentary style; and many of the punch lines are spoken by a hard-hitting narrator. "Before he is twenty-five, Virgil Starkwell will be wanted in six states for assault, armed robbery, and illegal possession of a wart. . . . Tragedy strikes. His grandfather is hit in the head by a baseball and thinks he's Kaiser Wilhelm. . . . Virgil tries to join the Navy but is judged psychologically unfit when he says an ink blot looks like two elephants making love to a men's glee club. . . . Virgil and Louise's simple wedding ceremony is followed by a deeply moving blood test. . . . The couple name their boy Jonathan Ralph, after Virgil's mother. . . . Food on the chain gang is scarce and not very nourishing. The men get one hot meal a day: a bowl of steam."

The jokes don't grow out of a give-and-take between the characters but are recited either in voice-over narration or by the characters as they face the camera, responding to questions posed by an anonymous interviewer. All the actors thus become stand-up comics, delivering their best lines directly to the camera.

*Bananas,* too, is an extended cabaret skit, a Woody

Allen vaudeville act. Instead of crime, the trigger this time is politics, with Woody switching from Al Capone to Fidel Castro, in rabbinical beard. Just as *Take the Money and Run* was made for laughs, so *Bananas,* despite its political window dressing, is first and foremost a madcap farce, with Woody in high comic gear tearing through one loony routine after another.

Woody is Fielding Mellish, a New York loser who has trouble getting dates and is stuck with a job as a products tester. To impress a girl friend who has rejected him, he flies off to revolution-torn San Marcos, is co-opted into the guerrilla forces, and while he's looking the other way is elected their leader. He returns to America in political glory to raise money for the new government, is accused of being a Communist agent, stands trial, and is acquitted when the judge suspends a sentence of guilty on the promise that Fielding will not move into his old neighborhood.

If *Take the Money and Run* is not primarily a social satire, then *Bananas* is assuredly not a political one. Allen is not Jonathan Swift, haranguing his audience with a comedy of moral commitment. His goal is to be nutty and appealing, and again his movie asks only that we like him.

At the end of *Sleeper* Woody says that he doesn't believe in politics; and true to his word, in *Bananas* he stands to the side, mocking the guerrillas as well as the *ancien régime.* The rebel leader, Esposito, proves to be as ruthless as Vargas, the tyrant he overthrows. "The official language will be Swedish," decrees Esposito, intoxicated with his newly won power. "Underwear is to be changed every half hour and to be worn outside. All children under sixteen will now be sixteen." Rebels, tyrants, leftists, rightists, radicals, conservatives: to Allen, any kind of politics is a lot of double-talk and ego boosting.

It's good for a few laughs but is decidedly peripheral to matters he really does care about—love and sex, and himself.

For all its epic potential *Bananas* is another movie about Allen's schlemiel persona, a hard-luck wise guy who falls into uncovered manholes, has bad breaks with women (his girl can get in the mood only if he'll say I love you in French: "I don't know French," he stammers, "what about Hebrew?"), and relies on his wit to bail him out of hot water. "Have you ever been to Denmark?" a potential girl friend asks. "Yes, I've been to the Vatican." "The Vatican's in Rome." "They were so successful they opened a branch in Denmark." Being funny, cracking wise, taking off on any subject that comes to hand—this is Woody's real goal in the film and accounts for the haphazard structure and the parade of comic routines. Woody throws in a scene of Fielding jabbering to an analyst which has nothing to do with the story, such as it is, but provides some good patter. "I was a nervous child, a bed wetter. I used to sleep with an electric blanket. I was constantly electrocuting myself. . . . I used to rub dirty sections of a pornographic book in Braille." He describes a dream in which priests carry him on a cross; another procession of priests, with another strapped victim, passes by, and the two groups start fighting for a parking space.

Later, at a fund-raising dinner, Fielding Castro comes on like a stand-up comic who's bombing. "Locusts are available at popular prices, and so are the women," he tells the stuffed shirts in the audience, who have come to hear about the wonders of San Marcos. "We lead the world in hernias. Columbus stopped there and contracted something that can now be cured by one shot of penicillin."

Though    Allen sends up love and sex along with

politics, there are moments in his character's on-again,
off-again affair with the pseudo-radical Nancy (who is
readier to give herself to causes than to him) where a
serious side of his sexual anxiety surfaces. A scene in
which Nancy rejects Fielding—the relationship isn't
working for her, something is missing—isn't funny,
despite the quips. "Maybe it's me," Nancy says. "Maybe I
can't give." "You don't have to. I give, you receive. Am I
not smart enough? Too short? Is it because of personality
or looks?" "No," she answers, "it has nothing to do with
the fact that you're short, or your teeth are in bad shape."
Fleetingly, beneath the jokes, we feel Fielding's sense of
abandonment and sexual failure. Our laughter freezes,
and the delicately played scene in a sunny Riverside Park
anticipates a strain of rueful, sardonic comedy that is to
dominate Woody's later work.

"My first two pictures were full of areas ruined by my
inexperience," Woody said in an interview in 1972.
"There wasn't enough pre-planning. But I don't think
anyone else would have made them for all their flaws and
immaturities. You can say they weren't factory-made
films . . . they're not machine-made. I do have a certain
kind of style, and it's my own."

*Everything You Always Wanted To Know About Sex\**
*(\*but were afraid to ask)* is also very much his own movie.
Woody was in earnest when he boasted that it's "a very
personal approach to sex. I don't think anyone else would
have made this same film. It's very far out. A unique and
bizarre view of sex." The movie is thus deliberately
mistitled, because it doesn't tell us everything *we* always
wanted to know about sex but rather shows us what kind
of weird sex fantasies have been rooting around in
Woody's head.

*Sex* was the least popular of  Allen's movies of his

early, *Hellzapoppin* style and the least well received critically. "A failed experiment in a career of unbroken successes," wrote Paul D. Zimmerman in *Newsweek*. "It was bound to happen," Vincent Canby lamented. "Allen could not go on being funny indefinitely. Allen fans everywhere can only groan, 'Woody, how *could* you?' " Yet from this corner, *Sex* is the most audacious film in the canon (so far). Wildly uneven, yes, but wonderfully risqué, as Allen sets out to outrage the kind of numbingly conventional middle-class sensibility that's revealed in Dr. Reuben's fatuous nonbook. It's a comedy of epochal bad taste as Allen takes on a roster of sexual fetishes and taboos. Macho heterosexuals, homosexuals, transvestites, nervous Jewish boys, frustrated wives, Kinsey-type sex researchers, people who sleep with animals, and breast worshippers, among others, go down for the count, clobbered by Allen's surreal wit.

It's Allen's one film so far (1981) where his humor takes on a genuinely scabrous edge. The revue-style format —the film consists of seven separate skits—allows Woody to work piecemeal, in spurts and drabs, and the result is his nerviest, raunchiest, most puncturing comedy to date.

In the opening skit, "Do Aphrodisiacs Work?," Woody comes on as a medieval court jester, spitting out puns and wisecracks in an insolent modern manner. "But seriously, ladies and germs." Sounding like Bob Hope, he attacks his listeners. "His Majesty keeps in shape by taxing the peasants," he chortles nastily. He's a bust; the king is not amused; the fool shuffles off in disgrace, delivering his best line when no one's around: "TB or not TB, that is the congestion. Consumption be done about it?" Maybe he's a lousy stand-up comic because he's so randy. "I would give my life for a bare bodkin, to see the queen's bare bodkin, or anyone's bare bodkin, or even one with a little clothes on it," he muses, Woody the sexual loser in Shakespearean drag. When he's finally about to score with the queen, he gets his hand caught in her steel chastity belt. "I will open the latch and get to her snatch," he says. But "the royal box is locked." Awakened by a loud banging, the king strides into the queen's chamber to find her and his jester in awkward embrace. "I don't look good in twain," the jester pleads; but off goes his head.

In the second episode, "What Is Sodomy?," a doctor (Gene Wilder) falls in love with a sheep. "You from the hills of Armenia, and me from Jackson Heights . . . I think it could work if we gave it a chance." His extramarital affair causes the doctor to grow distracted, and one by one he loses his wife, his home, and his job, winding up in a Skid Row flophouse drinking Woolite.

"Gina, your body to me is a cathedral," drools Woody, in Italian, to his chic wife (played by Louise Lasser), in the third segment, "Why Do Some Women Have Trouble Reaching an Orgasm?" But even as a Marcello Mastroianni type, Woody is unlucky in love, because his wife just lies there, "passive like a lox." He tries to excite her with a vibrator, and it bursts into flames. But all of a sudden, when they're shopping in a smart white boutique, his wife gets aroused, and they have sex right then and there. It's the beginning of a pattern, sex in public places. At a house party, under the table in a restaurant, at an auction—wherever there is a chance she will be caught and punished, she and Woody have sex with a vengeance.

Allen's offers a middle-class farce as a nonanswer to question No. 4, "Are transvestites homosexuals?" Sam (Lou Jacobi) and his wife go to dine at the home of their wealthy and stuffy in-laws. Very calmly, Sam excuses himself from the table, goes upstairs to his hostess's bedroom and proceeds to put on one of her dresses. When the door opens, and he is about to be discovered, he jumps from the bedroom window and runs into the street where his purse is snatched and a crowd gathers, as gruff-voiced, mustachioed Sam tries to hide behind the lady's coat that he's wearing. "Sam, you should have told me. I would have understood," his wife tells him, as they undress for bed, the misadventure concluded. "If you'd said, 'I'm sick, I have a diseased mind,' I would have understood."

In "What's My Perversion?" quiz-show contestants stump a panel of sophisticated questioners. A man who exposes himself on subways is followed, in a special segment, "Fetish of the Week," by a rabbi who likes to get tied up. To demonstrate his thing for the panel and the audience, a model beats him as his wife sits at his feet and eats pork.

Episode No. 6 asks, "Are the findings of doctors and clinics who do sexual research accurate?" Victor Shakapopolis (the name of the character Woody played in *What's New, Pussycat?*), the author of a book called *Advanced Sexual Positions: How To Achieve Them Without Laughing,* goes to the house of a Dr. Bernardo to find out. Dr. Bernardo explains some of his pet theories. "I think the penis should be 19 inches long. Clitoral orgasm should not be just for women. There is a connection between excessive masturbation and entering politics." He shows Victor his laboratory experiments. "I'm studying premature ejaculation in a hippopotamus. I want to take the brain of a lesbian and put it into the body of a man who works for the telephone company. I built a four-hundred-foot diaphragm: birth control for an entire nation at once. This will show those fools that called me mad."

The lab explodes (from all the hot air?), and the doctor's haunted-looking house goes up in a burst of flame. From the wreckage a gigantic tit emerges. Victor warns the sheriff, "Be on the lookout for a large female breast, about 4000 with an x cup. The tit shoots half and half." Hero to the rescue, Victor proclaims, "Don't worry, I know how to handle tits." He brandishes a cross in front of it, and the thing, mesmerized, follows him into the gaping hole of a giant bra. The sheriff is puzzled, though, because there is only one of them. "They usually travel in pairs," he says. Victor concludes from all this that when it comes to sex "there should be certain things left unknown—and with my luck, they probably will be."

The final segment of the film is entitled "What Happens During Ejaculation?" To demonstrate, Woody plays a sperm waiting to be shot out of an erect penis that's the size of a spaceship. "Do you guys know what it's like out there?" Woody, the perennial neurotic, asks his colleagues. "What if it's a homosexual encounter? What if he's masturbating? I'm liable to wind up on the ceiling. I'm due at my parents' for dinner." Woody's supervisor reminds him of his obligation: "You took an oath when you entered sperm-training school: to fertilize an ovum, or die trying." Woody consoles himself with the fact that at least the guy they're working for is Jewish.

"This is Mission Control. A fine job. Attention all hands. Attention gonads. We're going for seconds." And thus the film ends not with a whimper but a bang!

Allen's mock Rabelaisian romp is a parody rather than a celebration of sex. Sex, the film says, is dangerous, titillating, and unavoidable; it induces fetishes, obsessions, and perversions. It's a dirty joke that drives men mad. It's a trigger for catastrophe. In the skits in which he appears, Woody is yet again a sexual nervous wreck, abused and humiliated in his search for gratification. He gets his head chopped off; he gets shot into outer space as part of a chorus of sperms; he chases a tank-sized tit; he can make love to his wife only in public. A would-be hell raiser, he's forever bamboozled and victimized by his sexual itch. Poor Gene Wilder, lusting after a sheep; Lou Jacobi with an urge to put on a dress; and the contestants on "What's My Perversion?" are all prisoners of odd compulsions. No one escapes from the grip of sexual desire; and under its spell, everyone is nearly as batty as Dr. Bernardo.

Opening up his Pandora's Box of sexual kinks, Woody mocks and explodes common fantasies, preoccupations, fears, anxieties, and taboos. His bawdy, juvenile, surreal comedy has purgative powers; giving in to its humor is a way of restoring us to sexual sanity. And perhaps nowhere else in his work is Woody's own bedrock common sense more apparent than in this anarchic sexual circus.

Filled with parodies of movies—Antonioni dramas of ennui, romantic triangles, science fiction voyages, haunted-house thrillers—and of television and advertising, *Sex* is Allen's most visually sophisticated film of this early period. He experiments with a different use of color and a stylized decor for each episode, with the result that the film is that rare thing, a comedy that is both raucous and beautiful to look at.

*Sleeper* takes place two hundred years in the future, in a sterile Brave New World; *Love and Death* is set in Russia at the time of *War and Peace*. In both these far-out settings, Woody holds stubbornly onto his persona, remaining a jittery, sly, bespectacled New York Jew with sex on the brain. *Sleeper* is mock science fiction; *Love and*

*Death* is a mock romantic epic.   Allen burlesques the narrative conventions of each genre, making fun of his stories as he tells them. Scrambling the past as thoroughly as he garbles the future, he sends up Tolstoyan history as well as Huxleyan prophecy.

In both settings, by virtue of how he looks and the way he talks, Woody is an outsider, a lone court jester whose level-headedness makes him a true Martian in the mixed-up worlds through which he time-trips. He is a humanist and a romantic in societies where original ideas or the expression of spontaneous feelings are considered dangerous. In *Sleeper,* he is Miles Monroe, owner of the Happy Claret Health Food Restaurant on Bleecker Street and a clarinet player with the Ragtime Rascals, who entered St. Vincent's Hospital for a dyspeptic ulcer one day in 1973 and is defrosted almost two hundred years later. "This isn't a miracle of science, this is a cosmic screwing," Miles says (sounding just like Woody Allen). "I can't believe this. My doctor said I'd be up in five days. He was off by 195 years. . . . I knew it was too good to be true. I parked right near the hospital." In *Love and Death,* by means of another cosmic screwing, Woody is once again the odd man out, the black sheep in a family of hardy, dim-witted nineteenth-century Russian peasants.

Living in fear of their leader, just about everyone in the world of the future seems to be lobotomized. As Miles's girl friend Luna explains to him: "Sex is different here in the future. We don't have any problems, everyone's frigid, except for the ones whose ancestors are Italian." The patriarchal and militaristic Russian society is equally rigid and equally wary of the stray individual.   Allen thus uses the future as well as the past to reflect present foolishness, just as his own distance from the societies in both films echoes his contemporary alienation.

Still intent on giving us a good time, Allen protects both *Sleeper* and *Love and Death* from becoming comedies of ideas. Every big abstract theme—war and love and death—provokes a gag. "What does it feel like to be dead for two hundred years?" Luna asks Miles. "It's like spending a weekend in Beverly Hills." "I'm a teleological existential atheist," Miles says, using words merely for the sound they make. "I believe there's an intelligence to the universe, except for certain parts of New Jersey." In *Love and Death,* when he sees a field covered with the corpses of soldiers, he says, "Boy, that army cooking will get you every time." Before he is about to be executed, his character Boris says, "I'm wracked with guilt, consumed with suffering for the human race, and developing a herpe on my lip."

"I'm always joking, you know that," Miles admits to Luna, in a rare straightforward moment. "It's a defense mechanism." In both these episodic comic fantasies Woody avoids seriousness, using slapstick and wisecracks to undercut the potentially epic thrust of his stories. In both films he plays an alienated, goofy, saintly, picaresque character who does not want to be a hero but who is nonetheless pressed into heroic activity. In *Sleeper* Miles is enlisted in a revolutionary group which opposes the tyranny of the leader, and quite against his will he has the chance to become a political savior. In *Love and Death* Boris goes along with his wife Sonia's grandiose plan to save Russia by killing Napoleon. But Woody, as always, doesn't want to save the world, he only wants to find some safe, private place in it for himself. Significantly, both these fables end with Woody in retreat. In *Sleeper* he winds up with Luna, who asks him what he believes in, since he says politics and religion accomplish nothing, and since relationships don't last because people get tired of each other. "Sex and death," Miles answers. "Things which happen once in a lifetime. At least after death you're not nauseous."

The smart-aleck comment is his way of dodging commitment. What's important in *Sleeper*, as in *Bananas*, isn't whether one form of government has been replaced by another, or why the revolution has succeeded or failed, but that the comic hero and his lady friend end up together.

In *Love and Death* he escapes by dying. Caught, tried, and executed for his half-hearted attempt to rewrite Russian history, he again signs off with a joke, with in fact a full comic routine addressed to the camera: Woody the stand-up comic picked out by a spotlight from the enveloping darkness of his prison cell. "There are worse things in life than death," he assures us, from the special vantage point of the evening before his execution. "Think of death as cutting down on your expenses." On another major subject, he has this advice: "The quantity [of sex] is not as important as the quality, but if the quantity drops to less than once in eight months, I would definitely look into it."

*Sleeper* has more sight gags and pantomime than the earlier movies. Though wary of being compared to the silent clowns,   Allen wanted this time to try a more acrobatic kind of comedy, and he wrote a part for himself where how he moves creates almost as many laughs as what he says. In his first scene, after he is defrosted, he walks like a somnambulist, in jerky, erratic rhythms: Bergson's mechanical man come to partial life. He hops into a wheelchair and, like a madcap yet knowing Harpo Marx, he creates utter havoc in the hospital, barreling into stern authority figures as he wields the chair like a deadly weapon. Later he masquerades as one of the robot slaves that seem to do all the work in this denatured society. His face painted in clown white, his arms shooting out like semaphores, he moves like a windup doll.

Since Miles is a fugitive, always on the run, the movie is filled with chases and getaways that recall the pell-mell pace of the silent slapsticks. Woody climbs down a rope, hangs out of a window on a reel of tape, dons a suit with a whirling apparatus and tries to fly by flapping his arms, and steers a car that floats on water. Perhaps because he's an interloper, borrowing business that goes against the grain of his verbal comedy, he exaggerates sight gags and parts of the body—the mime's tools—to surreal proportions. Miles and Luna discover a field of gigantic fruit. Miles slips on a huge banana—a self-conscious pratfall that underlines Woody's aloofness from the true innocence of the original slapstick clowns. When the two characters sit down to eat, they dine on an enormous piece of celery. One of Miles's duties as a robot slave is to cook, and he turns out a giant, throbbing pudding that seems to have a life of its own, like the ambulatory tit in *Everything You Always Wanted To Know About Sex.* For the slapstick finale, Miles and Luna, posing as doctors, attempt to clone the dead leader through his nose. (The big tit and the spaceship-sized erection in *Sex* say something after all about sexual obsessions; but what does a nose "mean," apart from its pure absurdity?) Parts of the body blown up to nightmarish proportions, food the size of automobiles: what is this outlandish exaggeration but Woody's mockery of physical comedy?

"Man consists of two parts, his mind and his body," Boris concludes at the end of *Love and Death,* "only the body has more fun." But for Woody's comedy, it's the mind that counts more than the body, and his absurdist distortions of the body and of bodily needs for sex and food, in both *Sleeper* and *Sex,* reveal his temperamental distance from the nonverbal slapstick comedy where, at breakneck speed, people eat, make love, throw pies at each other, smash up cars, and collide with a world of objects. Measuring his own "head" comedy against the "body" comedy of an earlier tradition, Allen sprinkles *Sleeper* with self-conscious quotations from the work of the silent clowns.

*Love and Death* is a return to verbal comedy. The opening and closing monologues clearly establish Allen as the comic master of ceremonies. "How I got in this predicament I'll never know . . . executed for a crime I never committed," Woody's familiar voice wafts over us, accompanying pictures of clouds. "But isn't all mankind in the same boat? But I go at six o'clock tomorrow morning. . . . I have a tremendous yearning to be young again. . . . I remember Uncle Nikolai, with his laugh. God, he was repulsive." And with that, we're off and running, under Allen's control as he guides us through a mock *bildungsroman,* a farcical spiritual autobiography which follows Boris from birth to death and through all the important stages of his life, from mystical childhood experience to abortive first love to incidental war hero (he's shot out of a cannon and lands on a group of French generals) to lover of a fabulously sexy countess to the climactic moment when he has the chance to redesign history by assassinating Napoleon, and bungles it. Framed by Woody's opening and concluding monologues, delivered on the evening before his execution, the story is constructed as a grab-bag reminiscence, a pilgrim's progress toward "salvation" as, in the Bergmanesque final shot, Boris, alongside Death in a white sheet, dances down a lane of trees.

As both child and man, scrawny, freckled, bespectacled Boris offends the norm. Unlike his brothers, he's no strapping Russian peasant. The adult Boris makes his entrance in a ritualistic family dance, following his muscular, athletic, marvelously coordinated brothers into the center ring, and falling all over himself, his arms and legs entangled in comic disarray. Where physical control and expertise are demanded, Woody the eternal schlepper takes a pratfall, kicking up his heels only to land on his ass.

In *Sleeper* most of Woody's jokes are about bodies; in *Love and Death* he kids the mind. This is a comedy about intellectual affectation: big words and abstract concepts keep getting in the way of Boris and his sometime girl friend Sonia, who reluctantly becomes his wife. The two of them fall into pseudo-intellectual discourse when what they would really rather do is fall into bed. "Morality is subjective," he says. "Subjectivity is objective," she counters, in one of their several ongoing debates. They toss around some expensive words and concepts, like epistemology, teleology, ontology, eternal nothingness, pantheism, moral imperatives, the Oneness of the universe. "Could we not talk about sex so much?" Sonia finally says.

Allen  thus burlesques philosophical abstraction, as well as love and death and war and politics and religion and high culture. He quotes from and sends up Ingmar Bergman, T. S. Eliot, Eisenstein, Aquinas, Kafka, Dostoevsky, and Tolstoy. No subject is too lofty for Woody's reductive, deflating humor. "Are there girls?" the young Boris asks, in his first encounter with Death. "If I could just see a miracle," he says, hungry for spiritual exaltation. "A burning bush . . . or Michael Sasha pick up a check."

As the title for a comedy, *Love and Death* is rather daunting and indicates Allen's attempts to place his work in a larger, headier framework—despite his refusal to keep a straight face in the presence of God and death and the world of higher thought. If not exactly a comedy of ideas in the Shavian sense, *Love and Death* is nonetheless a comedy about ideas, and about intellect, in which Woody clearly respects as well as makes fun of the life of the mind. His mockery is in fact a form of tribute, perhaps the only kind that this professional skeptic and scoffer can handle.

In spite of his compulsive joking, then, his making light of history and prophecy, both *Sleeper* and *Love and Death* contain hints of Serious Artist at Work. Beautifully designed and photographed, both movies certainly *look* serious even if they rarely sound it. With Prokofiev's heroic score, and Ghislain Cloquet's sumptuous photography, there are glimpses throughout *Love and Death* of a different kind of film altogether, a true epic in which Allen's deflating comedy gives way to genuine romance, and irony shades into pathos.

But Allen sees to it that both movies remain, at heart, celebrations of zaniness. In their incongruities—Woody's contemporary New York Jewish comic sensibility pivoted against alien environments—and their zesty vaudevillian gags that slice up the story line into entertaining fragments, both pictures finally are closer to the absurdist farce of *Bananas* than to more down-to-earth comedies like *Play It Again, Sam, Annie Hall,* and *Manhattan.*

Since *Love and Death,* Woody has avoided setting his work in a fantasy future or mythical past, nor has he dispatched his character to exotic (dis)locations. Instead, in *Annie Hall* and *Manhattan,* he presents himself without any farfetched fantasy embellishments. It took Woody ten years as a film maker to arrive at a point where he could make a clean, subdued contemporary comedy of manners like *Manhattan.* Perhaps, without fully realizing it himself, as he experimented along the way with an assortment of comic styles and masks, *Manhattan* is the kind of movie comedy he was heading toward all along. It is his purest work, which shows what's left after the surreal zaniness, the time warps, and the self-inflating fantasies have been eliminated.   Allen said that he deliberately restricted the number of laugh lines, cutting out jokes that were too funny or that were not revelant to the characters or the situations. In this streamlined comedy, going for laughs is less important than preserving the truth of the characters. It's as if  Allen has gotten the nuttiness out of his system (for the time being at least), to make room for the somber, reflective quality that has been there, underneath the comedian's manic joke-telling, all along. In *Manhattan*  Allen quite literally has cleaned up his act.

The process of simplifying his comedy by bringing it closer to home began on stage in 1968 with *Play It Again, Sam* and continued with the film version of the play in 1972, with his appearance in *The Front* in 1976, and with *Annie Hall* in 1977. Unlike his earlier movies, *Play It Again, Sam* doesn't place him in an unlikely role or setting. It isn't about Woody robbing banks or leading a revolution but worrying about getting dates and, while he isn't looking, falling in love with the wife of his best friend. *Sam* is his first comedy to focus on what is to become his favorite, indeed his obsessive theme, the quest for the successful relationship, and presents Woody not in an outlandish Marxian farce, but on terra firma, suffering the pangs of sexual defeat and enjoying the thrill of sexual triumph. It sets Woody up in a new relationship to his audience, one based less on our sense of superiority to his character than on our identification with him in his state of sexual anxiety and romantic longing.

After *Sam* he didn't return to earth again until *The Front,* in 1976. In both contemporary films, he was directed by someone else, as though aware that he was trying something new and therefore needed an outside viewpoint. *Sam* at least retains echoes of Woody the zany stand-up comic who makes an art of self-mockery; there are scenes in the film where farce predominates, as in his nervous preparations for a date, when everything goes wrong, and he collides with every object in sight. In *The Front* Allen doesn't use any comic routines to support his performance, and there is no reference to Woody's fantasy life, as there is throughout *Sam,* where he communes with Humphrey Bogart and discovers, to his delight, that his life is beginning to resemble the story of *Casablanca,* one of his favorite movies.

In *The Front* we see Woody from the outside as he plays it straight in a story with a clear-cut beginning, middle, and end which, quite unlike *Bananas* or *Sleeper,* takes politics seriously. In this solemn, lesson-pointing morality drama, set against the political blacklist of the fifties, Woody plays a man of dubious morals who becomes a political hero when he refuses to cooperate with a committee of witch-hunters. In his own movies, Allen avoids this kind of heroism, and one of the alienating qualities of *The Front* is seeing him blossom in the course of the action into a full-fledged political saint.

Allen plays Howard Prince, a cashier in a neighborhood bar who moonlights as a bookie. A friend of his is a television writer who is blacklisted and who asks Howard to act as his front by signing his own name to the scripts.

At first he enjoys pretending to be someone else; he likes the attention he receives from producers, and he can certainly use the extra money he gets from this charade. As someone else, he even attracts an idealistic girl friend. But when Hecky Brown, a blacklisted comic, commits suicide, Howard begins to question the rules of the game he's playing. He comes out to his girl friend and then he speaks up to a congressional committee. "Fellas, I don't recognize the right of this committee to ask me any questions. You can all go fuck yourselves."

From being a marginal man eking out a life near the bottom of the social scale—a neurotic Jewish underachiever—Howard Prince (the name is carefully chosen) evolves into a man of principle who's sent to jail for refusing to cooperate. As this bum turned idealist, Woody never really escapes or transcends his usual image—he wasn't meant to. He was hired for who he is, and because he isn't called upon to do anything that he hasn't done before, he can slide gradually, without jarring us, into the somber climax. Toward the end, as the character begins to struggle with his conscience, Woody reveals a brooding quality that's always been the under-side of his giddy self-mockery. In a long close-up, as he reacts to Hecky Brown's funeral, his face is a mask of grief which carries no trace whatever of his familiar comic persona. But most of the time Howard Prince is a wisecracking schlemiel, and so the role requires no histrionics, no passages of virtuoso acting. Without uncovering any unsuspected depth or range, Woody performs decently throughout, in a subdued, at times even hushed style. In his scenes with Zero Mostel (who plays Hecky Brown), he is wonderfully yielding and generous, making no attempt to pitch his work at Mostel's high-strung level.

For all this, however, the film is deadly. The pacing is off, as the story lumbers along from one scene to the next; the fifties decor is handled with a stilted, enervating self-consciousness, so that the movie seems to be unfolding in a vacuum; and Woody isn't permitted to play off the frozen, smug, immaculate beauty of Andrea Marcovicci, his bland leading lady. Martin Ritt's heavy, slow-motion direction is abetted by Walter Bernstein's screenplay, which reduces the history of the blacklist to a simpleminded drama of the good guys (the liberals and the communists) versus the evil guys (the witch-hunters). The film never acknowledges the fact that the left-wingers sold their careers by giving their support to a vicious dictatorship; there are no enlightened anitcommunist liberals in the movie, no people who stood up to the congressional madness but who also recognized Stalin's moral and political bankruptcy. All the right-wingers are impossibly blank of face and voice, while the blacklisted writers and performers are unfailingly noble.

Because Ritt and Bernstein and Mostel and Herschel Bernardi (who appears as a cowardly producer) were all victims of the blacklist, they approached the project with strong personal feelings. But their film is stillborn. The stately pacing, the methodical underlining of every point, the obviousness and humorlessness of the writing and direction, turn an important and potentially stirring subject into a deadpan, uninformative political tract.

Many people who say that *Annie Hall* was the film that turned them on to Woody Allen dismiss his earlier work as self-indulgent, disconnected surreal farce. But *Annie Hall,* far from springing full-grown and all at once from the comic's imagination, is a movie with a past. Everything that Woody had done as a performer, from his club work to his commercial plays to his comic essays to his far-out movies, led up to *Annie Hall* and can be felt, palpably, as a presence within it. Far from representing an abrupt departure, or miraculous transformation, the film simply penetrates more deeply the same subject matter that has always concerned Woody: sex, intellect, art, neurosis, and above all, tying everything together, himself. It's just that this time, instead of packing his persona off to some fantasy landscape, he sets him on home ground, in the world of New York show-business hustle that he knows well, has conquered, and almost (though he can't quite admit it) loves.

The movie may be called *Annie Hall* but it is in fact intensely autobiographical and self-centered. What really makes it seem different from his earlier comedies is the very nakedness of its self-absorption; with fewer trimmings, in terms of decor or storyline, than any of the preceding comedies,   Allen offers up himself—his anxieties, successes, failures, regrets—as the central focus of his film. *Annie Hall* gets rid of most of the clutter of the other movies, and presents Woody on his own, holding us by the force of his personality. The line between   Allen and his persona had always been blurred; and in *Annie Hall* the distinction between Woody on stage and off is even finer. Everyone knew that Woody and Diane Keaton had had an affair, and that the film was a review of their relationship and its breakup. Art was clearly very closely imitating life, and   Allen did nothing to discourage such associations by casting himself as a famous comedian (named Alvy Singer) whose career, from gag writer to stand-up comic to television personality to big-time celebrity hounded on the street by bullying fans, is recollected in fragments spinkled throughout the film. We see him telling jokes at a political fund-raiser, in a television spot with Dick Cavett, and doing a gig at a college auditorium. We even see Alvy being interviewed to write material for a rotten comic as, in voice-over, Woody says: "This guy's pathetic. If only I had the nerve to do my own jokes."

For the true  Allen fan, the film is honeycombed with in-house jokes and references and with a résumé of Woody's opinions and preoccupations: his dislike of Los Angeles, his contempt for television, his love of movies, his obsession with death, his fatalism ("life is divided up between the horrible and the miserable"), his scorn for intellectual pretension, his ambivalence about analysis ("I've been seeing an analyst for fifteen years. One more year and then I'm going to Lourdes.") During the course of the movie, Alvy goes to see *Children of Paradise* and *The Sorrow and the Pity,* two of  Allen's  own personal favorites, and meets Annie outside the Beekman Theater to see Bergman's *Face to Face* (Annie is two minutes late, and so they can't go in, because he must see a film from the very beginning, or else he feels completely disoriented). As  Allen followers know, Bergman is his all-time favorite director. Woody reprises wisecracks from his nightclub routines: at the college concert we hear the one about how he flunked out of New York University for cheating on a metaphysics final by looking into the soul of the boy next to him.

This most self-referential of movie comedies opens with  Allen alone on screen, standing against a plain background and talking directly into the camera. To warm us up, he gives a few minutes of nightclub patter, opening with an anecdote about two old ladies complaining about how bad the food is at a Catskill Mountain hotel and how small the portions are. "That's how I feel about my adult life," he confides. He quotes Groucho's joke about not wanting to belong to any club that would have him for a member, and then applies this to his relationship with women. He tells us he's just turned forty: "I'm not worried about aging. I'll be the balding virile type, as opposed to the distinguished gray, unless I'm one of those men with saliva dripping from their mouths who wander into a cafeteria carrying a shopping bag and spouting about socialism."

After he's introduced himself, reminding us in effect of what we already know (that he's lonely and nervous and depressed, has trouble with women, and is a compulsive kibitzer), he mentions that he has just broken up with Annie. "Where did the screw-up come?" he asks, and most of the rest of the movie attempts to provide an answer, with Woody guiding us through a tangle of places and times as he recalls scenes from his childhood, reviews high points in his career, and alludes in passing to his two failed marriages. As the master of ceremonies, the teller of the story, Woody as Alvy Singer (*Annie Hall* is his song) seizes complete control over the proceedings, suspending characters and events in his own floating stream of consciousness. He moves the story from the present to the past, he interweaves fantasy and reality, he interrupts to talk directly to us, commenting on characters and incidents. He muses over scenes from his life—and Annie Hall is only one part of his reverie, title notwithstanding. At the end, after he finally breaks up with Annie in a health-food restaurant on Sunset Boulevard, Alvy incorporates the scene into a play he is writing; we see two young actors performing the parts of Alvy and Annie. He gives the affair a happy ending: "It's my first play," he apologizes, "and you want things to come out perfect in art because it's real difficult in life." Like that play, *Annie Hall* reworks life into art, changing it around so that it comes out "perfect."

Originally the film was even more self-absorbed than in its final version. Allen's title for it was *Anhedonia*, that "melancholy but noncontagious psychological condition that prevents its victim from enjoying himself," and it was a free-for-all, a series of loosely connected, mostly fantasy episodes, based on Woody's life and times. Much closer in spirit to the surreal quality of *Sleeper* and *Love and Death* than to the pared-down, basically realistic romantic comedy he wound up with, it was another showcase for Allen's fantasies about himself, with this time the reveries taking on a baroque Felliniesque cast. But as he and his indispensable editor, Ralph Rosenblum, got more deeply into the completed footage, he began to redesign the film, principally on the strength of Diane Keaton's warm, appealing performance. As in her other movies with Allen, she helps to bring his far-out comedy to earth, and he decided to structure the film around Alvy's relationship with her. Reluctantly, then, and only after the fact, Allen bases his comedy on a clash of personalities; *Annie Hall* emerges as a true comedy of character interaction rather than the succession of skits and gags that was Allen's usual way of putting together a movie. The wisecracks, the anecdotes, the one-liners are still there, of course, but they're scaled down and more closely connected to character than in the earlier films. When Woody tells his second wife that he heard *Dissent* and *Commentary* had merged to form *Dysentery*, he is not simply making a good joke, he is expressing his character's hostility at being at a party with a group of *New York Review of Books* intellectuals, around whom he feels uncomfortable and threatened. His witticism is a response to a particular situation and issues from a clearly defined character.

At the center of the jokes and assorted memories, *Annie Hall* is a story of an archetypal Jew who meets an archetypal *shiksa*. Annie's from Chippewa Falls, Alvy is from Brooklyn. Those in her family drink, eat skimpy plain dinners, are unfailingly polite to each other, and hate Jews; his relatives yell a lot and eat up a storm. She's convinced she's not too bright; he's very proud of his intellect. They're equally neurotic. And indeed their anxieties, insecurities, and social terrors draw them together in the first place. Alvy, though, begins to take advantage of Annie's lack of self-confidence. He dominates her, taking over her life the way Allen takes control of the film—on one level Allen has made a movie about his own bossiness. Treating Annie like an appendage to his own life and career, making her feel bad because she is not as bright as he is, generally reinforcing her insecurities rather than trying to counteract them, he is the Svengali to her Trilby. Alvy is attracted to her precisely because she is someone he can mold. As his disciple, Annie is expected to see the world as he does. He buys books for her (Ernest Becker's *The Denial of Death* is the central text on Alvy's syllabus) and encourages her to go to night school. But when she becomes interested in one of her teachers, he is bitterly jealous. Their relationship is based on the premise that Annie is an idiot; and once she begins to question that, once she begins, however tentatively, to strike out on her own, cultivating friends and developing interests, the affair is doomed.

Allen's earlier movies signaled us that beneath the comic self-mockery he was really a terrific guy, bright and sexy and in control. But in *Annie Hall* the melancholy, self-critical pose that had always been a part of his persona is no longer played simply for laughs and is no longer simply a charade. For the first time, on public view, Allen expresses a genuine unhappiness with himself. This time his neuroses cost him a relationship. His ego, his intellectual pride, his intense absorption in his work, his possessiveness, his wit (charming, but it can be cruel), his passive-aggressive tyranny—all these aspects of his persona, the underside of his character's immense likability, are held up as matters for analysis and regret.

*Annie Hall* uncovers a pathos that had always been lurking around the edges of Allen's farces. It deepens the Woody persona, presenting him as a complex, struggling character, introspective, rueful, "anhedonic" indeed—a character whose wit is shadowed by melancholy, and whose professional success is qualified by a nagging sense of personal inadequacy. For the first time on film Allen plays something of the loser he disingenuously usually claims to be. As the story unfolds, Alvy Singer is pretty much of a fool, for all his wit and charm. He's sexist, moody, impossibly self-centered. It's only from the standpoint of the present, as he surveys the past in enlightened retrospect, that he is wise; it's only after the fact that he fully realizes how lucky he was to have known Annie. "Relationships are crazy, irrational, but we keep going through it because we all need the eggs," he concludes, offering his benediction on all those who, like himself, have loved and lost.

Charming, accessible, beautifully written and acted and directed, *Annie Hall* was of course a tremendous hit. People who hadn't been looking suddenly declared Allen to be an accomplished film maker and no longer a mere comedian. Though Allen had always received good reviews, his zany, surreal comedies carried a cultist taint, and they were something of an acquired taste. But

*Annie Hall* was the kind of romantic, common-sensical comedy-drama that had something for almost everyone. Woody had transformed his own personal experience into popular entertainment, making familiar material—the story of a fizzled romance—seem fresh and winning. For his reworking of life into art he was showered with Oscar nominations and awards, with statuettes and certificates of excellence; he was hailed as a triple-threat genius, the greatest comic film maker since Chaplin, the Orson Welles of the seventies.

How could so much acclamation not make him a little dizzy? Even for so reserved a personality as    Allen, the dangers were great, and despite his natural tendency to disbelieve the extravagant praise, the immediate result of all the hoopla was *Interiors*, perhaps the single worst movie ever made by a major American film maker.

*Interiors* is so thoroughly misconceived, so absolutely hollow, that it almost calls into question the integrity of all the rest of his work. Like the clown who aspires to play Hamlet,    Allen decided to go straight. Having mastered a popular comic style, he now felt constrained by the limits of comedy; he wanted to crash through comic boundaries in order to see how his usual material would look from a different perspective, through a glass darkly. "When you do comedy, you're not sitting at the grown-ups' table," Woody said, in 1978, as he was planning *Interiors*. "You're sitting at the children's table."

Subjects and character types    Allen had always mocked are treated, in *Interiors,* in a solemn, portentous style, with nods to Ingmar Bergman, O'Neill, Ibsen, Strindberg, and Chekhov. Preoccupations and affectations previously lanced by his wit are now set up as worthy of the most sober scrutiny. Anxiety, alienation, guilt—all the ailments modern urban man is heir to, all the common currency of modern malaise—are discussed with utterly deadpan decorum. But Allen can't have it both ways (or at least he hasn't yet learned how to play both sides of the same subject with conviction); he can't treat being a neurotic as a subject of comedy in one film and as the stuff of domestic tragedy in another.

*Interiors* is about a distraught gentile family—a distant father, a castrating mother, and their wretchedly unhappy children, three sisters (it worked for Chekhov, Allen may have decided). The mother (named Eve: is this what Allen really thinks of women?) is an interior decorator who has run her house with iron control, managing to knock the daylights out of everyone. The father (Arthur) is repressed and vacant, and the daughters comprise a veritable thesaurus of modern ills. Renata (played by poor, miscast, agreeable Diane Keaton, who will apparently go along with anything Allen asks her to do) is a fidgety, successful poet married to an embittered hack novelist; Flyn, unmarried, is a glossy, cheap, television actress who knows she will never be any good; and Joey (played by a spectacularly charmless woman named Mary Beth Hurt) Can't Find Herself. She is driven by the need to express herself, but she doesn't seem to be good at anything.

Nobody in this family gets along with anybody else. The daughters have a long, entangled history of sibling rivalry; and no one, especially the Mr., can stand Mother Eve. He announces at dinner one evening that, having done his duty, having raised his family, he now wants time for himself. This throws Eve into a nervous breakdown. By the end, after much Sturm and Drang, she finally succeeds in committing suicide, while her husband has remarried, and the three sisters go on with their knotted

lives, their mother's death and father's remarriage presumably having constituted some kind of exorcism. "The
water's so calm," one of them says, as all three look out to
sea in the closing tableau. "Yes, it's very peaceful,"
Renata says, bestowing a final blessing.

The film offers an epidemic of complexes and anxieties, of anguished, solitary dark nights of the soul and
tormented discussions of the need for art and self-
expression in the face of man's mortality. Yet, perhaps
because they are well-to-do WASPs, everyone in this
high-neurotic family talks in measured tones, uttering
self-consciously constructed periodic sentences in genteel
voices.    Allen seems to be confirming the stereotype of
WASPs as forbiddingly formal, dead of face and voice,
glacially polite to and utterly estranged from each other.
(Do rich goyim really talk to each other like this?) Not a
one of them has a joke in him, or a spontaneous, joyous
moment. Life is unending psychological hell for these
appallingly humorless, self-centered characters.

No doubt growing weary of them himself,  Allen
near the end brings on a character from the outside
world—Pearl, Arthur's bride-to-be, who is clearly presented as an antidote to this poisonous family. Dressed in
red (get it?), she is a good-hearted, fun-loving anti-
intellectual, a broad who knows how to express her
feelings. "You only live once, but once is enough if you
play it right," she says. Entering the dark world of this
insular family, she is a walking psychic wonder, an earth
mother and savior who breathes life into one of the
daughters when the girl nearly drowns. You might think
that with this character Woody is introducing some Jewish
feeling and warmth to oppose to all the gentile frigidity,
but Pearl is played by Maureen Stapleton, who is about as
Jewish as Debbie Reynolds.

In an uncharacteristically chatty interview,  Allen said before the film's release that it deals with "the spiritual turmoil, the floating unrest that can only be traceable to bad choices in life. Also the apotheosis of the artist beyond his real worth. And how a lover can possess the loved one as an object he can control. . . . There's something of me in all the characters." Clearly, there are themes here that are important to  Allen: the connections between neurosis and creativity, the artist's need to gain control over people as well as over his work. *Annie Hall* is about just these subjects, handled in a penetrating comic style; but with *Interiors*  Allen doesn't have the vocabulary or, more crucially, the temperament to present his ideas about art and the artist in the form he chose, an intense claustrophobic chamber drama à la Strindberg and Bergman. The film is achingly studied, with the kind of pretentious literary flourish that has always provided grist for  Allen's comic mill. He appears to have so little confidence in his grasp of the material that he winds up explaining everything; the story unfolds like a series of psychiatric profiles neatly laid out for balance and contrast. Characters announce their positions and analyze each other to a fare-thee-well, while even the most casual action is given weighty symbolic import. The film is a round robin of these walking case histories offering summations to and about each other. "Eve created a world around us that we existed in. It was like an ice palace," announces her husband, near the beginning, telling all. "You act the part of an aloof artist. No one can get near you," Arthur tells Renata. "Poor Joey. She has all the anxiety of the artistic personality and none of the talent," Renata says. (And so much for poor Joey.) "I think you're too perfect to live in this world, with your perfect interiors. There's no room for any real feelings,"

Joey laces into her mother, delivering a tirade that drives the woman to take a one-way walk into the ocean. "You're not just a sick woman . . . there's been a perverseness and willfulness of attitude about many of the things you've done. At the center of a sick psyche, there is a sick spirit."

Time and again, in words and phrases, in anecdotes and images, there are echoes of Woody's comedy. Much of the movie sounds like  Allen, the master parodist, parodying himself. "I can't shape the real implication of dying. The intimacy of it embarrasses me," Diane Keaton says, sounding for all the world as if she's doing a deadpan sendup of the usual neurotic she's played for  Allen in the past. About her recent poem, "Wondering," published in *The New Yorker,* she says, "I find it now much too ambiguous." "I experienced nostalgic memories. I was compelled to write them down." "I feel like we're in a dream together." "I just experienced a strange sensation. . . . I had a clear dream where everything seemed so awful and predatory. I was here and the world was out there and I couldn't bring us together." "My paralysis set in a year ago." "I have a preoccupation with my own mortality." "The creative thing is very delicate." "I'm not responsible for your guilt feelings." Dreams and portents, guilt, paralysis, mortality—is  Allen kidding? You keep waiting for the comic payoff, the joke that will blast through all this pompous posturing, but as  Allen told *Newsweek,* "There are no intentional laughs." Except, fleetingly, with Pearl, there is no comic relief, as if  Allen was afraid the whole thing would collapse if he permitted his characters or his audience a full laugh or even an occasional smile.

During screenings of the film, there is always a nervous, continual rustling movement, as if the audience is not certain how it is supposed to be responding. Initial respectful silence is later broken by scattered titters and strangulated laughter—the real tension is not within the film but in the uneasy relationship between the film and the audience.

Fussy, repressed, and immaculate, Allen's style is as guilty of overcontrol as that of the batty mother who has wrecked everyone's life with her passion for order. The film is overloaded with visual clues of the characters' alienation and emptiness. Everyone lives in pristine, cream-white rooms, and dresses in gray and white, in perfect harmony with their emotional sterility. Pearl's whore-red dress is the only stab of color in the calculated bleakness. Sedately paced, filled with pregnant silences, its every frame beautifully composed, the film drips with prestige and Art.

*Interiors* is exactly the kind of rigidly schematic work that invites the high-toned academic analysis that Allen has always pooh-poohed. And that is just what Allen has begun to receive. Here is Professor Maurice Yacowar on *Interiors,* sounding like a parody of academic overkill: "The central characters represent different approaches to recognizing man's mortality. Specifically, they represent sensuality, romance, and art, which [Ernest] Becker [in *The Denial of Death*] enumerates as three ways to transcend his limited, mortal self if he lacks faith in God." And here he is on water imagery in *Interiors*:

On the thematic level, Allen achieves a related effect by intercutting shots of the sea, especially in the series that begins when Arthur first tells Eve that he plans to remarry. A natural force, the sea represents the powers over which man has no control, the power in which Eve will eventually immerse herself. In Allen's use of the sea there is also a sense of expanding awareness. After the opening shots of interiors and secure doorways, Allen directs us through the windows as the characters look out upon the sea and recall their past lives. For most of the film the characters are defined by the tension between their inner natures and their living spaces, that is to say between their true interiors and their merely designed interiors (or exteriors). But with increasing force and volume the sea asserts itself against these shallow preoccupations. After Eve has drowned, our last view of her stately beach house is dominated by the sickly yellow grass in the foreground; it diminishes the impression of stability that the house—and Eve's designs—made earlier and it mutely reminds us of the superior power of the sea.

There's a charming moment in *Play It Again, Sam* when Woody converses with "Humphrey Bogart" as he tries to make a play for Diane Keaton. He hands her a line, hoping she will bite; when, against all hope, she does, he turns in delight to his mentor and says, "She bought it." Well, the critics, most of them, "bought" *Interiors,* another of Woody's B.S. lines. For the most part, and astonishingly, he got away with it. Intimidated, the Academy of Motion Picture Arts and Sciences gave him a nomination as Best Director. In *The New Yorker,* Penelope Gilliatt wrote that the film represents a giant step forward for him.

Allen really has begun to be taken too seriously, which is the critics' problem, not his; but that he may believe some of the wild adulation *is* a threat to his work. It tripped him up on *Interiors,* but not on *Manhattan,* which has a confidence and élan that represent a healthy reaction to everyone telling you how good you are. Now it remains to be seen where  Allen's high critical standing, his enthronement as America's premier film maker as well as its most beloved comic, will carry him next: to more artsy hot air like *Interiors* or, as in *Manhattan,* to further experiments in deepening his comedy without sacrificing its entertainment value or breaking its back (See chapter 8 ).

*Interiors* was worth it if that is the price   Allen —and we—had to pay in order to get *Manhattan,* the most grown-up, most technically accomplished, most securely pitched, of all his films, a clean-looking, sober comedy-drama which is the true fulfillment of the blend of comedy and pathos promised in *Annie Hall.* It is typical of the way Allen's  works "speak" to each other that his best film emerged from his worst, as *Manhattan* is the phoenix that rose from the ashes of *Interiors.*

In *Manhattan,* as in *Interiors,*   Allen examines affluent, articulate, creative neurotics, but this time he is on home ground, in the city that he loves, among characters and settings he knows at firsthand. (And thankfully he is himself the star again.) Suffering from blighted relationships and from stalled, diverted careers, the characters—as in both *Interiors* and *Annie Hall*—are unhappy in the modern manner, taking pills to help them sleep and to help them get up, going to psychiatrists, unable to be alone and growing exasperated when they're with others. They're on a treadmill, and the main action in each of the films is to get them off it, leaving them, at the end, at a different stage of their neuroses.

Like the two earlier movies, *Manhattan* is a sexual and emotional musical chairs in which characters pair off, withdraw, get back together again, separate, in an almost ritualistic pattern of arrival and departure, reunion and retreat. In *Manhattan*  Allen  plays Isaac Davis, a success-ful television writer who leaves his lucrative, soul-denying position in order to write a serious novel (about Manhattan, the decay of culture, the death of the spirit, the joy of life in the city, among other things). Recently

divorced—his wife has left him for another woman—
Isaac is having an affair with a teen-ager named Tracy. He
meets and gradually falls in love with Mary Wilke, his
married best friend's mistress. When his friend Yale
breaks off with Mary, Mary and Isaac spend time together
and begin to appreciate each other. Isaac breaks off with
Tracy. His ex-wife publishes a damning account of their
marriage in which she accuses him of Jewish paranoia,
sexism, moral and intellectual superiority, and having
morbid thoughts about death. Mary and Yale get back
together. Mary breaks off with Isaac. Isaac goes back to
Tracy, to declare his love and need, but she tells him that
if they really care for each other, they can wait for six
months, until after she returns from studying acting in London. "You have to have a little faith in people," she says.

"We keep on having relationships because we need
the eggs," Woody tells us, in the parable that closes *Annie
Hall*. The characters in *Manhattan* all need the eggs, too,
as they stumble blindly or at best with only partial vision
from one romantic calamity to another, switching partners à la mode. A husband cheats on his wife, another
wife takes wicked revenge on her ex, an older man trifles
with the feelings of a minor, a woman who plainly doesn't
know her own mind goes from pillar to post. Isaac, Yale,
and Mary are all writers, but they are so absorbed in their
dating problems that their work deteriorates or gets
postponed. Isaac's promising novel, which he hopes will
absolve him of years of commercial hackwork, remains
unwritten; Yale can't focus on his critical study of Eugene
O'Neill; and Mary descends from reviewing an edition of
Tolstoy's letters for a prestigious quarterly to grinding out
a novelization of a popular film. Only Isaac's mean
lesbian wife has the peace of mind to write, tossing off a
humorless feminist analysis of her rotten heterosexual

marriage. And only Tracy, the youngest member of the set, has the maturity and wisdom not to give in to her feelings of the moment: she will go to study acting in London, as Isaac had earlier advised her to do, and her departure puts a stop, for a time, to the jiggling, hectic courting patterns.

Though they worry compulsively about themselves, forever investigating their relational problems, these self-detained characters nevertheless manage to commune with Manhattan. They are true walkers in the city. When they are depressed or anxious, when they can't concentrate on their work, off they go into the streets, seeking stimulation and diversion. (It's refreshing to see a movie in which city life actually saves people.) Isaac and Mary go boating on a lake in Central Park. He trails his hand through the water, in an impulsive romantic gesture, and comes up with a handful of slime: the city,    Allen seems to be saying, is not, thank God, the country. If it has few of the joys of nature to offer its residents, so what? It has restaurants and museums, theaters and bookstores and shops, as well as therapists. It has size and energy and architectural splendor, and only a country bumpkin could fail to respond to its medley of sights and sounds.   Allen's anxious characters thus play out their private dramas in a heroic, regal setting of a sharp, thrusting, clean-looking Manhattan, whose grandeur is enhanced throughout by the lush George Gershwin music.

For all its epidemic of neurotic symptoms, the movie has a celebratory quality. It is a lyrical comedy of modern (bad) manners, festive and life affirming. The gentle, romantic mood comes directly from Woody, who makes a bemused master of ceremonies. As both a participant in the action and its orchestrator, he is more forgiving than he has ever been before. Except for the dead-faced lesbians, whom he evidently both fears and detests, he regards the characters' foibles and blunders, their distractions and pretentions, with a kind of paternal indulgence, his point of view suspended somewhere between the intimacy of *Annie Hall* and the detachment of *Interiors.*

*Manhattan* offers a new, more grown-up version of the Woody persona. He's more relaxed here, and at least a little more settled, than in earlier fictional self-portraits. Isaac-Woody has a sense of himself, professionally and personally; a man with some real success under his belt, he's more sober and self-accepting, and this time we catch him in the middle of an affair, rather than on the outside of the love game, looking in. To be sure, he's still a wit, making cracks about his love life, his grievances, and the assorted foolishnesses of his fellow man. "I'm going out with a girl who does homework," he says, in mock disbelief. "There must be something wrong with me, because I've never had a relationship with a woman that's laster longer than the one Hitler had with Eva Braun." "When it comes to relationships with women, I'm the winner of the August Strindberg Award." Driving in a taxi with Mary, just as he realizes he may be falling in love with her, he says, "You look so beautiful I can hardly keep my eyes on the meter." Later, less enchanted with her, he tells Yale that Mary is "the winner of the Zelda Fitzgerald Emotional Maturity Award." After he meets Mary's former husband, whom she has always described as Apollonian, he calls him a homunculus. This more mature version of Woody's persona hasn't then misplaced his comic sting, but he does make fewer gags, and he doesn't fire them off at random, as a display of comic prowess, but in response to specific characters and events.

Isaac expresses a wider range of feelings than Allen's earlier characters. When he breaks off with Tracy, telling her that it isn't good for either of them to get involved, she begins to sob, and he says, "Don't cry," in a wonderfully gentle, caressing tone. It's a lovely moment that uncovers a real tenderness in Woody and that makes you understand why so many teen-age girls are crazy about him.

There are moments of sexual humiliation in the film, but the image of Woody as a sexual success is primary. Isaac's ex may have thought he was a flop, but she leaves him for a mannish-looking woman, which salves Isaac's ego; besides, Isaac has a stunning young mistress who adores him, and she's the wisest character in the film, the one with the most mature attitude toward the Manhattan dating dance. In addition, Isaac can claim a genuine, if short-lived, success with Mary. In his relationships with both Tracy and Mary, Isaac is more open than the character Allen usually plays; he's vulnerable, he isn't as compulsively and self-protectively witty, and he makes wrong decisions. Allen doesn't then stand aside in mocking judgment, as he does in most of his earlier work, and he lets Tracy have the final word.

Since Diane Keaton plays Mary, Isaac's relationship with her naturally recalls Allen's earlier movie romances. Mary is affected, and a full-time nervous wreck, and Isaac can't stand her at first. Yet he begins to see her intellectual pushiness as a symptom of her insecurity, and he grows to like her. He stops kidding her and begins to treat her as an intellectual equal, which is no doubt a first for Isaac, as it is (on screen at least) for Allen.

He also ends up respecting Tracy. Though at first he may have thought of her as a fling, he grows to see her as a person with needs and feelings all her own. When he runs to see her at the end, after Mary has thrown him over for Yale, he's being a coward, unable to face up to the prospect of being alone. But it's clear that he also really cares for her.

Although Isaac winds up without either Mary or Tracy, he has grown up in the course of the film. He's been able to respond to two women not as images, or as sounding boards for his jokes, or as objects to be molded and controlled, but as people with their own problems and struggles, their own strengths and weaknesses.

Allen's character, then, is not that of a clown, or a loser, or an outsider. He is in fact very much a member of a Manhattan in-group. His world is Manhattan's East Side, extending from the forties to the nineties, and with Bloomingdale's its central artery. Isaac eats at Elaine's (like Woody Allen himself), an Upper East Side restaurant patronized by the literati; and he takes his son for lunch at the Russian Tea Room. Before he moves to a smaller apartment (after he resigns from his well-paying television job), he lives in a smashing duplex. Clearly, Isaac is a man who has made it, in terms that the slick Manhattan society he is a part of would instantly recognize and acknowledge. There is certainly some provincialism and hubris in calling the film *Manhattan,* as Allen is speaking only for a privileged portion of it. His bounded little world has much in common with the world at large, to be sure, but it is also a distinct suburb of it, a separate place with rules and codes of its own. The film is self-congratulatory in showing us that Isaac (i.e., Woody) has penetrated this inner world of the big city, but it also contains an awareness of the limitations and pitfalls of the gilded ghetto. And so, like everything else about this appealing comedy, Allen's view of the Bloomingdale's set is nicely balanced.

*Manhattan* marks Allen's return to the comic fold, after his disastrous attempt to transcend it in *Interiors.* But it is comedy scored in a new key, one sounded only obliquely in the earlier pictures. Elegant and sedate, it is a far cry from the free-for-all vaudeville of much of his earlier work. There is nothing improvised or spur-of-the-moment about *Manhattan.* This is Allen's most meticulous movie, yet its studied black and white photography and stately pace do not intrude on its comic point of view. Allen's achievement with *Manhattan* has been to move his comedy beyond farce and surrealism to an unembellished contemporary reality and in the process still hold on to his humor.

It took Allen ten years to capture his own world on film in a straightforward way, and the career has been richer for all the detours and experiments. If Allen had started out with *Manhattan,* he might have had no place to go. Instead, beginning far from home, with curiosities like *What's Up, Tiger Lily?* and *Take the Money and Run,* he created for himself a wide-open field in which to explore comic possibilities. In a way *Take the Money and Run* is a mess that Woody has been cleaning up ever since. Behind *Manhattan,* then, is a decade of experiment and development in which Allen has had his growing pains as a comedian, writer, actor, and film maker, in public view. Though the source of his comedy has continued to be himself rather than the world out there, and though he has never transcended the limitations of that performing self, he has continued to change the style and tone of his comedy, and so those of us who have been with him from the beginning know that we can look forward to future jolts and surprises.

# 4

## The Same,
## Only Different

WOODY ALLEN is not an original. His comedy reverberates with borrowings and imitations that cut across the comic pantheon from silent movie slapstick to Borscht-belt satire, from Marx Brothers mayhem to Kaufmanesque acerbity. With echoes of Chaplin, Keaton, Lloyd, the Marxes, George S. Kaufman, S. J. Perelman, Robert Benchley, Bob Hope, Milton Berle, Henny Youngman, Mort Sahl, Wally Cox, Jerry Lewis, and Mike Nichols and Elaine May, his persona is a résumé of comic traditions of the last fifty years. His eclectic style is nonetheless distinct, for though he may remind us of other performers, he has never been anyone other than himself.

Allen isn't a pioneer, bending the comic muse into new and unexpected patterns; neither in what he says nor in how he says it is he a radical. His subjects, as well as his technique, are part of a comic mainstream. Mocking pretense and hypocrisy, slashing into contemporary follies, and telling jokes on himself (the schlemiel with a list of grievances who is foiled by every step he takes), he does what comedians have always done. A card-carrying traditional comic, he is simply better at his job than anyone else has been in the last twenty-five years.

Polonius's sage advice to Laertes—neither a borrower nor a lender be—has never made much of an impression on Allen, whose comedy is littered with quotes from and tributes to the work of his own favorite comedians. Allen may have flunked out of college, as he never ceases to remind us, yet in his chosen field he is an excellent student, a thorough historian of twentieth-century comic style. A true appreciator of other people's work, he has always been generous in citing sources and influences. Although in different interviews, at different times in his career, the names of his favorite entertainers change, two stand-up comics always appear near the top of his list: Bob Hope and Mort Sahl. The two are certainly different from each other—and different from Allen as well. It isn't so much their material or their personae that Allen responds to as it is their manner and technique, their sheer comic deftness as they work the house. Hope and Sahl are masters of comic timing.

In the fifties Mort Sahl was a preeminent political humorist filtering current events through the lens of his abrasive comic style. Like many social satirists, he was alight with a wild-eyed radical fervor—in his staccato, hepped-up delivery, he seemed bent on saving the world. Sahl opened stand-up comedy to larger issues than it had ever dealt with before. "He made it different for all of us who came after him," Allen said. "He changed comedy for all of us." His influence among aspiring comics in the fifties and early sixties was pervasive. His agitated style, his intellect, his keen social consciousness, his hip, fiercely antiestablishment stance—all these novel qualities helped to change the image of the Jewish comic from that of an older generation of aggressively middle-class Borscht-belt kibitzers like Milton Berle and Henny Youngman. Ironically, though, Woody's own brand of humor is much closer to that of the Catskills gag men than to Sahl's. Like Berle and Alan King, Allen sets his comedy in a world of personal gripes and casts it with familiar types like nagging mothers and crackpot wives. Allen plainly has never had Sahl's messianic streak. Politics is not his field, and he distrusts topical comedy. "I don't deal with current affairs for two reasons," he explained in an interview in 1965, just as he was gaining recognition as a stand-up comic. "One is that I don't know about them, so it's pointless. And also, these personal problems interest me more. I think they're unchanging. . . . Topical stuff is old news in a little while. It was an amusing comment at the time. But if you get into personal relationships . . . and less ephemeral matters, it won't be dated."

Allen, the would-be comic, studied Sahl's work from a performance rather than a content standpoint. "It's not the political commentary that is important, but the way Sahl lays his jokes down. He does it with such guile, such energy. He's my favorite performer," Allen said in 1977.

Sahl created a hipper audience for stand-up comedy, and it was to that audience—urban, sophisticated, politically aware—that Allen spoke, moving the mother-in-law school of comedy from the Catskills to clubs in Greenwich Village. Using Sahl as a model, Allen himself excelled in timing, though his rhythm is slower than Sahl's, more evenly paced. And like Sahl as well, his voice often drips with scorching irony and sarcasm. But apart from these stylistic similarities, and the fact that both are nervous, big-city Jews, and therefore outsiders in gentile America, the two have little in common. With politics as his focus, Sahl is an essentially impersonal comedian, while Allen takes himself as his subject and is among the most personal and self-referential of comic performers. Sahl's evident neuroticism, reflected in the compulsive aspects of his style—his chain smoking, the rat-tat-tat speed of his patter—never becomes a part of his act as it does with Allen. Never calling attention to the obvious fact that he's a nervous wreck, or playing off his nervousness for comic effect, Sahl concentrates on attacking what's wrong in the world rather than what's wrong with himself.

In both the manner and the matter of his comedy, Allen is closer to his other idol, Bob Hope, than to his *landsman* Mort Sahl. Yet what could Woody and Bob have in common? Hope is an Establishment gentile, with no ethnic traces in voice or manner or appearance. Despite his famous ski nose, he is a handsome man, in a quite conventional way; there is nothing intrinsically comic about his face or physique. He looks like what he is: an arch-conservative Republican. Also unlike Woody the Schlepp, Hope moves well. In the musical numbers with Bing Crosby in their series of *Road* movies, Hope is the more agile dancer; he is the more athletic and graceful, despite his heavier frame. There is nothing about Hope then that in any obvious way tags him as an outsider or as a comic figure, and so his character is a wholly manufactured product, whereas Allen's persona developed naturally from the comic possibilities of his appearance and ethnic background. "Hope was the guy next door," Allen has said, "the man from the electric company. You really believed him. He was not a clown in the sense of Chaplin or Keaton. . . . He was much more real than Groucho."

Yet in the character he created, out of whole cloth as

it were, Hope, like   Allen after him, plays an inveterate womanizer, a coward, a braggart, a fall guy forever getting swindled by sharpshooters and landing in scrapes, in often exotic locales, yet forever calling upon a native shrewdness to free him. Like   Allen, Hope plays a loser who ends up being a winner; though he's the perennial comic patsy, he is often fantastically lucky. He's a hayseed who falls into wonderful adventures, encountering a series of beautiful and usually designing women along the route. Though he is often duped, victimized, taken advantage of, played for a sucker, Hope gets even by the sting of his wit. He is a supreme put-down artist—a wicked man with an insult.

On film Hope's insolence is always held in check; but as a master of ceremonies (on the Academy Awards shows, for instance) he makes no attempt to conceal the pleasure he takes in his comic assaults. He is so self-assured that he usually knows when to stop (unlike a Don Rickles), though there are moments when a genuine nastiness shoots through the comedy, and our laughter freezes. Woody can be brash and snotty too, of course, as he takes potshots at people and things he can't stand. But Woody's aggressiveness has to break through his schle-miel façade, whereas Hope's springs in a more direct way from his persona.

In May 1979 Bob Hope was the guest of honor at a benefit for the Film Society of Lincoln Center. For the occasion,   Allen selected and (along with Dick Cavett) narrated a seventy-minute compilation of clips from Hope's movies, which he called "My Favorite Comedian." Unlike   Allen's , Hope's films have never been taken seriously, and Woody wanted to rescue them from the critical doldrums as well as to point out why he has always admired Hope. "Hope's bantering style—the fantastic ad-lib style, the verbal interplay—reached a point of graceful spontaneity rarely equaled in films," Allen says, during his voice-over narration. "The lightness is everything. The puns, the asides, the fast one-liners, the great quips that appear throughout his work, are quick, bright, and delivered very lightly." Dick Cavett mentions Hope's superb articulation, which enables him to speak rapidly, piling joke upon joke in a dizzying comic rhythm. The two commentators point out recurrent themes and character traits in Hope's movies. "A constant ploy is Hope pretending to be somebody he's not," Allen says. "He is always vain, a womanizer, a coward's coward, but always brilliant," Allen notes, sounding as if he is describing his own persona. "He's the superb brash imposter," Cavett says, and cites Hope's "immaculate playing of comic panic" when he's caught in one of his acts.

Allen concludes the tribute with footage from a film of his own, *Love and Death*—a scene at a ball where his sword gooses a Russian aristocrat, and where he makes a date with a ravishing countess. "This excerpt from *Love and Death* is not an imitation," Allen points out, "but an influence. It appears throughout my work, a pale reflection [of Hope] but I'm in there trying."

While he has always claimed a close kinship with stand-up comics like Hope and Sahl, seeing his own work as growing directly out of theirs, Allen has been reluctant to have his comedy measured against other comic traditions, particularly that of the silent clowns. "I don't want my pictures to be compared with Keaton or Chaplin," he said in 1975. "You can't compare. I'm working forty years later. I'm a product of TV and psychoanalysis." Allen is of course a talking clown, not a mime; he has no great gifts as a physical comedian, and so the central impulse of his work—his quick verbal wit—is vastly different from that of silent comedy. But there are routines throughout his movies that recall the comic world of Chaplin, Keaton, and Lloyd: Woody performing a fey Chaplinesque dance in *Bananas;* getting ready for a date and then going out the door without his pants on, trying to play the cello in a marching band, and hobbling to keep up with a chain gang on bikes, in *Take the Money and Run*; making a shambles of a first date, overturning chairs and falling against collapsing bookshelves, in *Play It Again, Sam*; marching out of step with other soldiers during combat training, in *Bananas* and *Love and Death*; turned into a human cannonball in *Love and Death*; moving like a robot, attempting to fly, and hanging perilously from the window of a futuristic skyscraper in *Sleeper.* Guns explode in his hands, chairs crumble at his touch: Woody is victimized by objects, and he's out of step with his environment.

Although Allen's images of comic mischance get their laughs, they have a studied, self-conscious quality, as though he is including them for a change of pace, as a respite between verbal riffs. Compare any of his physical gags to the opening monologue in *Annie Hall,* where he stands still and looks directly into the camera. Here he is on home ground, in the comic arena in which he is the contemporary master, and he takes charge with an authority that he never has when he's doing mime.

A scene in *Sleeper* in which he makes an escape by climbing down a rope indicates his distance from the slapstick tradition. Any of the silent comics would have turned the moment into a miniature ballet, with man and rope engaging in a dance of opposing wills. In the world of silent comedy, things are as animated as people, and the rope would have a personality of its own—stubborn, combative, tricky.   Allen doesn't build the moment into an image of physical grace and control masquerading as comic ineptitude, or of comic exasperation leading to victory. It is no more than a perfunctory interlude—and we don't even see its outcome, Woody finally landing on the ground after battling with the rope. The silent comics insisted on performing their own stunts, whereas Woody dangling in midair from that rope looks as if he's faking it against a studio backdrop.

"When Chaplin and Keaton were making films, the world was very physical," Allen said, in 1977, at the time that *Annie Hall* was released, and he was being hailed as the finest comic film maker since Chaplin. "Now things are electronic, not so physically oriented. The conflicts have moved from the exterior to the interior. . . . The playing area has moved from outside to inside. We have to find good ways of dealing with this in comedy." Allen's interior, mental comedy—a product of the age he lives in, the age of "TV and psychoanalysis" —reverses the world view of the silent comedians. Concentrating on the inner rather than the outer man and focusing on talk rather than action, it nonetheless contains echoes of their work.

Not surprisingly, Chaplin is Allen's favorite. "I like Chaplin better than Keaton," he has said. "Chaplin took risks. And frequently those risks didn't come off; and he came out as pompous, maudlin, and embarrassing." One of those risks, *City Lights,* is Allen's favorite film comedy, because of its blend of laughs and pathos. Using Chaplin as model and inspiration, Allen in his own way has tried to extend the possibilities of comedy, mixing satire with sentiment, and cutting through comic detachment by appealing to audience empathy. He has tried to find a contemporary equivalent for the romantic and lyrical strain that runs through Chaplin's work. But of course his own style is quite different from Chaplin's, and the specifically Chaplinesque element in his work is fleeting: a scene in *Bananas*—a deliberate steal from *Modern Times*—where Woody tests some newfangled equipment that goes haywire; an extended sequence in *Take the Money and Run*—shades of *Monsieur Verdoux*—where Woody tries but fails to kill a woman who's blackmailing him. The last scene in *Manhattan* recalls the ending of *City Lights,* where the formerly blind girl for the first time sees the tramp and recognizes him as her savior. In the last shot, Chaplin, face front, registers a mixture of feelings—love, uncertainty, rejection, loss, wonder, puzzlement, transcendence, in an image that has become one of the most famous in the history of films, an image that is a kind of summary of Chaplin's magical presence as the tramp. In the way the shot is set up for the camera, as well as in its dramatic context, the ending in *Manhattan* evokes some of the pathos of *City Lights,* Woody's expression, like Chaplin's, containing a wonderful, busy mingling of emotions. In desperation, he has come to his former teen-age girl friend, to ask her to stay with him. She tells him to wait, to have a little trust in people, and he looks at her, in the film's final, lingering close-up, with appreciation and bemusement, and also a little wonder: the student has become the teacher, the pupil is wiser than her instructor. It's a marvelous moment, Woody transfixed, moved, hurting, stopped in his tracks. Maybe, that last shot suggests, there's happiness yet for his hapless, embattled character; maybe he has finally broken through the compulsive sexual circle in which he's been entrapped.

Like Chaplin, Woody is small. But in the way they dress, and in how they use their bodies, they are altogether different. Woody dresses to conceal his body, while

Chaplin's costume calls attention to his. His costume is outside of time, or of any specific reality; the tramp, while intensely human, is not quite human in any immediately recognizable way. In appearance he's a creature of the theater rather than one drawn from life. Being of no particular time and place, he belongs to all time; being no age's exact contemporary, he belongs to the ages. Woody dresses in a deliberately nondescript but contemporary style which, unlike Chaplin's getup, makes him look like a real person, absolutely nothing out of the ordinary. Chaplin speaks eloquently with his body; Woody is mostly mute with his. Chaplin uses his smallness for comic contrast, setting up the tramp against burly authority figures, like the huge cop who terrorizes him in film after film. The tramp's stature becomes an emblem of his outsider status, and his being alone in the world. Woody rarely uses his physique for anything more than easy laughs—his body doesn't become a meaningful symbol the way Chaplin's does.

"I could probably deliver lines better than Chaplin can, because I don't think he talks very well," Allen said in an interview in 1970. "But I would like to develop into a better physical comedian," he added, almost as an afterthought. "I think I have the instincts, but not the grace to do it." In the decades since the statement, however, Allen has worked only sporadically on using his body as a comic instrument.

Penelope Gilliatt has called Woody Allen a Jewish Buster Keaton, and you can see what she means. Buster is the most resourceful and logical ot all the great comedians. Though he is confronted by a world that keeps tricking him, changing the rules when he isn't looking, and that tries to crush him, he remains unfazed. In a famous sequence in *Sherlock, Jr.,* Buster walks into the action of a movie that is being shown at the theater where he is a projectionist. Common-sensical Keaton assumes of course that the world on film will obey natural laws, only to find himself in the middle of a landscape where, through the magic of film editing, time and place are in constant flux. Buster sits on a tree stump, only to have the setting change to a snow-covered field. He sees a river and dives into it, but between the moment of his dive and his entry into the water, the scenery shifts once again, through a flick of the editor's scissors. Seemingly unconcerned about either the immediate past or the immediate future, Buster meets each baffling transformation patiently and resourcefully. Woody's world is often equally unfriendly. He too is thrown into environments that refuse to cooperate with him and that answer his sweet reasonableness with potentially annihilating illogic.

Yet Woody confronts reversals and sudden catastrophes with an aplomb that recalls the great Keaton's. In his own way, underneath his show of helplessness, he is as cool and as sane as the Great Stone Face. (Like Bob Hope and of course unlike Buster, he often talks himself out of jams, meeting the unexpected with a verbal skill that parallels Buster's physical adaptability.) Woody meets misfortune with a face that is often as blank as Keaton's. Right beneath Buster's implacable façade, emerging once in a while in almost subliminal flashes, is the look of a man in pain, the look of a man about to crack (and who, in real life, did). Woody's comic mask—his silly face—isn't as deeply mysterious as Keaton's, but it too contains dark possibilities. For both him and Keaton, as for all great comics, comedy encompasses at least a hint of tragedy.

Woody's old-fashioned, horn-rimmed glasses, like Harold Lloyd's, brand him as an outsider, a potential patsy. Making them look cowardly and a little absent-minded, their glasses are an invitation to bullies and sadists. The nice guys as comic dupes, sweet-natured and gullible, Woody and Harold are always in hot water. Being a silent clown, Lloyd saves himself through physical daring, scaling a department store, unforgettably, at the climax of *Safety Last*, for example, while Woody escapes through his gift of gab. Though Woody is eminently sane while pretending to be nuts, Lloyd is so deeply normal that he can't even play at being crazy. He is the most regular of all the great screen comics, a clean-cut go-getter who aspired to if he didn't always attain all the trappings of the American dream. In appearance and character, he is a quintessential WASP; and when he added a voice to his persona, he sounded like James Stewart, as he delivered quips in a flat, Middle American drawl.

When Lloyd, Chaplin, and Keaton spoke, their comedy was less expressive. As Chaplin especially realized, sound was a threat to the kind of comic worlds they had created (except for the garbled nonsense song at the end of *Modern Times*, Chaplin didn't speak on screen until 1940, in *The Great Dictator*). But the comedians who dominated the early years of talking pictures absolutely required voices. Groucho, Mae West, and W. C. Fields had voices perfectly pitched for comic attack. Snarling and biting, with their stiletto sharpness and their reserves of irony, all these famous voices were ideally inflected for insult and innuendo. Marxian comedy—Groucho's rapid-fire delivery, Chico's accented gibberish, even Harpo's silence, which played off against his brothers' compulsive stream of words, and which was broken by his beeping horn and his harp—is unthinkable without sound.

Compared to the great, stabbing comic voices of early sound movies, Woody's lacks edge. It's soft and light and scarred with a deep regional accent. But Woody is a slyer put-down artist precisely because his delivery isn't as assured or as obviously cagey as those of the vocal stylists of the thirties. An insult hurled out of Woody's thin, meek voice is more startling than one that issues from Groucho's sneer or Fields's growl.

In spirit and in his particular gifts as a comedian Woody is closer to the first great clowns of talking pictures, the Marxes, than he is to any of his nonspeaking forebears. Like the Marx Brothers, his is a comedy of verbal twists and turns, of primarily mental rather than physical acrobatics. It's comedy that delights in agile wordplay, as it creates a series of verbal cartoons. Like the Marx comedies, Allen's work ripples with puns, nonsequiturs, mock epigrams, verbal riffs where language sails off into surrealist flights of fancy. Like Groucho, Allen is an ace verbal strategist who overturns language, pummeling and kicking and stretching it in order to impede communication. Juggling language is for Allen, as for Groucho, a form of self-defense, a powerful weapon that is a way of calling attention to everyone else's stupidity. A wielder of words, Allen, like Groucho, uses language to keep the world at bay.

In some ways Woody Allen is the Marx Brothers rolled into one. He has some of Groucho's sass, his ready, lethal wit and leering sexuality, some of Harpo's childlike sweetness, Chico's adolescent mischievousness, and (yes) Zeppo's leading-man appeal. Like the three clownish Marxes, he both inherits and creates chaos wherever he goes. But unlike them, Woody for the most part goes it alone. Groucho needs a dupe or a partner in comic crime, whereas Woody needs only himself. He plays off his own craziness, whereas the Marxes stir up everybody else's and, unlike Woody, don't want to take the trouble to think about themselves. There is no equivalent in Allen's movies of Margaret Dumont, that imperially sedate, endlessly patient and trusting Mount Everest of a woman whose mere presence provides the brothers with their ripest target. Dumont's airy propriety is the field against which the Marxian madness rebounds and collides —she's the perfect foil for Groucho's smirking rudeness, Harpo's and Chico's childlike naughtiness.

The Marxes set out to wreck wherever they are, while Woody falls into trouble or stirs havoc inadvertently. Unlike Allen, Groucho is a devilish emcee, an aggressive maker of mayhem who takes delight in dismantling whatever environment chance and luck have thrown him into. Whether he's president of a college or of a mythic, war-torn country, whether he's masquerading as a doctor or an opera impressario or a noted explorer, he barrels his way through, producing an uproar with the collusion of his dotty brothers. He's the lord of misrule, forever one-upping the enemy with his steady stream of words, his chop-logic, his mockery of politeness and social convention: Never give a sucker an even break is Groucho's motto as well as W. C. Fields's.

Allen has never quite had the anarchic, freewheeling style of the Marxes. Perhaps because one part of him has always wanted to be an insider, he has never pierced social convention with as devil-may-care an attitude; and he has a romantic, even a sentimental streak that is entirely missing from Groucho's and Chico's characters (though not Harpo's). Groucho especially didn't have a kind bone in his body. Misanthrope and misogynist, he was as merciless in his comic assaults as W. C. Fields. Allen may often treat women like sex objects, the way the Marxes do, but he is also a romantic who wants to fall in love. Diane Keaton, after all, is a real person, not a sex symbol or, like the majestic Dumont, an object of derision.

The Marxes do and say things which we in the real world do not dare to. Their freedom from social restraints, their epic rudeness and vulgarity, provide a vicarious release for our own aggressive instincts. Their antisocial comedy plays on audience fantasies of being violent, cruel, disreputable, low-down—of letting go. Although his comedies (especially his early ones) flirt with anarchy,　Allen really likes and needs order. His comedies have points to make, whereas Marxian farce isn't meant to be interpreted.

Like the Marxes,　Allen creates comedies that are a sequence of sketches that take off, typically, from a glaring contrast between character and setting. The Marx Brothers on a college campus, in *Horsefeathers,* or involved in high-level politics, in *Duck Soup,* make as much sense as Woody playing a bank robber or leading a South American revolution. In *Bananas,* the most Marxian of his comedies (the title strikes a playful echo of *The Coconuts,* and the political shenanigans recall *Duck Soup*), Woody confounds his story at every turn. Like his forebears, he is set on tearing up his story line, ripping it apart with constant invasions of visual and verbal gags.

Combining the verbal anarchy of the Marxes with overtones of Chaplinesque romanticism,　Allen's comedy is in some ways a throwback, a return to earlier comic traditions. But except for his indebtedness to Bob Hope, he found very little to emulate in movie comedy since the last Marx Brothers farces in the forties. What happened to American film comedy in the approximately two decades prior to　Allen's debut?

In the fifties and sixties, the movies produced no

major comic stylists or traditions. The best work was being done on television and in cabaret, and perhaps because theirs was a comedy of skits, none of the major performers in either medium tried to adapt his work to the requirements of full-length movie narratives. The most popular (or at least the most visible) movie comic of the fifties was Jerry Lewis, adored by the French but among American critics as much a dirty word as Doris Day. Lewis played the perpetual adolescent clown with a bleeding heart. Goofy, adenoidal, both victim and architect of chaos, and girl crazy, Lewis was at heart a burlesque comedian—his style was broad and pushy, and he had none of the ease of great farce performers like the Marxes. Well aware of Lewis's low critical standing, and conscious too of the echoes of Lewis in his own work, Allen has been generous in his comments about him. He appreciates Lewis as a *landsman,* a Jewish boy who made good, a Borscht-belt comic with whom he shares close cultural and ethnic ties.

Like Jerry, Allen has a little-boy-lost winsomeness that arouses maternal and often sexual sparks among female fans. Both comics are physically awkward, ugly-handsome schlemiels whose loser image is mixed with hefty doses of self-congratulation. Jerry is clearly as neurotic as Woody—as much of a worrier, as self-absorbed, as unable to relax—yet he doesn't use his evident maladjustment for a self-reflective kind of comedy, and as a result his work isn't as probing as Allen's. He plays his *mishegoss* merely for silliness. Lewis apparently can do nothing in moderation—his sentimentality is as garish and jittery as his clowning, so that finally not only his character but the quality of his work as well seems adolescent.

Yet like Allen, Lewis has always been very serious

about what he does. For years he offered a course in film making at The University of Southern California and then published a book, *The Total Filmmaker,* based on his lectures. Whatever one may think about the level of humor in films of Lewis's like *The Bellboy, Ladies' Man, The Errand Boy, The Patsy,* and *The Nutty Professor,* they are the work of someone who knows something— who knows in fact a good deal—about how to create images on a screen. Unlike the Marxes, and very much like  Allen, Lewis cares what his comedies look like.

Widely hailed as the film maker who rescued movie comedy from a dry period of almost two decades, as the first writer-director of movie comedy since Preston Sturges with a distinct sensibility, Woody Allen is the undisputed comic king of the seventies. But where is the competition?

Mel Brooks is often cited along with  Allen as a major comic film maker of the seventies whose work has helped to revive a languishing American genre. Certainly there are similarities between Brooks's comedy and Allen's , similarities that reflect their early training as part of Sid Caesar's comic committees, their passionate love of movies, and their New York Jewishness. But Brooks, unlike  Allen, seems to be almost exclusively a parodist. His range, so far at least, has been remarkably narrow. *Blazing Saddles,* his most popular film, is a spoof of Westerns; *High Anxiety* takes off on Hitchcock; the sources of *Silent Movie* and *Young Frankenstein* are indicated clearly enough in their titles. Though earlier work of his like *The Producers* and *The Twelve Chairs* suggests that he might try other kinds of comedy in the future, he has made his mark as a film maker whose inspiration is other movies. In Allen's work, "the movies" are only one of a multitude of cultural references movies" are only one of a multitude of cultural references both high and low, both academic and popular, whereas Brooks seems permanently stuck at the Saturday matinees he attended as a child. Locked into a comic evocation of Hollywood's golden age, his work seems out of touch and in the end trivial. Movies about movies, his spoofs are certainly funny in places, but the laughter doesn't ring with the social and psychological overtones of Allen's comedies about himself.

Unlike Brooks, who makes entire films as parodies of popular genres,   Allen uses quotes from other movies only fleetingly, catching disparate movie images on the wing. At the beginning of *Play It Again, Sam,* Woody (playing a film critic) sits in a theater watching *Casablanca.* He's in a stupor, wide-eyed with wonder and admiration, transfixed by the images on the screen—it's a charming moment that presents him as a genuine buff. His comedies always have included tributes to and parodies of many kinds of movies. *What's Up, Tiger Lily?* sends up James Bond thrillers. *Take the Money and Run* takes off on more arcane styles—the biographical gangster dramas of the thirties, with their sober narration and documentary pose, as well as the spontaneous interview style of *cinéma vérité.* Along with overtones of Marxian comedy in *Bananas* are references to *Battleship Potemkin* and to dream imagery in the work of Ingmar Bergman. *Everything You Always Wanted To Know About Sex* is a surreal sendup of a potpourri of genres, from haunted-house thrillers and domestic triangle melodramas to science fiction journeys and dramas of modern angst in the Antonioni style. *Sleeper* kids futuristic science fiction extravaganzas, while *Love and Death* mocks the overblown style of the Hollywood epic, with further quotes from Eisenstein. And the noncomic *Interiors* is palpably

Examining the face that launched a thousand quips, in *Take the Money and Run* (1969).

Woody Allen as a convict? Comic incongruity, in *Take the Money and Run*.

Losing control: comic chaos, in *Bananas* (1971).

Two sides of Woody: playing for laughs (above) and playing for pathos (with Diane Keaton and Tony Roberts), in *Play It Again, Sam* (1972).

The Fool (Allen) bewitched by eros: attacking the Queen (Lynn Redgrave) in *Everything You Always Wanted to Know About Sex\* (\*but were afraid to ask)* (1972).

Woody as intrepid comic hero in a surreal world: saving Diane Keaton (above), gathering dinner, in *Sleeper* (1973).

Woody playing with images of death (above), about to be shot out of a cannon and love, courting Diane Keaton, in *Love and Death* (1975).

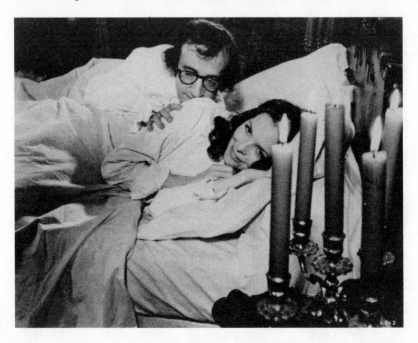

Sharing the frame, on screen (above), absorbed by a kooky new friend Annie Hall (Diane Keaton), and on the set, laughing at someone else's joke (with Helen Ludlam, Keaton, and Colleen Dewhurst). *Annie Hall* (1977).

In *The Front* (1976), directed by Martin Ritt, Allen's generosity to co-player Zero Mostel is evident in this still.

Ersatz Ingmar Bergman: pretentious mise-en-scène in *Interiors* (1978), with Keaton, Kristin Griffith, and Mary Beth Hurt.

Woody and Diane take the air on the far East Side of *Manhattan* (1979), Allen's loving tribute to his hometown. Gordon Willis' seductive chiaroscuro photography transforms the Big Apple into an urban wonderland.

A more sober Woody Allen (above) dominates *Stardust Memories* (1980) while
with a touch of nostalgia reminders of Woody embroiled in moments of comic
frustration (as in the scene below) are inserted throughout the film.

Who are these world-famous figures? The one in the middle is *Zelig* (1983), human chameleon.

Clothes make the man: Allen's biggest schlemiel of the eighties, *Broadway Danny Rose* (1984).

Who is the interloper? A movie fan (Mia Farrow, in dark hat) enters one of her favorite movies, "The Purple Rose of Cairo," unnerving its cast and disrupting narrative momentum (1985).

Another Allen version of *Three Sisters*. Centered Hannah (Mia Farrow) and neurotic Holly (Dianne Wiest) surround Lee (Barbara Hershey), who shares qualities of each. The calculated contrasts in *Hannah and Her Sisters* (1986) are typical of Allen's group portraits of the eighties.

Allen in another unmasked moment: receiving bad news in *Hannah and Her Sisters*.

On the job: Allen lines up a shot with his cinematographer Carlo Di Palma (second from right), for *Radio Days* (1987).

Half of the cast for *Radio Days*: the family of avid radio listeners. The "other" cast is the radio stars the family hears but never sees.

The directors of *New York Stories* (1989) in front of New York's Plaza Hotel. Allen is bracketed by Francis Coppola (left) and Martin Scorsese.

Allen as the Oedipus wreck, Sheldon Mills, of "Oedipus Wrecks" in *New York Stories,* overpowered as usual by his mother (Mae Questel).

A misdemeanor in *Crimes and Misdemeanors* (1989): Allen's courtship of Mia has an unhappy ending.

A crime in *Crimes and Misdemeanors*: despite appearances here, Judah Rosenthal (Martin Landau) will arrange to have his mistress (Anjelica Huston) killed.

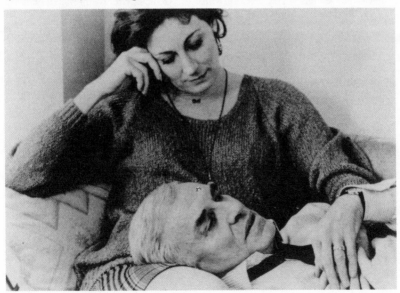

Woody Allen clearly has the attention of his actors, Mia Farrow and Alec Baldwin, as they prepare for a scene in *Alice* (1990). Is there something else besides concentration in Farrow's penetrating gaze?

A study in contrasts: a waif (Mia Farrow) and a prostitute (Lily Tomlin), adrift in the studio-bound dream world Woody Allen created for *Shadows and Fog* (1992).

The end of the road, on screen and off: The split between Judy and Gabe Roth (Mia Farrow and Woody Allen) is apparent in this shot from *Husbands and Wives* (1992).

A scene in a restaurant, a recurrent setting in Woody Allen's stories from Manhattan. But in this shot from *Manhattan Murder Mystery* (1993), Diane Keaton, Alan Alda, Anjelica Huston, and Woody Allen don't seem to be having much fun. Neither is the audience.

"Don't speak!" an actress (Dianne Wiest), transfixed by her own grandeur, commands a bedazzled playwright (John Cusack), in this scene from *Bullets over Broadway* (1994).

In *Mighty Aphrodite* (1995), Kevin (Michael Rapaport), like the audience, is enchanted by Linda (Mira Sorvino). In adding a touch of class to her character, a porn-star prostitute, Sorvino outwits sexual stereotyping.

In *Everyone Says I Love You* (1996), his unlikely musical, Woody Allen sets a big production number in an unlikely setting, the Fifth Avenue emporium of jeweler Harry Winston.

The great Judy Davis, coming apart as only she can, while the object of her rage, Harry Block (Woody Allen), tries to reason with her, in *Deconstructing Harry* (1997), Allen's fiercest comedy of the decade.

Is this a posed or a candid shot of Woody Allen and "the notorious Soon-Yi" in Barbara Kopple's ambivalent documentary, *Wild Man Blues* (1998)?

Notice the panoramic compositions in *Celebrity* (1998), Woody Allen's underrated chronicle of a society bitten by fame. On the top: a spoiled movie star (Leonardo DiCaprio) is surrounded by photographers and an anxious journalist (Kenneth Branagh, right, holding envelope); on the bottom, a supermodel (Charlize Theron) is on display.

Hattie (Samantha Morton), a mute, eloquently expresses her irritation with jazz artist Emmet Ray (Sean Penn), her egoistic lover more attentive to his guitar than to her, in *Sweet and Lowdown* (1999).

Would you trust these guys to rob a bank? Woody Allen, Michael Rapaport, Jon Lovitz, and Tony Darrow plot in plain sight in *Small Time Crooks* (2000).

a film in the Bergman style, a family passion play on the order of *Face to Face* and *Persona.*

Tossing these references to past movies through his comic blender adds to Allen's heavily allusive style. But the parody is merely an aside— Allen striking comic sparks in his response to other people's work—rather than, as it often is for Brooks, an end in itself: the point of his comedy. Brooks is an archivist, spinning movie-based fantasies that refer to other movies more than to life. He scores off a variety of movie genres, sometimes striking genuine comic gold, as in isolated moments in *Blazing Saddles* and *Young Frankenstein,* particularly, but more often his work seems derivative—a distinctly secondary kind of humor.

Brooks's methods and Allen's are similar in ways that go beyond their delight in kidding antediluvian movie conventions. Like most comedians filling out full-length narratives, both work piecemeal, with fitful inspiration and spotty results. They begin with an initial comic premise or idea—a takeoff on Western movie clichés, the notion of Woody as a bank robber—and then build their films as variations on a sustaining theme. Because Brooks is wilder than Allen, as both a personality and a director, his comedies are more hit-and-miss. Brooks plainly doesn't know when enough is not only enough but far too much. The most noticeable act of self-destruction in his work is the finale of *Blazing Saddles,* where actors from the sound stage next door burst onto the set of his film to mingle with his cowboys and Indians in a frenzied free-for-all that is meant to show up the artifice of moviemaking but that ends up merely dismantling the movie. The chaos of the ending looks like the desperate maneuver of a film maker who doesn't know how to get off the stage.

Brooks doesn't have  Allen's self-censorship or basic good judgment; his comedy is sometimes based in fact on flaunting his *bad* judgment, on elevating messiness and bad taste to aesthetic criteria. So far Brooks hasn't been able to duplicate on film the comic inspiration apparent in his recordings starring the Thousand-Year-Old Man. Rich in *Yiddishkeit,* overflowing with droll, mocking Jewish wit, this is a skillful piece of character acting, in addition to being a gold mine of one-liners. On film, though, Brooks is lackluster. Unlike  Allen, who's not much of an actor but who is masterful at playing the character he's created, Brooks doesn't seem to have a self to play; he's a curiously featureless movie actor, unable even to capitalize on his lopsided looks. It's no accident that he hasn't cast himself in his best work. Zero Mostel and Gene Wilder star in *The Producers,* and Wilder appears as well in *Blazing Saddles* and *Young Frankenstein.* Wilder, who also in a sense "stood in" for Woody in the romance with the sheep episode in *Everything You Always Wanted To Know About Sex,* is a true comic actor rather than a comedian who transports a ready-made personality from film to film. As opposed to Brooks's hyper, blasting style, Wilder's is understated—he gives his characters suggestions of a private, inner life. You feel that he could turn serious at any moment, and the tension between comic high jinks and incipient drama lends his work a layered quality that Mel's simply doesn't have.

For all his shortcomings, however, there is no question that Brooks is a comedian who makes films rather than a comedian who simply uses film as a vehicle for his jokes. In the past decade there is no one else except Allen  who has compiled a comparable record. Sporadically, since the late sixties, sharp social satires like Mike Nichols's *Carnal Knowledge* or Paul Mazursky's *Bob and*

*Carol and Ted and Alice* announced a director with a fresh comic approach. But Nichols seems to have abandoned movies for the stage and was determined at any rate not to be typecast as a mere comedy director. And Mazursky has deserted the wry comedy-of-manners style that was so appealing in *Bob and Carol* to make high-minded social commentary like the hollow, preening *An Unmarried Woman*. At the end of the seventies, with *Animal House* and its flood of imitators, the wacky satire purveyed on television's "Saturday Night Live" has begun to make an impact on movie comedy; but it's unlikely that this anything-goes, revue-sketch style will lead either to a true renaissance of film comedy or a long-lived trend. Practically on their own, then, Brooks and Allen have kept the comic muse alive at the movies throughout the seventies.

Having absorbed influences from a variety of sources, Allen has begun, now that he is a clearly Establishment figure—a comic landmark—to exert some influence of his own. Comedies are beginning to emerge which are unmistakably in the Allen style. Two 1980 offerings, one a film, the other a play, and both written by collaborators and friends of Allen's are distinctly Allenesque. *Simon,* written and directed by Marshall Brickman (who worked with Allen on the screenplays of *Sleeper, Annie Hall,* and *Manhattan*), is a far-out comedy in which a schlemiel hero, one of the world's natural victims, is thrown into a wild adventure. *Marie and Bruce,* a play written by Wallace Shawn, a member of the Allen gang at Elaine's, starred Louise Lasser, the ex–Mrs. Allen.

An untenured professor at Columbia, Simon is a visionary with a crackpot scheme for turning the planet into a spaceship and moving it to another solar system, when the day comes that we run out of food and water and air. Silly Simon, toying with cosmic destiny, becomes the hero of a brainstorm concocted by a think tank of high-powered lunatic scientists who call themselves the Institute for Advanced Concepts. They present Simon (who has been selected by computer—the voice of Louise Lasser—as the perfect dupe for their plan) as a visitor from another planet. They tell him that his mother was a spaceship and that he himself is a recipe, or perhaps a toaster. Under attack, as in Allen's comedies, is the insulated academic mind. Sounding off about other planets and spouting quotes from Wittgenstein, Simon is too immersed in the world of higher thought to be able to cope with the world as it is, and his transformation into an alien is a sly comment on his being out of it in the first place.

Like many of Allen's comedies as well, *Simon* is a power fantasy translated into broad comic terms. Escaping from the clutches of the Institute, Simon takes over a national broadcasting system, delivering to the nation his views on life and death and the future of the cosmos. Like one of Allen's schnooks, Simon is thus thrown into an outlandish situation where all his repressed fantasies of being able to change the course of history are realized with spectacular impact. Poor Simon, out-of-touch academic, victim of a fiendish brain trust, turns the tables on his victimizers—and ends up with the Nobel Peace Prize. Behind this mock apocalyptic comedy are echoes of Woody at the head of a banana-kingdom revolution, Woody the hero of a Brave New World, Woody attempting to rewrite history by assassinating Napoleon. Underneath the comic persona, then, of the meek, put-upon Jewish boy, all but strangled by his upbringing, is a hero and tyrant lying in wait—Brickman's burlesque, like many of Allen's, is a fantasy of Getting Even. *Simon* says, like   Allen, that the meek, the neurotic, and the Jewish shall inherit the earth.

Like Allen's  comedies, *Simon* has wide-ranging satiric targets. Besides academics, it takes swipes at cultists, scientists, and newscasters. It's a comedy of references and code words—of promiscuous name-dropping, in the Allen manner. The subjects attacked are both large—media manipulation of public opinion—and parochial—when the excited, power-crazed hero takes over the airwaves, constructing a World According to Simon, he outlaws giving children names such as Free, Muzak in elevators, and politicians in cone-shaped party hats.

Alan Arkin plays Simon with an edge of barely suppressed hysteria. His antic style suggests that the jokes could curdle at any moment and that comic distress could topple over into psychic collapse. His high-strung performance—the sense that he is playing for real—gives the movie a surprisingly mordant undertone.

If *Simon* recalls earlier Allen farces, Wallace Shawn's *Marie and Bruce* points to a later, darker style, though Shawn goes further than Allen had yet dared to in the direction of comic bitterness. The play is one long marital squabble between a slovenly, catatonic, overweight, terminally depressed housewife and her passive-aggressive husband, the two of them partnered in a perfectly poised sadomasochistic relationship. Hell is other people, Sartre said, and *Marie and Bruce* is determined to prove it.

Though Shawn's comic voice is shrill and hard to take, Woody Allen was a hovering presence throughout: in the scrawny husband's deceptively mild manner that is as lethal as it is self-protective; in the battle between a hysterical woman and a controlling, withdrawn man, which recalls Diane Keaton and    Allen in some of their films together; and in the appearance of Louise Lasser, Allen's    former co-star and former wife, television's Mary Hartman grown corpulent and pitching her neurotic comedy in a fierce, truly unsettling key that stifled all laughter. Lasser's presence in the play, and Shawn's association with the Allen entourage (he was the homunculus in *Manhattan* and a member of the brain trust in *Simon*) aroused speculation that *Marie and Bruce* was a dark, a pitch-black, comedy version of the short-lived, stormy Allen-Lasser marriage.

As he inherited traditions of nightclub humor and movie comedy, so    Allen stepped into another well-defined groove when he began to write comic essays for *The New Yorker*. Consciously, and with wonderful self-assurance, he began to stake his claim as the heir to a small but distinguished tradition in American letters, the comic sketches of writers such as Robert Benchley, James Thurber, and S. J. Perelman. In exquisitely crafted pieces these writers adopted a pose of comic complaint that was urbane, caustic, incisive—that was, in short, *The New Yorker*.

   As he surveys contemporary foolishness, Benchley is calmer and more genteel than Perelman. Benchley casts himself as a well-bred Connecticut WASP, standoffish, puzzled by the inconveniences and absurdities, the small, nagging discomforts, of modern life. Writing from the vantage point of an insider clucking in dismay at invasions of his privileged WASP domain, he regards all departures from the status quo as signs and portents of revolution. "Scientific research has disclosed the fact that the effect of harsh noises on the brain is more deleterious than that of drugs, and nowhere near so pleasant while it is happening," sniffs Benchley, the urbane grouch. And here he is, with typical elegance, about to launch a tirade against one of his pet peeves:

Nobody would like to see the Brotherhood of Man come to pass any more than I would, for I am not a very good fighter and even have difficulty holding my own in a battle of repartee. I am more the passive type, and I would be glad to have everybody else passive too.

But I am afraid that it can't be done. I am afraid that there are certain situations in which a man finds himself placed by chance where there is nothing left for him to do but hate his fellow man. It isn't that he wants to hate him, but certain chemical reactions take place in his system.

Take, for example, the case of a dining car . . .

Like Benchley, Perelman appears in his essays as a man of enviable and steadfast reasonableness variously perplexed and amused and enraged by an unending assortment of idiocies. Although he sometimes maintains Benchley's posture of lordly disapproval, he more often descends from imperial heights to enter into the fray, words a-flying. Perelman is an upstart and rascal who will take on anyone or anything, from dumb Hollywood movies to classic Russian novels, from Schrafft's to Dashiell Hammett to world affairs. Perelman recognizes no sacred cows.

He is at heart, like  Allen, an absurdist. As in the routines he constructed for Groucho Marx, Perelman delighted in undermining the process of communication. He made a mockery of logic and of rational discourse, and by exposing its clichés he could make any spoken or written style look ridiculous. Perelman's reductive strategy was to chop language up into clichés, nonsequiturs, outrageous puns, and to pile implausibility upon absurdity until his initial comic premise, his point of departure, was nowhere to be seen. Perelman's freewheeling, punning, parodistic style, and the thrust in many of his pieces toward pure fantastication, have certainly had a deep impact on Allen. Like Perelman, Allen is drawn to surreal farce in which he creates a comic world where the timeless and the narrowly topical clash in hilarious counterpoint, and where just about anything goes, no matter how far-out and farfetched, so long as it is good for a laugh. Here, for a taste, and with a premonition of Allen in the humor, is Perelman on one Mr. Saidy:

Mr. Saidy was a hyperthyroid Syrian leprechaun, and a man of extraordinarily diversified talents. He was an accomplished portrait painter in the academic tradition, and his bold, flashy canvases, some of which were stored in our stockroom, impressed me as being masterly. John Singer Sargent and Zuloaga, whom he plagiarized freely, might have felt otherwise, but since neither was in the habit of frequenting our stockroom, Mr. Saidy was pretty safe from recrimination. In addition to the painting, playing the zither, and carving peach pits into monkeys to grace his watch chain, he was an inventor. He had patented a pipe for feminine smokers that held cigarettes in a vertical position and a machine for extracting pebbles from gravel roofs.

And here he is again showering us with a cornucopia of absurd details:

Do you happen to know how many tassels a Restoration coxcomb wore at the knee? Or the kind of chafing dish a bunch of Skidmore girls would have used in a dormitory revel in 1911? Or the exact method of quarrying peat out of a bog at the time of the Irish Corn Laws? In fact, do you know anything at all that nobody else knows or, for that matter, gives a damn about? If you do, then sit tight, because one of these days you're going to Hollywood as a technical supervisor on a million-dollar movie.

You may be a bore to your own family, but you're worth your weight in piastres to the picture business.

Yes, Hollywood dearly loves a technical expert, however recondite or esoteric his field. It is a pretty picayune film that cannot afford at least one of them; sometimes they well-nigh outnumber the actors . . .

Some of Perelman's extravaganzas may seem like free-for-alls, charged by improvisatory fits, but Perelman, like Benchley—and like    Allen—is an immaculate writer. In his sketches the world may be turned inside out and upside down as it spirals headlong into utter and inspired chaos, but Perelman always keeps steady watch over his prose. He is in firm command of the lunacy he sets in motion.

Absorbing influences from many sources, Woody Allen's comedy is a patchwork quilt made up of pieces of Groucho, Bob Hope, Chaplin, Keaton, Perelman, Bergman, Jerry Lewis, Eisenstein, Sahl, and old Hollywood movies. Eclectic, allusive, imitative, his comedy is nonetheless the exclusive property of a funny-looking, freckled, lank-haired schlemiel as modern hero.

# 5

## The Jewish
## Connection

Y OU don't have to be Jewish to appreciate Woody Allen.
But it helps. For along with Bob Hope and Mort Sahl,
Chaplin and the Marx Brothers, Ingmar Bergman and
Sergei Eisenstein, Allen's inescapable Jewishness has
been a major influence in his work. As a Jewish comic, he
inherits a rich oral and literary tradition that runs from
the low-brow self-mockery and mother-in-law gags of
Borscht-belt jokesters to the complex modernist stories
and novels of a group of writers that includes Isaac
Bashevis Singer, Saul Bellow, Bernard Malamud, Philip
Roth, J. D. Salinger, Norman Mailer, and Joseph Heller.
Allen shares with all the Jewish humorists, from the
lowliest Catskill comic to the Bellow-Malamud-Roth
literary triumvirate, an ironic sense of self and the world,
and a joy in language.

The central link among the major works in this
literary and comedic tradition is the concept of the
schlemiel as hero. Allen's persona may well be the most
popular version of a comic type whose personality traits

are deeply embedded in Jewish culture. Isaac Singer's Gimpel the Fool, Bellow's Herzog, Malamud's Fidelman, Roth's Alexander Portnoy, and Heller's Yossarian are among the most famous literary schlemiels who, like Woody's character, are outsiders and victims, the butts of jests both local and cosmic. Mangled by their families, unlucky in love, they slide from one upset to another. Failure is their lot, ironic complaint their response. They are all brilliant talkers, spraying their enemies with a shower of words. Isolated by their "foolishness," they see life from a slightly crooked and decidedly idiosyncratic slant. Often saying or doing the unexpected, they have special insights. Like Lear's fool, they know more than anyone else, even if they sometimes present what they see in a deliberately cockeyed style, making us work hard to grasp the truth.

Swindled, duped, insulted, an outsider even in the close-knit *shtetl* where he lives, married to a whore who bears children that are not his, Singer's Gimpel is the prime schlemiel in the modern Jewish literary pantheon. Yet no matter how ill-treated he has been, Gimpel loves his wife, grieves at her early death, and continues to believe in the trustworthiness of others. His childlike innocence and his affirmation in the face of defeat ultimately transform him into a sainted character, a kind of local shaman who tells magical stories and who is able to confront his own death with a smile. Perhaps Gimpel isn't such a fool, after all?

Bellow's Herzog is a modern-day, big-city schlemiel, a brilliant man who's made a mess of his life. Twice-divorced, his early academic promise unfulfilled, the victim of his second wife's murderous rage, deceived by his best friend, duped by shyster lawyers and psychiatrists, Moses Herzog, professor at large, takes refuge in writing letters, wherein he communicates to friends and enemies, to intimates and strangers, to people from his present and his past, the wild tangle of feelings that has welled up within him. He is choked by his assorted grievances, but he gets through, surmounting the rotten luck that bedevils him with his stubborn romantic faith and his compulsively probing, alive intellect.

Malamud's Bronx-born Arthur Fidelman is an artist on the loose in Italy who keeps taking pratfalls in his doomed quest for control over his life and his work. His professional and erotic misadventures transform him into something of a madman-saint who tells stories drawn from his own private underworld. Experimenting with increasingly strange and abstract art forms, he becomes finally a nonartist—a craftsman in glass—who is a lover of both men and women.

Portnoy is the schlemiel not as a visionary, nor as an intellectual misfit, not as town scapegoat or marital victim, but as the compleat modern sexual neurotic, a nice Jewish boy who suffers from sex on the brain. With baroque erotic fantasies spinning in his head, he uses sex as a means of defiance and retaliation, a way of getting even with his overbearing mother and his constipated father.

Heller's schlemiel, Yossarian in *Catch-22*, is a sane man in an absurd world; he's the voice of reason calling out in the war-maddened wilderness. While everyone else goes in circles, Yossarian stands to the side, a latter-day Jeremiah cracking jokes in a doomsday epic. Though he seems to be a victim, in truth he plays a cooler game than any of the other soldiers and their officers, concealing his real wit and nerve beneath his fool's mask. Like most other schlemiels, Yossarian too meets a happy end, rowing out to sea, a free man at last.

These famous modern literary schlemiels—to whom Woody Allen is obviously a spiritual cousin—have in common then both their penchant for catastrophe and their ability to survive it. They are all comic antiheroes, bumblers and schleppers, who turn out to have wisdom and endurance. Always in hot water, at odds with the world, they may look like dumb clucks with no mazel, but they're shrewd. Whether divinely simple like Gimpel or terrifically neurotic like Portnoy, they use their appearance of being foolish or incompetent as a strategy for survival. All of them, like sly, knowing, ironic Woody, claim the last laugh.

Like Woody as well, the schlemiels of modern Jewish letters are wonderful performers who treat their lives as theater. They tell their own stories (most of them), speaking typically in a voice of Jewish comic complaint, cataloguing their *tsuris*—the history of injustice that trails them—with irony and bitterness. They are self-styled comedians whose subject is themselves. Like Woody, the Herzogs and the Portnoys of the modern Jewish novel have busy inner lives. They're compulsively analytical, self-absorbed, and self-conscious. They are intellectuals and philosophers whose minds are ablaze with lofty ideas, theories, and convictions while their bodies itch for women, and who are as victimized by their powerful emotions as they are by their abstract thoughts. Schlemiel comedy is thus a mingling of sex and philosophy, as the search for sex shares the stage with the quest for the meaning of life.

Fast talkers, they have at their command all the weapons of the stand-up comic. Their tirades are littered with one-liners, barbs, invective, self-mockery, stinging sarcasm. In love with language, and with their own wit,

Portnoy, Herzog, and Yossarian use words as attack and defense, as artillery and shelter. The busy swinging rhythm of their speech is the visible sign of their dynamic interior lives and their intellectual energy. Portnoy talks up a storm to his waiting, listening analyst; Herzog writes delirious, inflamed letters. At times they seem to be drowning in the steady rush of their invective. Roth and Bellow, in particular, write with an incantatory rhythm that recalls the energy and color of Yiddish, a wonderfully inflected language the sound and movement of which suggest torrential feelings.

The self-centeredness of the schlemiel heroes influences the form of the stories they star in. All of them—and this is certainly true of Allen's movies as well—are picaresques, made up of a series of mostly comic sketches at the center of which is the antihero's struggling, witty mind, his modern neurotic consciousness. Like Allen's movies, the novels and stories are extended monologues which advertise their hero's sensibility. Portnoy's bawdy, revved-up, self-consciously clever outpourings to his psychiatrist take on the beat of a marathon stand-up comedy routine:

> . . . if my father had only been my mother! and my mother my father! But what a mix-up of the sexes in our house! who should by rights be advancing on me, retreating—and who should be retreating, advancing! Who should be scolding, collapsing in helplessness, enfeebled by a tender heart! And who should be collapsing, instead scolding, correcting, reproving, criticizing, faultfinding without end! Filling the patriarchal vacuum! Oh, thank God! thank God! at least *he* had the cock and the balls! Pregnable (putting it mildly) as his masculinity was in this world of goyim with golden hair and silver tongues, between his legs (God bless my father!) he was constructed like

a man of consequence, two big healthy balls such as a king would be proud to put on display, and a shlong of magisterial length and girth.

Portnoy, like Woody in his films, is clearly installed as the master of ceremonies who supervises the order and content of the scenes, and whose sensibility permeates the air.

Fragmented and anecdotal, like Allen's movies, the picaresque schlemiel novels leap among the comic hero's memories and obsessions, gliding in and out of the present. Attempting an almost Joycean stream of consciousness as they give free play to their characters' embattled thoughts, novels like *Portnoy's Complaint* and *Herzog* seem as disordered as the fevered minds of their protagonists.

The typically divided, contradictory hero of the modern Jewish novel is a quicksilver compound of intellect and lust, rational skepticism and irrational fantasies. He is caught somewhere between the religious and social tradition in which he has been raised, and which he still clings to in part, and modern nihilism; escaping from the ghetto and a ghetto mentality, he is still in search of a place of his own—he's a man in solitary exile and yet he retains memories of the stable social structure that always has been the basis of traditional Jewish unity.

Portnoy, Fidelman, Neil Klugman (in *Goodbye, Columbus*), all want to escape from their families. Portnoy goes to Israel, Fidelman to Italy, Neil hopes that falling in love with a Jewish American Princess will lift him out of the Newark ghetto in which he lives. But their flights are not successful, and no matter how brash and modern and hedonistic they try to be, they are trailed by remnants of Jewish orthodoxy.

As in the paintings of Chagall and the parables of Kafka, a world of mysticism and the supernatural encloses the daily life of the characters, particularly in the work of Singer and Malamud, where the spirit world is made flesh and enters into the action to test the characters' faith. There are lingering mystical strains in the work of other major Jewish writers, Salinger and Bellow especially (less so in the more purely secular Roth), where characters, cut off from orthodox tradition, nevertheless are in search of meaning beyond the merely daily and temporal and physical. Hence, the great distrust of the body, the fear and titillation with which sex is regarded, in most of the contemporary Jewish stories. Sex is necessary, is joyous, troublesome, an eternal quest—but it is not enough, Bellow-Malamud-Roth sing, almost in unison. Yet intellect, the life of the mind, isn't sufficient either, especially when it is strictly academic and therefore abstracted from vital human concerns. Herzog, Professor of the Romantic Movement, is troubled by the nagging thought that his scholarly work is removed from the flow of contemporary life and thus fatally irrelevant.

A distrust of faith on the one hand and of "pure" intellect on the other courses through the work of these modernists, and what resistance they all have to the possibility that man is no more than his body. The quest shared by all the Jewish writers straddling the gulf between orthodox belief and heterodox defiance is to find some acceptable way for modern neurotic man to mingle with Chagall's angels.

Tossed back and forth between the aspirations of the intellect and the desires of the body, Jewish antiheroes make uneasy sensualists. They are all, these Portnoys and Herzogs (and Woodys), more at home with their thrusting, restless minds than with their hungry, persistent, bothersome bodies. Sex for them is distracting, unnerving, forbidden, at the same time that it is vital and exciting. Though they are often presented as funny-looking, women are attracted to them. (Like Woody says, speaking up for the modern schlemiel, he's basically a stud.) But they seem destined to be unlucky in love, perhaps because their sexuality has so strong an adolescent streak. On the one hand, their immature sexuality turns women into objects and appendages, and on the other, it tends to attract women of the smothering kind, women who want to gobble them up.

Outsiders to both the sustaining religious and social traditions in which they were raised, temperamentally alienated from the dominant WASP culture, the Herzogs and Portnoys of modern Jewish literature are men in the middle, wriggling painfully toward emotional freedom. Shadowed by the threat of psychic breakdown, they naturally make uneasy comic heroes, and their stories are modern comedy poised precariously on the rim of modern tragedy.

A great pitched battle is thus waged in contemporary Jewish letters between the writers and their Jewish identity, and between their defiant, isolated, intellectual protagonists and the indelible ethos of the part-nurturing, part-castrating Jewish community in which both the writers and their fictional alter egos grew up. Many of the writers, particularly Roth and Allen, have been accused, in their satires of American Jewish folkways, of Jewish anti-Semitism. Ambitious, upwardly mobile Jews intent on making it in mainstream America, they have been charged with sacrificing their heritage. But in attempting to deny or take flight from Jewish tradition, artists like Roth and Allen in fact continue to be passionately engaged with it, conducting an ongoing dialogue with

Jewishness as a state of mind and a way of life. Certainly there is ethnic hostility in their work, directed not only at Jews but even more fiercely at the dumb goyim. Here is Alexander Portnoy on the subject of Jewish parents:

> . . . What *was* it with these Jewish parents, *what,* that they were able to make us little Jewish boys believe ourselves to be princes on the one hand, unique as unicorns on the one hand, geniuses and brilliant like nobody has ever been brilliant and beautiful before in the history of childhood—saviors and sheer perfection on the one hand, and such bumbling, incompetent, thoughtless, helpless, selfish, evil little shits, little *ingrates,* on the other!
>
> . . . YOU FUCKING JEWISH MOTHERS ARE JUST TOO FUCKING MUCH TO BEAR! I have read Freud on Leonardo, Doctor, and pardon the hubris, but my fantasies exactly: this big smothering bird beating frantic wings about my face and mouth *so that I cannot even get my breath*. What do we want . . . ? *To be left alone*! If only for half an hour at a time! Stop already *hocking* us to be *good*! *hocking* us to be *nice*!

And here, with strong premonitions of Alvy Singer on the subject of Annie Hall and her family, is Portnoy on the *shiksa*:

> I am so awed that I am in a state of desire *beyond a hard-on*. My circumcised little dong is simply shriveled up with veneration. Maybe it's dread. How do they get so gorgeous, so healthy, so blond? My contempt for what they believe in is more than neutralized by my adoration of the way they look, the way they move and laugh and speak—the lives they must lead behind those *goyische* curtains! . . . O America! America! it may have been gold in the streets to my grandparents, it may have been a chicken in every pot to my father and mother, but to me, a child whose earliest movie memories are of Ann Rutherford and Alice Faye, America is a *shikse* nestling under your arm whispering love love love love love!

If Jews or the goyim are offended, so be it: comedy isn't supposed to be polite.

Like all good satirists, Roth and Allen sting; but like most satire, theirs contains a genuine attraction to the subjects under attack. Their jabs at Jewish manners bespeak affection, however grudging and slanted, and spring more from familiarity than animosity. Their attempt to come to terms with being Jewish in WASP America is an epic quest, not yet completed.

Allen's movie persona—sex-obsessed, witty, ironic, irreverent, plagued with ego problems, and struggling to find a place for himself—thus resembles the characters in the modern Jewish novel of manners. He seems at times to have stepped out of one of Malamud's short stories, recalling one of the author's solitary odd creatures who inhabit dim furnished rooms and engage behind closed doors in who knows what unnatural practices. Sometimes he's like one of Roth's high-strung young men rebelling against an aggressively middle-class upbringing. (Woody's parents, remember, like the *nouveau riche* Patimkim family in *Goodbye, Columbus,* believe above all in God and carpeting.) Like Roth's ambitious young heroes trying to escape the burdens of having grown up Jewish and middle-class, young Woody crossed the bridge from the provinces to the beckoning lights of Manhattan. Introspective, private, on guard, compulsively analytical, Woody, like a Bellow hero, lives deep within his mind.

No matter how far he may stray from home, Allen like Bellow, Malamud, and Roth is clearly thinking in Jewish. Jewishness—as a fact of life, a sensibility, a state of mind—is a crucial element in his image and in his comic themes. Like the major Jewish novelists, Allen is both a moralist and a fabulist, hurling his characters from the real world into a fantasy one, making the incredible

credible, bringing the otherworldly down to earth, and lifting the earthly into surreal orbit.

Allen's most popular theme—the ongoing battle of the sexes—is dramatized as a conflict between Jew and gentile. Like Alexander Portnoy, Allen stands before the otherness of the goyim with a mixture of awe and condescension; and like many Jewish romantics and lechers, he is drawn to *shiksas* whose pretty blond blandness represents both forbidden fruit and the incarnation of the American dream. The composite, idealized *shiksa* who haunts the fantasies of avid Jewish boys, in life as in art, with her regular features, her ingrained coolness and formality, and her inevitably neutral name, is perfect of form and devoid of content. She is everything that the Mrs. Portnoys of the world are not—God forbid that Alex, or Woody, should marry a woman who's like his mother. The fear of marrying her sends the Jewish sons of the world into their fevered search for the perfect *shiksa,* a girl who will not berate, cajole, henpeck, or emote, who will not, above all, instill guilt or fan the flames of anxiety, but who *will* put out and let him be.

The ideal totem for the jittery Jewish playboy varies of course from man to man: for Portnoy, it is The Monkey, dumb, pliant, hot to trot. For Woody, it is Diane Keaton. Now Keaton is as deeply and intensely goyish as Woody is Jewish; and to ignore this, or to deny it, is to miss an important part of Allen's comedy. Tall, lanky, with even features and a bland voice, Keaton is the real thing, a dyed-in-the-wool California gentile. There isn't a trace of ethnic coloring in her voice or demeanor or in the way she carries herself. But she has stayed around as long as she has because she rises above stereotype; she manages to escape from Allen's attempts to place her in a cultural straitjacket. She may appear at first to be bland

and ordinary, but on acquaintance she emerges as her own person, charming, vulnerable, mixed-up.

To be sure, the chief way Keaton breaks through the stereotyped *shiksa* mold in which Woody casts her is in being so very neurotic. She demolishes the strong (mostly Jewish) preconception that gentiles are people with frozen faces and manners, colorless voices, and lobotomized emotions. Keaton may come from the sticks (as in *Annie Hall*), but she holds her own with urban Jewish neurotics. Tongue-tied, insecure, changeable, she is a full-fledged dizzy dame, and a far cry from the pristine *shiksa* who is paradoxically a creature of erotic enchantment in the fantasies of many Jewish males. Part of the reason she and Woody get along so well, in movie after movie, is because they share neuroses. Both take pills, have vomiting spells, go to therapists, are prey to anxiety attacks. Both are great worriers and great nags. But for all the nervous symptoms they have in common, differences in style and tone do come between them, as the split-screen dinner scene in *Annie Hall* makes clear. On one side, Alvy's family has a noisy get-together, with everybody yelling at the same time as they gobble food in enormous greedy portions in what amounts to a burlesque of Jewish emotionalism and vulgarity. For blatant contrast, everyone in Annie's family dines with impeccable manners, speaking in tones so quiet you can hear the sound of knives and forks being placed on the fine bone china dinnerware. The Jews shout about death and money as they eat; the Halls talk only about superficial, impersonal matters—swap meets and fishing, the world of the Great Outdoors that gives Woody such a headache. The Halls have very little on their plates, picking at what a Jewish mother would call plain goyish crap, and, of course, they seem to be drinking their dinner. (Mrs. Hall is played by

Colleen Dewhurst, who, with her hoarse, gravelly, deeply mannish voice, sounds like a drunk.) Huddling at the end of the table is Granny Hall, a mean-faced, dried-up old crone, obviously a real Jew hater, who, Woody imagines, regards him as an intruder; he projects himself into the snippy old bat's fantasy of him as a bearded rabbi. When they go to a deli, Annie orders pastrami on white bread with mayonnaise as Woody looks at the waiter in dismay, lifting his eyebrows to comment on gentile stupidity. When Annie refers to her Granny Hall, Woody does a mock feint: "*Granny* Hall?" he repeats in disbelief. Later he makes fun of the name of Annie's brother, Duane (which he pronounces in three elongated syllables). To Woody-Alvy, Annie's world is straight out of Grandma Moses, or Grant Wood, and too goyish for words. But he and Annie cut through their preconceptions about each other to arrive, for a time, on screen as in life, at a working relationship. "The real Jew" and the real *shiksa* set up house together.

Keaton's transformation, in Allen's eyes and in our own, from archetypal supergoy to real person is reenacted in each of their films together. In *Play It Again, Sam* (the first of their co-starring vehicles), Woody at first takes her for granted; she is his best friend's wife, and he hardly notices her. But as he spends more and more time with her, he begins to see that she is sensitive, warm, down-to-earth, altogether a companionable fellow neurotic, the girl that he has been looking for, in short. She's not a type like the others he has dated or tried to pick up, she's genuine and emotional and she helps to make him less twitchy. But Allen does cast her as a woman who needs to be improved (by him), and in the teacher-student aspect of their relationship, which keeps being played out over and over, another ethnic conflict is revealed.

One of the recurrent themes of contemporary Jewish novels is that of the bright young Jew straying from the fold in order to upgrade the inarticulate, intellectually raw *shiksa*. Woody thinks of himself, however often he may deny it or scoff at the type, as an intellectual, the inheritor of a fierce Jewish respect for learning; and Diane, in film after film, is the dumb goyisheh who benefits from contact with his brains. The subject of her not being intelligent enough for Woody is sounded repeatedly—it is one of the major problems they have in *Annie Hall* (she tells Alvy, in a moment of gentile self-abasement, that she is beginning to get more of the references in his comedy routines), but it is present in *Sleeper* and in *Play It Again, Sam*, too, and in a different way in *Interiors* and *Manhattan*. Keaton is obviously an intelligent woman, and just as obviously insecure about how smart she really is. So she is a ripe target for Woody's intellectual superiority complex.

*Love and Death* subverts the smart-Jew, ignorant-gentile scheme that underlies the romantic comedies, with not such happy consequences for Woody. Unlike her dithering characters in *Annie Hall* and *Sleeper,* here Keaton doesn't lean on Woody. Intelligent and independent, her Sonia treats Woody-Boris cavalierly, making him suffer for his infatuation with her. Sonia is always more interested in someone else than she is in him, and she agrees to marry him only when she thinks he's going to be killed in a duel. Male chauvinist that he is, Woody seems to be making a connection between the character's wit—her ability to hold her own against him—and her promiscuity, as if it is only dumb *shiksas* who are the marrying, faithful kind.

Keaton's other intellectuals, in *Interiors* and *Manhattan,* also contain a sting of disapproval, as her mentor looks on edgily, poking fun at her newfound competence.

There is some cruelty in Allen's attitude toward her in both these films, as if the fact that she left him at the end of *Annie Hall* (and offscreen as well) has provoked a lingering desire to get even. In *Interiors* and *Manhattan*, the *shiksa* isn't dumb anymore, and she isn't as likable either. Keaton's character in *Manhattan* is like Annie Hall after she has completed all her night-school courses. Although she's a free-lance writer doing think pieces for intellectual quarterlies, her smartness doesn't rest easily on her (or on Woody either). She's defensive about being in the intellectual know, she parades her advanced ideas in a way that is grating and that in fact marks her as an outsider to *The New York Review* crowd.    Allen makes fun of Diane playing at being a New York intellectual, though beneath the pose he allows us to see her vulnerability, as well as her true intelligence. Mary Wilke is a complex role, one that shows Diane growing away from her director.    Allen's character in the film doesn't have the kind of impact on her that Alvy claims over Annie, or that Miles has over Luna. In *Manhattan* Diane isn't in awe of Woody's mind, having a keen mind of her own; and at the end of the movie she goes her own way, giving up Isaac to return, masochistically, to her married lover. It may be no accident that Diane doesn't appear in    Allen's next film: perhaps the student has outgrown her teacher.

In *Manhattan*    Allen moves Diane up in the intelligence scale in a way that is convincing, though clearly the tension between them on this issue has not been resolved. But in *Interiors* he sabotages her by casting her as a highbrow poet who publishes regularly in *The New Yorker*. Perhaps Diane is so much a prisoner of the image Allen    has created for her that we can't buy her for a moment as a serious poet; but no actress, even one trailing clouds of intellectual glory, could turn this factitious part into a believable character. (It is perhaps a measure of her trust in  Allen that she would have attempted a role which she no doubt saw was not for her.) In *Interiors* all the qualities of Diane's character that Allen  usually kids—the nagging self-doubts, the inarticulate stammering speech patterns—are played straight: she is a *serious* neurotic this time, beleaguered and washed out, unable to sleep, suffering from writer's block, wrangling with her husband, a failed novelist, and bickering with her sister and her mother. To underline the seriousness of it all,   Allen makes her look remarkably rumpled and unattractive, creating a deliberate visual shock after her fresh-faced charm as Annie Hall. And to indicate how brilliant the character is, he gives her thick, unsayable lines which sound like a translation from a foreign language.

The question of how smart a dumb *shiksa* can be thus appears throughout the Allen-Keaton movies. For both performers, off screen as well as on, it is obviously a subject loaded with anxiety. The bright Jew needs his adoring, naive gentile and can't take it when she discovers how intelligent she really is. And so in varying ways, in the later movies,   Allen makes her intellect undermine her attractiveness, turning her into a nerve-racking as opposed to a comic and likable neurotic.

Although Diane Keaton has worked for other directors, she has yet to make a substantial impact in her non-Allen films. She's fine in *The Godfather* in a secondary role—the door that closes on her at the end of the first part demonstrates the peripheral place of women in the Mafia hierarchy. Michael Corleone, heir-apparent to the Godfather throne, chooses Diane for much the same reasons that Woody does, because she is decidedly not his mother, she is an outsider, a pale WASP whose all-American blandness is measured against Italian passion. In *Looking for Mr. Goodbar,* Keaton's major non- Allen film so far, she is disappointing. She is at her best in moments which Annie Hall could handle: teaching deaf children, courted by a shy social worker she is not really interested in. Here the stammers, the appealing modesty and uncertainty that seem to be her stock-in-trade, work their usual magic. But Keaton seems plainly too normal and refreshing for the dark sexual milieu in which the story unfolds—the character's sexual self-destructiveness, her bitterness and despair, are beyond her. Diane's neuroticism is daffy and appealing, not sinister, as it is meant to be in this film.

If Keaton has yet to exorcise Woody completely, Allen   hasn't gotten over her either. He hasn't outgrown the *shiksa* syndrome; hence the Mariel Hemingway character in *Manhattan,* who is another Jewish male fantasy, a statuesque gentile, carved in the American grain (Ernest Hemingway's granddaughter, for goodness' sake!), and only seventeen. Unlike Diane, she is not dizzy; she is more knowing about the world and about herself than the mixed-up East Side adults among whom she is thrown. But clearly this girl does not fast on Yom Kippur; and for Woody that is part of her appeal. She is from a different culture, and according to prevalent Jewish concepts, from a different emotional world as well: she is WASP coolness to his Jewish twitchiness, WASP self-possession to his outsider's insecurity. Hemingway more nearly than Keaton conforms to a clear-cut stereotype. She has an innate dignity and calm that surely come from generations of economic and social security. Hers is breeding that can't be bought and that is not easily available to a group of people one generation removed from the indignities and hardships imposed by their immigrant status.

Mariel Hemingway is an American blue blood, and in desiring her—having an affair that is sure to make him the envy of his neighborhood—Woody shows that his fantasies haven't changed. The difference in their ages allows him once again to play the savior, whereas if she were his own age, he would have to relate to her on a grown-up basis. Yet because she is so young, it's only kid's play for Woody, and therefore safe. Since Woody courts two *shiksas* in *Manhattan,* both of whom leave him, perhaps it's time for him to move on.

But of course he's had no better luck with Jewish girls. Janet Margolin, who plays his wife in *Take the Money and Run* and his second wife in *Annie Hall,* Carol Kane, who is his first wife in *Annie Hall,* and Louise Lasser, his girl in *Bananas* and his wife in one of the episodes of *Everything You Always Wanted To Know About Sex\* (\*but were afraid to ask),* are all Jewish. His two wives in *Annie Hall,* who are seen only fleetingly, are whiny and demanding and hovering, confirming every Jewish boy's worst fears of ending up married to a woman who resembles his mother. Only Janet Margolin in *Take the Money and Run* is sweet, though a little fussy (she nags Woody about what he should wear to a holdup), and she's a rotten cook, serving him a dinner with the meat still in its plastic wrapping. She doesn't really get in Woody's way, though, because in this first film the girl hardly exists as a character at all.

Louise Lasser presents more of a challenge. On film at least the second Mrs. Allen doesn't go for Woody in a sexual way. She says to Fielding Mellish in *Bananas* that there is something missing for her in their affair. When he returns, in bearded disguise, reborn as a South American political hero, she likes him better, though after he reveals himself to her, she admits that she thought there was something not quite there for her again. In *Sex* Louise is a bored Italian aristocrat (typecasting!) who can get it on with her husband Fabrizio only in public places, where the sense of danger and possible discovery fire her passion. In both tussles with Lasser Woody plays a sexual victim, humiliated by his partner. Woody as himself isn't good enough, or exciting enough, or interesting enough, for Louise's Jewish American Princess, perhaps because Woody is too close to home for her. Louise in both movies becomes interested in him only when he isn't himself, decked out (in *Bananas*) in an outlandish getup that happens to meet her character's pseudo-radical political fantasies, or (in *Sex*) when he's not in her bedroom.

As a comic team Woody and Louise had no place to go beyond *Bananas* and the skit in *Sex*. Both, obviously, are serious New York Jewish neurotics. The ethnic contrast between Woody and Diane has mystery and possibility: she is as intrigued by his Jewish "otherness" as he is caught by her gentile exoticism, whereas Woody and Louise were, in a sense, on to each other from the beginning. Their sexual battle simply had less give to it than Woody's rifts with Diane and besides pointed toward an emotional heaviness that   Allen was not prepared to face, for right beneath the surface of Lasser's zonked-out, catatonic style is the intimation of genuine psychosis. Where Keaton's comic style is brisk and refreshing, Lasser's has thunderous rumblings. And unlike Keaton, whom  Allen was able to mold, Lasser is a formidable comic antagonist who physically and verbally is able to tear Woody apart. No wonder he cut her from his act!

Woody's troubles with women, his courtship patterns, his mating calls, his sexual tugs-of-war, are all attributes then of his inveterate Jewishness. He's like a sex-starved hero out of Philip Roth or a Jewish version of Gatsby lusting after and idealizing his unavailable Daisy. His sex comedy is tinged with Jewish guilt, humiliation, and self-mockery. Sex, finally, causes him more grief than pleasure.

Curiously, Allen slights another crucible of Jewish neurosis, the parent-child relationship. Parents (like the father who went to sleep after reading a kidnapper's ransom note) figured in Woody's stand-up comedy. In interviews early in his career, Woody made jokes about his parents, casting them in the roles of quintessential Brooklyn bourgeois who did everything in their power to see to it that their children would become garden-variety neurotics. But parents have all but disappeared in Allen's movies. Allen dismissed as merely coincidental —an irony of no importance—the fact that parents in both *Take the Money and Run* and *Bananas* wear masks. Virgil Starkwell's parents conceal their identity behind Groucho masks, while the parents in *Bananas* are covered by surgeon's masks (they're performing an operation as Fielding comes to bid them good-bye, on the eve of his departure for San Marcos). Both sets of parents are presented as low-comedy Jewish stereotypes, quarrel-some, breast-beating, guilt-inducing. They're briefly glimpsed caricatures, as is Alvy Singer's mother in flashback scenes in *Annie Hall*. Instead, then, of creating his own Mrs. Portnoy, a full-scale, operatic rendition of the hovering Jewish matron, Allen has practically erased her from his comic diagram. His pursuit of girls seems to leave him little time for mothers.

From Henry Roth's *Call It Sleep* to *Goodbye,*

*Columbus* and Heller's *Something Happened,* most of the major Jewish novels are set within the framework of the family. The beleaguered hero—Herzog, Portnoy, Augie March—is seen most typically in the role of son, husband, father, brother.   Allen, in his movies, as in his life, avoids entangling family alliances as much as he can; his recurrent role is that of boyfriend, or would-be lover, a part that gets riskier and that begins to look more and more like avoidance, as he gets older (see *Manhattan*). His comic vision is rooted in his hero's solitariness, not in his membership in a family or community. His one family drama, *Interiors,* the one film of his (up to 1980; see chapter 8) that is not about an isolated comic hero, is set, revealingly, not in a Jewish family, about whom he would have a ready familiarity, but in a pack of well-heeled gentiles, about whom, on the evidence of the film, he knows absolutely nothing. Didn't Allen trust himself to try a Jewish family drama, or did he think only well-off gentiles were worthy of the solemn Bergmanesque style he imposes on the characters? Chillingly polite, these pale Christians treat each other like strangers. Allen creates them from the outside, as if he is observing a pageant of well-bred WASP suffering.

Allen's  attempt to pass for WASP in *Interiors* only shows how firmly rooted his genius is in the soil of his own Jewish persona and background. Straying from self and home, he lost his touch, and turned out a shallow, would-be masterpiece, a work of strained seriousness. All that gentile restraint and formality, when what has been rippling beneath the surface of his work all along is a big, noisy, unashamedly ethnic comedy of manners, a Jewish comic epic such as no one else in current movies is equipped to make, a film equivalent of *Herzog* and

*Portnoy's Complaint,* in which   Allen releases a flood of pent-up Jewish humor that is both piercing and healing. Instead of the stingy goyish stale cake of *Interiors,*   Allen ought to have fed us a Jewish banquet.

# 6

# The Tricks of the Trade

A BRILLIANT borrower and adapter rather than innova-
tor, Allen runs a conventional comic gamut, from
irony to satire to parody and burlesque, from comic
realism to surreal farce. His techniques range from a
low-keyed comedy that depends on audience recognition
and empathy to a comic style of outlandish exaggeration.

Like those of all successful comedians, Allen's
laughs grow out of the mastery of comic formulas. Yet the
underlying rules and regulations must of course never
show; the best comedies, after all, often seem like a series
of inspired improvisations, as one laugh generates a chain
of others. And so the comedian who is in command of the
tricks of his trade must seem as if he doesn't really know
what he is doing, as if his routines are the result not of
study and practice—of consciously crafted technique—
but of the free, spontaneous flow of his native wit.

Drawn to comedy when he saw Bob Hope in *The
Road to Morocco* in 1942, Allen has long been a serious
student of its methods. As he examined the way his

favorite comedians constructed their jokes, he noted a recurrent pattern, one that he has used as the basis of his own work and that can perhaps best be described as the comic gap. All comedy, from one-liners to full-length narratives, grows out of gaps, discrepancies, disparities between what a character says and what he really means, between who he is and what he does, between what a character thinks of himself and what we think of him, between what characters know and see and what we know and see, between the objective truth of a situation and the characters' slanted, partial, lopsided perception of it, between the subject of comic ridicule as it is in reality and as the comedian exaggerates and distorts it.

It's often the case that the wider the gap, the bigger the laugh. Take the classic slip on a banana peel (which Woody kids not in *Bananas* but in *Sleeper,* where he slips on a giant one). A banana lies on the sidewalk. We see it. The character doesn't. We know what's coming. The character doesn't. Which is often the way comedy works. The comic potential of this incident depends, of course, on who does the tripping. If a forlorn person, an unfortunate, slips on the banana, the accident is of a piece with the rest of his life, and only sadists are likely to laugh. But if some *grande dame,* her nose in the air, her lorgnette swinging around her neck, slips, the contrast— the gap—between the victim and the mishap is greater, and most of us will be delighted with this image of imperial dignity confounded.

Comedy feeds on such incongruities, and traditional as it is, Woody's comedy is a festival of them. His work is built on variations of the all-important comic surprise, in which words, actions, and appearances are unexpected, anachronistic, seemingly inappropriate. His comedy is filled with gaps between Woody's would-be stud image and his goofy, unheroic looks, and between Woody and his often unlikely environments. The basic comic premise of his earlier movies depended on far-fetched casting: Woody as a Clyde Barrow-type bank robber, or a political hero, or a Tolstoy intellectual. (Imagine the reduction in comic surprise if Woody's roles in *Bananas* or *Sleeper* had been played by Charlton Heston!) No matter where he is, or who he is playing—an Elizabethan court jester, a sperm, an Italian aristocrat—Woody remains himself, wearing glasses and talking in Brooklynese. The more out of place he is, the "steeper" and more far-out the comedy.

In creating his persona   Allen followed a traditional comic pattern of placing himself at a distance from the norm. Comic characters are extreme, obsessive, in some way limited; they cultivate their eccentricities. They don't play straight with the world, as they practice subterfuge, take detours, go in circles. Some humor or conceit or folly, some quirk of character or appearance, sets them apart and makes them see themselves and others through a cracked glass. It is often the business of comedy either to improve their vision, if they are salvageable, or to hurl them into everlasting darkness if they are not. Over the course of his comedy,   Allen has "corrected" his character, narrowing the distance between him and the world, making him by degrees less rigid and hence capable of a greater variety of responses.

Woody's character thus comes at us at a tangent, on the curve of a comic arc. Floundering in preposterous settings, and cut off by the force of his preoccupations, he is an outsider. And even when he comes home finally, landing on firm ground in *Annie Hall* and *Manhattan,* after his Woody in Wonderland adventures, he still says and does the unexpected, thereby maintaining the comic gap. Allen's work abounds in verbal incongruities as in his dry, shuffling, stammering style he issues audacious statements and turns language and logic inside out with rapid-fire reversals and absurdist juxtapositions. Woody is a clever creator of verbal chaos, and the central element of all his comedy is verbal surprise. His goofy word salads, his neologisms and nonsequiturs, his verbal bombshells that explode pretense and hypocrisy, often contain good sense. His mockery of logic has a cunning logic of its own. Two prime examples of Woody's use of inversion and paradox occur in *Sleeper*. At the end of his futuristic adventure, Luna says to Miles, "You don't believe in science, or political systems, or God. What do you believe in?" "Sex and death," Miles answers, without blinking an eye. "Things which come once in a lifetime. At least after death you're not nauseous." His answer is—and is not—a true response to Luna's question. Part serious, part absurd, it shoots past reality—the way people really talk to each other—to discover a slanted reality of its own. It's a smart-alecky, jokey way of presenting the truth. Woody *does* believe in sex and death, after all; what's absurd is not the sentiment but the supporting details, the remark that sex comes only once, and that after death you're not nauseous. Woody's seemingly inappropriate comment is a way of neutralizing his genuine anxieties about sex and death.

Earlier in the film, after his defrosting, a doctor questions Miles about various icons and artifacts from the past. Miles's poker-faced explanations overturn, and deflate, reality. He identifies Charles de Gaulle as a famous French chef. Bela Lugosi, in this almanac according to Woody, was the mayor of New York: "You can see what it did to him." Billy Graham was "big in the religion business, he knew God personally. They used to go out on double dates together." Norman Mailer is identified as a writer who "donated his ego to the Harvard Medical School," F. Scott Fitzgerald as "a romantic author, big with English majors and nymphomaniacs." The girls in *Playboy*, Miles assures the doctor, didn't exist: "They were made of rubber. You blew them up." The doctor shows him a picture of Nixon, saying, "We suspect he may have been a President but he did something so terrible that his name was erased from all the history books." "Yes," Miles says, deadpan (and in 1973, too!), "They had to lock up the silver whenever he left the White House."

Woody's verbal dexterity, as these two examples indicate, confounds sense and expectation. His ready wit, a means both of camouflage and attack, is his chief weapon in his war against the world. Spouting incongruities, he scrambles sense in order to make a point, to take a swipe at narrow-mindedness, to undercut affectation. Mismatching the form and the content of what he says, he throws his adversaries off guard, and so seizes control of his environment, as in his verbal vaudeville in *Sleeper*, while seeming to play the fool.

Making the wrong or inappropriate or nonsensical comment is thus Allen's means of satirizing a character, an idea, a point of view or state of mind. Throwing verbal monkey wrenches into his patter is his way of mocking seriousness: no subject is immune from his barbed, debunking wit.

Allen has several favorite deflating techniques: he tosses isolated words and phrases into inappropriate contexts; he promiscuously mingles local references with universal concerns, undermining big issues like God and death by linking them with daily irritations; in a seemingly straightforward manner, he compiles lists the last items of which veer off into surreal absurdity; and he parodies the process of logical thought by wandering off into delirious tangents.

Delighted by the sound of words,  Allen creates gaps between words and their setting. Rabbi Ben Kaddish is the greatest *noodge* of the medieval era, he tells us, in one of his comic essays. A famous writer named Metterling is known as the Prague weirdo. Woody fondly remembers his father in *Love and Death*: "He was an idiot, but I loved him." Waking up two hundred years after an operation in *Sleeper*, he says he's the victim of a cosmic screwing. The spies in *What's Up, Tiger Lily?* search for an egg salad so good it could make you *plotz*. Woody refers to a woman he meets in *Love and Death* as the noted Spanish countess and *meeskeit*. In *Manhattan* he calls Diane Keaton's former husband a homunculus. "Do you accuse me of jejunosity?" he asks Sonia in *Love and Death*. "Manyness and oneness are studied as they relate to otherness,"  Allen writes in his Philo I course description. "Students achieving oneness will move ahead to twoness."

His pleasure in making words stand out is apparent in his usually inappropriate choice of names for his characters. Some, like the waspy Virgil Starkwell, are obviously unsuitable for a Jewish fellow from Brooklyn. Others, like Victor Shakapopolis (which Woody uses twice), sound too exotic. Fielding Mellish of *Bananas* is just right, the WASP lift of Fielding counterpointed by the ethnic plop of Mellish. Woody has a comic reaction when, in *Annie Hall*, he meets a woman with a similarly schizophrenic name—Alison (pure goyish) Porchnik (pure Jewish). Albert (The Logical Positivist) Corillo, Mendy Lipsky (alias Mendy Lewis, alias Mendy Larsen, alias Mendy Alias), Gaetano Santucci (also known as Little Tony, or

Rabbi Henry Sharpstein), and Little Petey (Big Petey) Ross comprise the dramatis personae in Allen's "Look at Organized Crime." His detective hero doesn't have a straight all-American name like Sam Spade but is called Kaiser Lupowitz. The real hero of Russian history, according to *Love and Death,* is Sidney Appelbaum.

Injecting words and phrases where they don't belong, peppering his dialogue with Yiddish, sudden insults, jargon, neologisms, anachronisms, and funny names, Allen tests words for their ability to startle us and to overturn expectations. His jugglings with words are a miniature version of the comic gap and point toward the wild disproportions and incongruities that supply much of the fuel for his comedy.

He belittles big themes by talking about them in a careless, offhanded manner, while little matters, concerns of merely local significance, he treats with mock solemnity. Great abstractions like God, death, the afterlife, and the future of the world are shredded as they pass through Allen's comic blender, while he subjects the discovery and use of the fake ink blot to sober scholarly analysis. Demolishing the insularity of higher intellectuals as well as the intransigence of the bourgeoisie, Allen satirizes a provincial mentality that can't conceive of issues larger than what to wear and the price of eggs on the one hand and a philosophical habit of mind that exists in airy, rarefied isolation on the other.

"Is there an afterlife, and what kind of night life do they have?" "Will there be aspirins in hell?" "Eternal nothingness is O.K. If you're dressed for it." "If only Dionysus were alive; where would he eat?" "If man were immortal, do you know what his meat bills would be?" "How is it possible to find meaning in a finite world given my waist and shirt size?" "Can we actually know the universe? My God, it's hard enough finding your way around in Chinatown." "Is there anything out there? And why? And must they be so noisy?" "The Cartesian dictum 'I think, therefore I am' might be better expressed 'Hey, there goes Edna with a saxophone!'" "Eschatological dialectics [is] a means of coping with shingles." Waking up in a world of the future, Woody (in *Sleeper*) says he knew it was too good to be true: he had found a parking place right outside the hospital. Epic time travel and the problems of parking; God and carpeting; aspirins and the hereafter; eschatology and shingles—through these mad minglings  Allen knocks the universe down to size, seizing control of the infinite by reducing it to minute proportions. While his thoughts sail aloft, scaling the heights of philosophical speculation, he trips on banana peels. The life of the mind is interrupted by the claims of the body, as the mundane intersects the eternal.

Allen pierces God and death—the two subjects that needle him—by placing them in unexpected and reductive contexts. In *Love and Death* he holds vaudevillian conversations with God, working Him the way a skilled comic works an audience. "Not only is there no God," Allen  states in his comic essay "My Philosophy," "but try getting a plumber on weekends." "The universe is merely a fleeting idea in God's mind—a pretty uncomfortable thought, particularly if you've just made a down payment on a house." "Do you believe in God?" one character asks in "Notes From the Overfed." "And if so, what do you think He weighs?" "If God is everywhere," the obese, mock Dostoevskian narrator of this story concludes, "then He is in food. Therefore, the more I [eat] the godlier I [will] become." In "Mr. Big," a buxom blonde, Heather Butkiss (a.k.a. Claire Rosensweig), whose figure "described a set of parabolas that could cause cardiac arrest in a yak," employs private eye Kaiser Lupowitz not to locate a long-lost honey, or a missing husband, but to find Mr. Big, that is, God. On his hunt Kaiser interviews a Rabbi Itzhak Wiseman ("a local cleric who owed me a favor for finding out who was rubbing pork on his hat"), who tells him that Jews are the chosen people in return for a price (He soaks them plenty), and talks to His Holiness the Pope in Giordono's Italian Restaurant in Newark, who says he doesn't know if God exists but "what's the difference? The money's good." Lupowitz figures it out: God *does* exist, but Heather (a.k.a. Claire) killed Him: "You posed as a pantheist and that gave you access to Him—*if* He existed, which He did. He went with you to Shelby's party and when Jason wasn't looking, you killed Him." "Kaiser, you wouldn't turn me in?" "Oh, yes, baby. When the Supreme Being gets knocked off, *somebody's* got to take the rap."

"What's death like?" Sonia asks at the end of *Love and Death.* "It's as bad as the chicken at Tresky's Restaurant," Boris says. "What's it like to be dead for two hundred years?" Luna asks Miles in *Sleeper.* "It's like a weekend in Beverly Hills." The august Doctor Helmholtz, a pioneer in psychoanalysis and a contemporary of Freud's, proved that "death is an acquired trait." "It is impossible to experience one's own death objectively and still carry a tune," Woody says. And at the end of *Love and Death,* he advises us to think of death as "cutting down on our expenses."

Being brash and nervy in the face of ultimate issues like God and death is Woody's way of dealing with the inexplicable. Belittling helps to relieve anxiety. If Woody tries to trim the feathers of God and death, he blows up sex out of all realistic proportions, making it larger than life size. An erection has the dimensions of a spaceship. A huge single breast stalks the countryside. The idea of sexual performance haunts Woody, so how better to indicate this concern than to present the sexual act (as he does at the end of *Bananas*) as exactly that—a performance, a bout, an arena sport narrated by Howard Cosell in which the challengers rate themselves and each other.

God, death, sex, immortality—these are not logical issues, and as  Allen demonstrates, they resist attempts to treat them in rational down-to-earth terms. In the same debunking style he dismantles the notion and process of logic itself. A technique he uses to send up logic and order is to make lists which plummet from poker-faced sobriety to hallucination. "Illicit activities engaged in by Cosa Nostra members included gambling, narcotics, prostitution, hijacking, loan-sharking, and the transportation of a large whitefish across the state line for immoral purposes." "Before he is twenty-five," the narrator of *Take the Money and Run* intones, "Virgil Starkwell will be wanted in six states for assault, armed robbery, and illegal possession of a wart." He interrupts the action in *Love and Death* to set up a syllogism. "What would Socrates say about killing Napoleon?" he asks, in his droll, deadpan style, looking directly into the camera. "Those Greeks were all homosexuals. They must have had wild parties, and taken a house together for the summer in Crete. (a) Socrates is a man; (b) all men are mortal; (c) all men are Socrates, that means all men are homosexuals. . . . I'm not. Some are heterosexual, some bisexual, and some don't think about it at all and become lawyers."

Allen thus delights in setting up a seemingly logical framework only to fill it with chop logic and surreal nonsequiturs as the mind of the speaker or writer becomes gradually unhinged, shooting off into utter delirium. On life: "For life is change and fat is life, and fat is also death." On epistemology: "So then, to know a substance or an idea we must doubt it, and thus, doubting it, come to perceive the qualities it possesses in its finite state, which are truly 'in the thing itself' or 'of the thing itself,' or of something or nothing. If this is clear, we can leave epistemology for the moment." On film: "Film is a young art and as such is not truly an art but an art within an art employing the devices of mass communication in a linear, nonmodal, anti- or nondiversified, creative otherness which we will call density. If a picture is dense, it has density." On explaining *Alice in Wonderland*: "The March Hare was Shakespeare, the Mad Hatter, Marlowe, and the Dormouse, Bacon—or the Mad Hatter, Bacon, and the March Hare, Marlowe—or Carroll, Bacon, and the Dormouse, Marlowe—or Alice was Shakespeare—or Bacon—or Carroll was the Mad Hatter. A pity Carroll is not alive today to settle it. Or Bacon. Or Marlowe. Or Shakespeare. The point is, if you're going to move, notify your post office." On the future of man: "More than at any other time in history, mankind faces a crossroads. One path leads to despair and utter hopelessness. The other, to total extinction. Let us pray we have the wisdom to choose correctly."     Allen spreads confusion—beginning with an appearance of order, setting out to define and to explain, to clarify and put in perspective, he gets side-tracked, tucking asides within asides, parentheses within parentheses, as logic and sense scatter, dwindle, and eventually evaporate altogether.

In Allen's comedy, the absurd and the surreal exert a continual pressure on the attempt to maintain order. Statements and actions that begin with an outward show of reasonableness topple from logic to lunacy, with characters, language, and the world collapsing amid the spiralling incongruities. Things, ideas, concepts are tossed together in bizarre combinations. "Yeats and Hygiene, A Comparative Study" reads an entry in Allen's course announcements. "The poetry of William Butler Yeats is analyzed against a background of proper dental care," promises another course. Allen's Rapid Reading program offers a dizzying trip into the comic beyond.

This course will increase reading speed a little each day until the end of the term, by which time the student will be required to read *The Brothers Karamazov* in fifteen minutes. The method is to scan the page and eliminate everything except pronouns from one's field of vision. Soon the pronouns are eliminated. Gradually the student is encouraged to nap. A frog is dissected. Spring comes. People marry and die. Pinkerton does not return.

A rabbi who leaps on top of a man in a frenzy and carves the story of Ruth on his nose with a stylus; a girl who looks like a herring; a man wandering the Urals and emotionally involved with a panda; a man who stutters, but not when he speaks, only when he writes; a doctor who attends a séance at which a table not only rises but excuses itself and goes upstairs to sleep; a man who dates a Cornish hen; a beagle who goes to a Park Avenue Jungian veterinarian who, for fifty dollars a session, "labors valiantly to convince him that jowls are not a social drawback"; a goldfish who sings "I Got Rhythm"; a horse that can recite the Gettysburg Address; a pope who talks like a gangster; a sea monster with the body of a crab and the head of a certified public accountant:    Allen's comedy is filled with these delirious impossibilities. He creates a lopsided world in which the dignity of man is under constant attack from surreal rearrangements.

And yet one of the main contrasts of his comedy is the bland response of his characters to the extraordinary sights and events that assault them. When they should be shocked or dismayed, when the world defies natural laws with a lunatic vengeance, they react with perfect, maddening nonchalance. Notified of a huge breast on the loose, a sheriff gives orders for its capture as though this event were merely par for the course, all in a day's work. Woody holds up a bank, handing the teller written instructions about what to do; and how does this holdup victim respond? With fear and trepidation? Hardly. Without blinking an eye, in a tone of utter, numbing blandness, he starts to argue with Virgil Starkwell over the legibility of his handwriting, insisting that "gun" has been misspelled as "gub." An orchestra saws away producing no sounds; no one at the banquet (in *Bananas*) takes notice. A group of convicts chained together knock on the door of a rural house, as if it were Avon calling. The rube woman who answer the ring treats them with hick politeness and affability, not for a second indicating panic or even discomfort. "I thought they were an unusually close-knit family," she later says. Even when the action isn't far-out, the characters' responses are surprising. Woody brings cake to the dictator of a South American country, who explodes because he prefers a different kind of cake. Virgil Starkwell meets an old friend, they chat amiably, and then the fellow says to Virgil, in a flat, neutral tone, as though he were talking about the weather, "By the way, I'm a police officer, and I have to arrest you." Sonia's husband (in *Love and Death*) lies dying. "How long has he got?" she whispers to the assembled priests. She's hungry, the old man is holding up her evening. "Where shall we eat?" she asks after her husband finally expires. "Riker's," the nineteenth-century Russian cleric suggests, mentioning the name of a now-defunct New York junk-food chain. In *Take the*

*Money and Run* a man who reports how he helped to capture a famous criminal continually interrupts himself with irrelevant details, talking about what he had for breakfast, what he took to the laundry. In *Play It Again, Sam* Woody goes up to a girl looking at a painting in a museum, makes some comment on it, and the girl launches into a diatribe about eternal nothingness. He visits a woman who talks hot—she seems like a sure thing, even for the luckless Woody; he pounces on her, she rears up in offended dignity, saying, "What do you take me for?" In *Annie Hall* Woody goes up to an old man, out of the blue, and asks him how he and his wife maintain their sexual interest in each other. "We use a large vibrating egg," the man explains, utterly deadpan. Woody asks a chic WASP couple what the secret to their successful relationship is. "I'm shallow and vacant and don't have any ideas, and he's the same," the woman answers in a cool even tone.

With its lopsided responses, its reductions and enlargements, its escalations into pure dotty fantasy, its anachronisms, disparities, and dissonances, Allen's comedy reflects the world like a fun-house mirror. Nothing is presented on a realistic scale: actions are either bigger or smaller than in life, either exaggerated or diminished for comic effect. Large themes are spoofed, small matters are inflated—and seldom do characters match their manner to the matter at hand. No wonder characters in Allen's movies are forever missing each other, failing to connect; no wonder his heroes are always on the prowl, the perfect, enduring relationship forever eluding them.

No matter what the tone or the form his comedy takes, from irony and satire to comic romance, from parody and burlesque to farce, his continuing ploy is to sprinkle anachronisms over his story and characters, seasoning his comedy with incongruities in order to undercut foolishness, hypocrisy, pretension, vanity, obsession, and convention, both his own and others'; to insult those he dislikes, and to instruct those he thinks are salvageable. His surreal farces, his parodies of popular genres, and his satires of modern big-city mores all depend on surprising comparisons and on abrupt departures from and intrusions on reality.

His comic stance—the tone of his work—is as stapled with shifts and paradox as his comic technique. Allen is a moralist and social commentator, a cynic, an infidel, and also a romantic, living in hope that the right girl is out there somewhere. "Don't cry," he tells Mariel Hemingway softly in *Manhattan,* when he breaks off with her. The tone is wonderfully soothing, caring, gentle— qualities he has always had and which have contributed to his enormous appeal. Woody is a classic case of a passive-aggressive personality, throwing his darts with a fetching shyness and nervousness. His is wit that can slay, if he chooses to let it, although the stinging, wounding side of his humor emerges only sporadically. You always feel that there are reserves of cruelty that he keeps locked up inside.

All comedy, to one degree or another, has this same cutting edge. Comedy is subversive, in some way hostile to the status quo. It attacks, simplifies, reduces; it is infantile, regressive, anarchic, and contemptuous; it is antisocial and sometimes even violent. Its intent is to sting, to berate and needle, sometimes for purposes of correction and improvement, sometimes merely for the sake of unsettling, letting out the demons of restraint and propriety. While containing all these negative impulses, Allen's comedy is yet notable for its air of bemused sweetness. How gentle a satirist he is, and yet how much hostility lies twitching beneath that quiet, winning exterior. How much self-contempt, and contempt of others, palpitates beneath that boyish, charming grin.

From the beginning Allen's comedy did more than simply make us laugh. It held up a mirror (whose reflection, to be sure, was distorted through Woody's wild comic imagination) to our own insecurities, our own feelings of exclusion and inadequacy. Despite its earlier exaggerations, Allen's comedy has always radiated little shocks of recognition. If much in the earlier films was far-out, set on the lunar landscapes of Woody's mind, much also made an appeal to our sympathy and identification. Woody was always inviting us to see pieces of ourselves in him—and it's precisely this human aspect of his work that insured his widespread popularity. The ultimate paradox of Allen's comedy is that all its incongruities, fissures, displacements, reversals, and transformations both realistic and magical, only confirmed, after all, that Woody is one of us. (See chapter 8 for a discussion of how Allen's work has changed its spots since 1980.)

# 7

## Climbing Parnassus:
## The Do's and Don'ts
## of Movie Comedy

A S A WRITER and director of movie comedies, Allen has
had to decide what subjects to make jokes about, how
to tie the jokes together into at least a semblance of a
story line, and what kind of visual style to give his
material so that it will look like a full-fledged movie rather
than a series of comic turns and asides awkwardly
transplanted from another medium. Making comedy
work on film poses special problems, and Allen has had
to jump hurdles in three areas, as comic actor, author,
and director.

The movie comedian is cut off from his audience.
Because his performance is frozen permanently on celluloid, he can't measure himself against the answering
response of a live crowd, and so he has to calculate in
advance, and without benefit of feedback, how to pace
himself, and at what level to pitch his delivery. Like
Allen , most comedians got their start someplace else—
in vaudeville or radio or on stage—before they began
appearing in movies, but while most comics discovered

that they had to tone down their stage performances for movies, to subdue the theatricality of their style,   Allen has had almost the opposite problem. His first performances were not on the vast stages of vaudeville houses but in intimate nightclubs where only a microphone separated him from the encircling crowd. These small rooms were an ideal environment for  Allen's low-key delivery, and he found when he began to act full-length roles on stage and film that he had neither the stamina nor the vocal technique. He had to learn to speak up and to vary the pitch and inflection of his voice, which has a tendency to become dry and monotonous. He found that the differences between telling anecdotes to a nightclub audience and acting a sustained role in front of movie cameras were enormous.

"If you don't have gags going for you, you've got nothing,"   Allen said after he had completed *Bananas*. Yet movies must have a tighter framework for the gags, the wisecracks, the comedian's shtick, than nightclub sets. "Once the gags stop, you don't care about the sitting-room scenes,"   Allen said referring to *Duck Soup*. In his own work, he has tried, with increasing success, to make us care about what is going on underneath the gags; to sustain audience interest *between* the jokes, as it were, by creating characters and situations that go deeper—that count for more—than the number of laughs they are good for.

Creating gags to fit into a story line and then spacing them over the course of a full-length movie in such a way as to maintain a comic atmosphere as well as the goodwill of the audience are two enormous hurdles for the comic film maker, as Woody discovered. In later work like *Annie Hall* and *Manhattan*   Allen changes his attitude toward the all-important gag, the skit or comic routine, the bright idea, which is the basic unit of all comedy construction: instead of bombarding us as in *Take the Money and Run* and *Bananas,* he restrains himself by using fewer one-liners and comic bits and by making closer connections between comedy and character. The jokes in the earlier movies were all-purpose and therefore essentially impersonal—the vestiges of  Allen's career as a professional comic—whereas gags in the later work spring primarily from character.

Movies are dangerous to the comic spirit not only in their demand for full-length narratives but also in their reality. The camera confers solidity on what it photographs; movie audiences expect to see a real world on the screen. The essence of comedy, however, is that it departs from reality; comic characters and events are exaggerated, theatrical, if not exactly larger than life (in a heroic sense) at least *different* from life. Comedy is a stylized form; the movies are "real": how is the comic film maker to accommodate the former without undermining the latter?

As he was learning how to write and to deliver and to photograph jokes for movies, and how to flesh out an initial comic premise for a story that lasts from approximately eighty to ninety minutes,  Allen probably asked himself these questions: How much can comedy say? How neatly can it say it? And how pretty can it look and still retain a comic aura?

Whatever his ostensible subject matter—crime or politics or sex or old movies or religion or modern manners— Allen himself is at the center of the comic framework. The laughs bounce off his persona. Through the continuing chronicle of his own (mostly) erotic misadventures, he is a revealer of middle-class madness and anxiety. "Selections From the Allen Notebooks" and "My Philosophy," the titles of two of  Allen's comic essays, describe all his work, for through his comedy he tells us what's on his mind. Even in his early far-out farces and burlesques Allen's work bristled with ideas and the promise of higher intentions. For all his self-mockery, Allen casts himself as something of a sage, a nebbish with the eyes of a hawk, who through his wit makes stabs at defining the meaning of life. "Women, attitudes toward and relationships with," is the largest entry in the Allen index, but surrounding and embellishing the central ongoing sexual comedy are references to other major Allen themes like psychiatry, God, death, art versus life, New York versus Los Angeles, integrity versus selling out, and the burdens and costs of Making It. In his comedy the life of the mind invades that traditional subject of laughs, the desires of the body: speculations on God and death and art darken Woody's dating problems.

How serious can comedy be? is clearly a question Woody has continued to ask, with mounting concern. To what extent, and in what ways, can comedy explore themes traditionally the province of the noncomic writer? Underlying the quest is Allen's lingering distrust of comedy ("When you do comedy, you're not sitting at the grown-ups' table"). Insecure about how big his comedy can be, he treats monumental subjects in a vaudevillian style, knocking them down to his own comic measure. He clearly enjoys the challenge of taking on themes not usually considered appropriate for comedy: calling a comedy *Love and Death* shows Allen's interest in tempting the fates. But so far in his movie comedies, if not in his essays and one-act plays, the Big Themes have appeared only fleetingly, as appetizers to the main course, Allen holding forth on love and sex. As *Interiors* indicates, however, he is drawn to treating serious subjects not surreptitiously, on the sly as it were, in a style of brash comic insouciance, but in a sober way, as the focus of a full-length narrative.

With *Interiors* out of his system there is every sign that Allen's comedies will now absorb heavier doses of the grim subjects that bedevil him. Ironically, though, before he made *Interiors,* which among other things is about the problems of the artist, the pains and rewards of creativity, he handled the theme with greater insight within the framework of a comedy, *Annie Hall.* Clearly he is preoccupied with the connections between a creator's life and his work (all his comedies speak to the point at some level): how does a writer make creative use of his experiences, transforming them in order to arouse laughter and provide insights which general audiences can relate to? *Annie Hall* proved that this theme is accessible to comedy, can in fact become a sustaining comic motif.

For all its cosmic fallout, its hints of grandiloquence, its feints in the direction of Higher Seriousness, Allen's movie comedy so far has been mostly about love and sex, as Woody pursues, conquers, and is rejected by women. (Love and sex certainly aren't synonymous in the courtship rituals which Allen's comedies chronicle. Sex can eradicate love, and love can transcend sex. Woody, caught in the middle, seeks refuge and distance in therapy, in being funny, and in showing off his psychic scars, the results of his excursions into the romantic jungle.) The battle of the sexes—not God and death—has been his ongoing theme, presented in a variety of formats, from the outrageous knockabout farce of *Everything You Always Wanted to Know About Sex** (**but were afraid to ask*) to the subdued stylized realism of *Manhattan.* An immaculate treatment of love and sex, *Manhattan* in fact feels like the end of a cycle for Allen—it's the most sober, the most grave and beautiful handling of what is, at this point in his work, the same old thing. In visual style and in mood it hints at a grander, headier comedy to come. (Again, see chapter 8.)

How Woody the stud makes out is the focus of the comic autobiography that Allen's movies reveal. So no matter where his stories take place, in no matter how outlandish or fantastic a setting, Woody and his sexual bravado and sexual defeats occupy center stage. Subjecting his dating problems to a series of variously lofty and visually striking frames, Allen has been skillful in disguising the sameness of his material.

Love and sex, the central pulse of his comedy, the springboard for most of his jokes, are subjects about which Allen has a lot to say. He keeps returning to them not only because they are good for laughs but because they arouse in him a tangle of contradictory feelings which have yet to be pacified. For Woody, women, at different times, represent salvation, refuge, and downfall. They can be objects of lust, beautiful empty vessels, true friends and companions, and foils that inspire his best comic zingers. They are bait, competition, reward; they are trouble, and they make life worth living. They complete and they distract. His best films, *Annie Hall* and *Manhattan,* are about how and why relationships between men and women don't last.

Why doesn't Woody get it right? He's witty, charming, seductive, quite the ladies' man, in truth; and from the evidence offered in the films, quite a titan in bed. Women laugh at him, think he's cute, become dependent on him—and so do we. But something keeps getting in his way, as his movies tell us over and over. Is it his ego? His need to be appreciated and to be in control? His compulsive cynicism? His acerbic wit? Or is it just human nature that makes people get on each other's nerves? It is all of the above, Allen's comedies suggest, which prevent him from capturing a happily-ever-after relationship. But Allen is a romantic at heart, and he keeps trying; his quest for the latter day Holy Grail—the relationship that works, and keeps on working—has been, so far, the fundamental subject of his movie comedy.

Tragedies end in a period; comedies end with a question mark. Proceeding toward a preordained resolution, tragedies have a tight linear movement; comedies depend on at least an appearance of chaos. Tragedies have a single focus, intense and claustrophobic; comedies are often episodic and sprawling. In tragedy we know where the story is headed; comic form is loose, seemingly improvisational, filled with unexpected dips and swerves. Tragedy presents a rigorously ordered world view, whereas comedy pelts us with images of anarchy and irrationality. Unlike tragedy, which traditionally ends in the finality of death, comedy typically concludes with renewal and promise—the open road down which Chaplin's tramp strutted at the ends of his adventures is an ideal image of comic open-endedness. In comedy, who knows what tomorrow will bring? For the comic hero, unlike the princes of tragedy, almost nothing is irreversible; the comic world is filled with unexpected possibilities. Think of all the improbable things that happen to Woody: he goes into St. Vincent's Hospital for a minor operation and wakes up about two hundred years later. He meets Napoleon. He subdues a giant tit. He gets shot out of an erect penis. He even wins the heart of a gorgeous teen-ager! (And to top it all, the nebbish from Brooklyn becomes a world-famous, world-class clown!) The comic world is in a state of constant flux, laying traps for the comic protagonist one minute, covering him with unlooked-for glory the next. Buster Keaton entering into the movie screen in *Sherlock, Jr.,* where the laws of space and time are upended, is an apt metaphor for the topsy-turvy world that comedy creates.

If the course of tragedy is a direct line toward the unavoidable, a collision with fate, that of comedy is the circle. Comedy tells its stories in curlicues and zigzags rather than in the clean unbroken rhythm of tragedy. Like the stories in which he stars, the comic hero goes in circles. The same damn things keep happening to him over and over. He never seems to learn or to prosper from his experiences; for him to mature too much, after all, might well be the death of his comic status. So Woody, typically, plays dumb, not letting on that he knows as much as he really does or that he is radically different from the guy we first became acquainted with in the mid-sixties. Like most comic stars, he is locked into a fixed persona, a character who can absorb only a limited number of changes.

The experience of tragedy, in life as in art, alters us. Oedipus, knowing what he knows at the end of the play, is not the same lordly, self-assured ruler he was at the beginning. Instead of transformation, comedy offers repetition. Being unfazed and therefore essentially untouched by his adventures is the secret of the comic hero's endurance; it is why, despite calamity, he goes on at the end, ready and in effect asking for more of the same.

Stories are important to the tragic form; in movie comedies they're merely excuses, providing the string for a necklace of comic baubles. Of course there are comedies with intricate, well-ordered stories, but this type of comic structure rarely has worked well on film. A Feydeau farce, a Jonsonian humors comedy, a Molière or Restoration comedy of manners, with their mechanically timed entrances and exits and their spiraling mix-ups, are alien to the spirit (as well as the requirements) of movie comedy. Movies had to discover their own kinds of comic narratives—and stories set in one room, with a tightly woven plot and with a neat, complicated interweaving of character and event, were simply too claustrophobic for the more open dimensions of the film frame. As pioneers in movie comedy like Mack Sennett and Chaplin quickly realized, the tight, artificial form of the classic literary comedies was not congenial to films. Silent comedy thus smashed comic form as it had been handed down for centuries in the theater by taking comedy out of closed interior spaces and placing it outside, in the real world, and providing it with episodic stories as wide open as the settings.

What we remember from Chaplin and Keaton, or the talking comedy of the Marx Brothers, is not a tidy, well-told story but isolated routines that epitomize and celebrate a comic persona: Chaplin making a dinner out of shoelaces in *The Gold Rush,* roller-skating blindfolded, and singing gibberish in *Modern Times,* executing an elegant pas de deux in the boxing arena in *City Lights,* balancing the globe on his fingertip in *The Great Dictator.* Chaplin's comedy is a series of such privileged, inspired moments which can be enjoyed on their own, apart from any narrative context.

Even more than the silent clowns, the Marx Brothers and their writers blithely disregarded concepts of narrative plausibility and continuity, constructing their films as a sequence of vaudeville sketches. They grabbed at anything to take their minds (and ours) away from the story, throwing in harp and piano solos or full-dress production numbers like so many bolts from the blue. For them, stories were only an interference. All they required was a setting where they could work their comic chaos: the opera, an ocean liner, a college campus, a mythical country in political turmoil, a doctor's office, the horse races. Who can remember the story line of any of the Marx pictures? Who wants to? And yet who can forget such comic turns as the overcrowded stateroom in *A Night at the Opera,* the mock auction for land in *The Coconuts,* the mirror scene in *Duck Soup*?

Like those of Chaplin and the Marx Brothers, Woody's comedies unfurl as a series of misadventures unified only by the continuing presence of the comic hero. Episodic and picaresque, with one routine following another, Allen's stories are a parade of comic ideas loosely draped around an initial pretext. Allen's earliest movies especially, the prehistoric *What's Up, Tiger Lily?* and *Take the Money and Run,* use a scattershot approach, shooting off a barrage of verbal as well as visual one-liners. Triggered by a basic comic idea—Woody in the incongruous guise of a bank robber or heading a guerrilla revolution—he and his co-writers ricochet from one skit to another in a disordered narrative style that is typical of the best movie comedies. Some of the gags take off, while others bite the dust as story, characterization, and unity are sacrificed in the frenetic quest for laughs. If the jokes come fast enough, a comic rhythm and momentum are maintained even if some of the business fizzles.

*Bananas,* a junk pile of comic bits and pieces shakily stitched together by Woody's presence and by the merest wisp of a narrative thread, is the best of Allen's early ragamuffin style. It opens with a parody of the "Wide World of Sports" as Howard Cosell moderates a live, on-the-spot assassination. "We've seen a series of colorful riots beginning with the traditional bombing of the

American Embassy," Cosell drones, in his distinctive, obnoxious style. The President of the Republic of San Marcos is shot, as expected. Cosell pushes through the crowd, to chat with him and to wish him luck, as the titles flash onto the screen, accompanied by rapid-fire gunshots. After the titles we are introduced to Fielding Mellish, an obscure products tester, who demonstrates an exercizer designed for busy executives. Fielding starts out very sure of himself, but the machine quickly goes haywire as his oblivious boss continues with a bland sales pitch to a prospective customer. "Machines hate me," Fielding confesses to a co-worker. "Why did I quit college? I was in black studies. By now, I could have been black."

He tries to score with Norma, the office nympho, but she is busy. Frustrated, he goes to a bookstore to buy some porno magazines. (*The National Review* and *Airport* are shelved in the porno section.) With a portly matron standing nearby, Fielding pretends to be interested only in highbrow journals, calling out the names of the respectable publications he plans to buy, while hiding the girlie magazines underneath. But his cover is blown when a loudmouth counterman asks his boss what the price of *Orgasm* is. On his quick exit from the store, Fielding gives the shocked matron a squeeze.

On the subway ride home a gang of toughs attack an old lady with crutches who is sitting next to Fielding, who cowers behind his newly purchased copy of *Commentary*, pushing the crutches away from him. The doors open, and in a momentary heroic burst he pushes the thugs onto the platform. As he rests against the closed doors in a glow of triumph, they open again unexpectedly, the thugs rush in, Fielding faints, the old lady reads *Orgasm* (as fast music, evocative of silent comedies, accompanies the action).

On the way home Fielding directs a driver into a

parking space, motioning him on, and on, and on, until the car smacks into another car. Fielding says fine and hurries on.

At home he takes out meat. It starts to hop. There's a knock on his door. He unlocks one lock, then another, and another. It's Nancy, asking him to sign a petition in support of the rebels of San Marcos. The two of them quickly fall into an intellectual discussion. "Eastern philosophy is metaphysical, redundant, abortively pedantic," Fielding says, flirtatiously. "The Danes have an instinctive feel for the human condition," she says. "Hmm, that's wise, that's very pithy." "Yes," she agrees, "pithy. It had great pith." "Yeth." "Well, lithen— listen. . . ." He tries to set up a date. But she's busy. One night she has her women's lib group. "Does that mean you're hostile to the male sex?" Fielding inquires. Another night she may bomb a building. To impress her with his radical *bona fides*, he says he's planning to picket an embassy. (Shots of Fielding, his glasses fallen off, jostled by a crowd and with a hose twisted around his neck.)

When he finally gets Nancy into his bed, she turns out to be a *kvetch*. It's too hot, there's not enough light, there's too much light, "Say 'I love you' in French."

"I was a nervous child," Fielding, lying on the couch, confesses to his therapist. He recalls a dream in which he's carried on a cross on Wall Street by cassocked priests who challenge another cross-carrying group for a parking place.

"There's something missing for me," Nancy tells Fielding. "Is it personality or looks or I'm not smart enough?" he asks, all in a jitter. "No," she says, "it has nothing to do with the fact that you're short, or your teeth are in bad shape." "Do you have fun when you're with me?" "No," she says. "And it's not because I don't love you. I need a leader. . . . I am interested in so many vital political things. I want to go and work with pygmies in Africa, with lepers in a leper colony." "I love leprosy," Fielding says, "I like cholera, I like all the major skin diseases."

Crestfallen, Fielding confides to a co-worker. "She needs a leader. Hitler?"

In San Marcos, almost as soon as he checks into a rundown hotel, Fielding receives an invitation to dine with the President. He hears a harp, but it isn't a heavenly message, it's only a harpist practicing in the closet.

He brings President Vargas a plum cake. "I like cherry cake, not plum," Vargas squawks. "They don't make cherry on Tuesday," Fielding explains. "Are you tense?" Vargas asks Fielding during dinner. "No," he says, eating his wineglass. "Could you keep it down? I'm getting a headache," Fielding says to a silent orchestra. The waiter brings the check. Fielding asks who had the roast beef, who the corned beef and cabbage.

The plot: Vargas plans to kill Fielding but make it seem as if the rebels did it and thereby to turn America against the guerrilla forces that are threatening to unseat him. Fielding escapes and winds up in the rebel camp, where he must hide out until the revolution, six months thence. "But I have a rented car!" he shrieks.

Fielding undergoes combat training. Practicing the art of camouflage, he hides in a bush—and gets peed on. Instructed in snakebite remedies, he protests, "I cannot suck anybody's leg whom I'm not engaged to." "I just got bitten by a snake," screams a busty woman, her hand to her chest. The entire camp runs after her, offering their services.

Fielding is dispatched on a food-gathering mission to

a neighborhood diner. He orders 1,000 grilled cheese sandwiches and 300 tuna fish sandwiches, 700 regular coffees, 1,000 7-Up's, 500 Cokes, cole slaw and mayo on the side. The proprietor doesn't flinch, a few minutes later delivering the order in a sea of green paper bags.

Fielding and a woman rebel eat their sandwiches on an oceanside cliff, *Tom Jones* style, as eating becomes a metaphor for sex. They strip. There's heroic martial music ("Victory at Sea"?); fade-out; the woman lies smoking, obviously becalmed and satisfied by Fielding's performance.

"I've made provisions for reinforcements from UJA," Vargas announces. "Are we for or against the government?" a CIA agent asks, on board a plane to San Marcos. "The CIA isn't taking any chances. Some will be for, some against."

Rebel soldiers storm the steps of Vargas's palace, as Hasidim with cups ask for donations. A baby carriage rolls down the steps in homage to *Battleship Potemkin.*

Vargas makes a reservation for one at the Miami Beach Hotel.

Esposito sets himself up as the new dictator of San Marcos. "These people are peasants," he mutters. "They're too ignorant to vote. There will be no elections until I decree. The official language will be Swedish." He orders executions of Vargas's men in the public square. Fielding assigns numbers to the victims, as if they were waiting their turn in a bakery.

Esposito is overthrown, and Fielding is installed as leader. He is sent, in Fidel Castro beard, on a fund-raising trip to the United States. At a dinner, he tells a dignified crowd that locusts are available in San Marcos, at popular prices, and so are the women. "We lead the world in hernias."

In disguise, he meets and beds Nancy, who tells him, "You remind me of a stupid clown. He was a real idiot." She says sex with him was a religious experience; he confesses to being Fielding Mellish. "Omigod, I knew something was missing."

On the evening news, Roger Grimsby reports that Fielding Mellish has been accused of being a subversive, a Commie front preparing a takeover of the country. Grimsby also reports that the National Rifle Association declares that death is a good thing, and that New York garbagemen strike for a better class of garbage.

Grimsby reports from Fielding's trial. Fielding, representing himself, calls this a mistrial. "This is a sham of a mockery of a sham. There's not a single homosexual on the jury." "Yes there is," the judge snaps. "Oh really. Is it the big one on the end?"

The first witness, a cop, calls Fielding a New York Jewish intellectual Commie crackpot. Fielding counters by asking him if he ever had sexual relations with a girl with big breasts.

J. Edgar Hoover, a big black woman, is called to the stand. A man storms in, confesses he did it, only to find out he's at the wrong trial. Miss America is called to the stand to sing an aria in Italian. A juror drinks from a goldfish bowl. The jurors pass a joint. Fielding questions himself, jumping from the floor to the stand at a steadily accelerating pace. The judge orders Fielding to be bound and gagged. In this state he questions an extremely nervous-looking woman, who understands his mutters perfectly.

Grimsby calls a commercial break. A handsome priest assures us that we will be forgiven if we smoke New Testament cigarettes.

The judge suspends a sentence of guilty on the

promise that Fielding will not move into his old neighborhood.

Fielding and Nancy go for a walk on the Brooklyn Heights Promenade. "Do you love me?" she asks. "Can you define love?" Fielding counters, sailing off into mumbo jumbo about otherness and wholeness and not being jealous of the thing one possesses.

"The action is swift, rhythmic, coordinated," Howard Cosell announces, as he narrates Fielding and Nancy's wedding-night bout. "He needs a little seasoning, but he's not the worst I've had," Nancy responds to Cosell's prodding questions. Fielding anticipates he'll be ready for another match next spring, as a subtitle announces that the astronauts have landed on the moon and established the first all-Protestant cafeteria.

Disjointed, fragmentary, hectic, above all vaudevillian, *Bananas* is thus a procession of wacky verbal and sight gags. Grafting revue humor and the tricks of stand-up comedy onto a picaresque story, Allen makes a mad dash for his laughs and gets most of them. Story and characterization are sacrificed for jokes, wisecracks, puns, anachronisms. *"Bananas* was only coincidentally political," Allen said at the time the film was released. "I really had no point I was trying to make in the whole thing. I was just trying to think of a funny idea. It could just as easily have been an idea about crime again, or bank robberies."

He maintained a freewheeling atmosphere on the set. "Funniness is organic," he said. "What you write is not what you shoot." He improvised and followed suggestions from his actors; he didn't rehearse scenes or know in advance where he was going to put the camera. He shot some scenes over and over, changing the comic business and much of the dialogue. And when he began the editing process he "annihilated" the film, altering, rearranging, and deconstructing his footage. Typically, he had trouble finding an ending. "It was either a chase or a courtroom scene. Either would have worked very well. We couldn't afford a chase."

Like most writers of picaresque movie comedy, Allen has always had trouble getting offstage. The endings to *Take the Money and Run, Bananas,* and *Sleeper,* in particular, have the look of desperation. How do I get out of here? Woody all but asks us. Having indulged in a comic free-for-all, he doesn't know how to round off the action neatly in a final comic point. For *Take the Money and Run* his character is back in jail, coyly asking for a bar of soap (a verbal reminder of one of the best gags in the film, when Virgil carves a gun out of soap, only to have his weapon dissolve as he bluffs an escape during a rainstorm). But putting the character back in jail seems less a thematic point than an admission of storytelling defeat, Woody going in circles. To give *Bananas* a trace of narrative unity, Allen brings on Howard Cosell for a "Wide World of Sports" encore. *Sleeper* doesn't really end at all, as Woody and Diane have a conversation about sex and death while they are stranded in the middle of an uncompleted comic action. *Love and Death* ends, peculiarly, with a lovely long shot of Woody dancing with Death down a row of poplars: awfully high-toned as the finale for a farce.

By the time of *Annie Hall* and *Manhattan,* though, Allen has learned how to take a curtain call. *Annie Hall* concludes with a visual résumé of the high points of the film. This shrewdly calculated coda ( Allen working closely with his editor, Ralph Rosenblum) is an homage to Diane Keaton which enlarges her performance (it probably helped her win the Oscar) and also makes us nostalgic about what we have just seen. *Manhattan* too ends with a beguiling grace note—a close-up of Woody looking at Mariel Hemingway with a mixture of tentativeness and love, a distinctly Chaplinesque blend of comedy and sentiment that leaves us with the feeling that what we have seen has been meaningful as well as moving.

All of Allen's movies from *What's Up, Tiger Lily?* to *Love and Death* follow the same episodic, open-ended format in which the gags rather than the story are what's important. The films represent a showing off of comic technique; taking us along for a ride, they ask that we suspend all the usual concerns for narrative sense and continuity. The timing of individual jokes, and protecting the overall comic rhythm, take precedence over the story line or character development. It's the comedian's sensibility that's on display, not his skill in fashioning a well-made plot.

With *Play It Again, Sam, Annie Hall, Interiors,* and *Manhattan,* Allen abandons a burlesque framework for stories about relationships. These four movies are character studies of why and how a group of people either do or do not get along with each other.

Betraying its shifts of focus during the planning stages, from a movie about Woody and his rich fantasy life to one that is primarily about not Annie, exactly, but Woody's attitudes toward her, *Annie Hall* is as structurally untidy, as disjointed and pockmarked, as the earlier farces. Moving from the present to the past, sometimes placing the characters as overseers of past action, jumping from New York to Los Angeles, weaving fantasy in and out of reality, and using a number of film gimmicks like split screen and animation and subtitles, the film is a structural hodgepodge. *Manhattan* alone among   Allen's comedies so far tells its story in a straightforward style, in a narrative sequence not invaded by fantasy or memory. Although it is immaculately organized—a first for Allen —*Manhattan* is still more a series of perceptions about its mixed-up characters, more a mood piece about modern dating rituals, than a full-fledged conventional story.

Unlike the earlier movies, then, *Annie Hall* and *Manhattan* are primarily comedies of character rather than comedies of incident. What keeps them moving is not so much comic misadventures, as in *Bananas* or *Sleeper* or *Take the Money and Run,* but the ongoing relationships among the cast of characters, who might by this point be identified as the Woody Allen Repertory Company. *Annie Hall* and *Manhattan* focus on the kinds of relationships that were at least a marginal element in the earlier comedies of the open road: Woody and his two sidekicks, the sweet, kooky, lost girl (usually played by Diane Keaton, or a Keaton type) and the cool, intelligent best friend (Tony Roberts and Michael Murphy are interchangeable in the role) whose conventional handsomeness sets off Woody's famous homeliness. Seemingly better adjusted than Woody, his best friend nevertheless has problems too. In *Play It Again, Sam* he neglects his wife for business, talking compulsively on the phone in a nonstop high-level businessman's jargon. In *Annie Hall* he is a New York actor gone Hollywood; he's sold his artistic promise for the financial rewards of commercial claptrap, and he's been infected by the faddish Coast mentality, mellowing out, eating health food, putting on a gas mask to shield himself from the sun while driving. In *The Front* he faces a blacklist because of his Communist associations. In *Manhattan* he is a stalled academic, unable to meet either professional commitments (a major critical study of O'Neill) or personal ones (he carries on an affair with Diane Keaton while reserving most of his affection for his wife). But whatever his failings, the best friend has a warm spot for Woody. He goes with him on long walks through the city, a pastime that takes up much of the action in *Manhattan*; and he's there with good advice, offering sensible correctives to some of Woody's paranoid flights, like his conviction in *Annie Hall* that an imagined foe was mocking him when, in asking a question, he said "D'Jew?" instead of "Did you?"

Tony Roberts and Michael Murphy are among Allen's best friends offscreen too. As in *Annie Hall* Allen and Roberts call each other Max, a name that started when, to avoid being recognized in public (as if that were possible), Woody asked his friend to call him Max. Allen's trust in these two men shows in their work together; their scenes have an easy, natural flow, and the cool tone of the two actors nicely balances Woody's neurotic delivery.

Allen casts his friends in the running role of the girl too, as if he can work well only with actors he knows intimately. Himself intimidated by celebrity, he has said often that he is wary of working with stars; apart from the ones he uses in cameo roles, almost the only stars are the ones he created, like Louise Lasser and Diane Keaton.

The Allen Girl (usually then a real-life girl friend or an ex-wife) laughs at his quips, is amused by his awkwardness, finds him adorable, and usually leaves him. It's the same girl, more or less, the same response, the same relationship, over and over, though pitched in different keys and set in a variety of backgrounds. Like the best friend, Woody's women perform in a low key, in a style of comic inflection that is in fact recognizable as the Allen touch. Listen to the way dialogue is delivered in all of Allen's movies, and you'll hear the same mellow tones, the same cadences and nuances, over and over: the stammers, pauses, overlappings, the hesitations that give a lifelike dimension to the characters even in the wackiest settings and circumstances.

Apart from these few intimates—the best friend, and the joking, yielding, indispensable girl friend—Woody is not generous in sharing his acting space. His comic colleagues and antagonists have less presence than those of the silent clowns—there are no ensemble comic turns in his films, no equivalent of the group comedy of the Keystone Kops or the ensemble anarchy of the Marx Brothers.    Allen typically goes it alone, striking sparks with only a few carefully chosen characters whom he relegates to distinctly supporting roles. Sometimes the movies suffer from this peculiar reticence, the deadpan quality that's forced on the supporting players. Think of the characters in *Sleeper*; except for Woody and Diane, all the citizens of the film's futuristic society are utterly expressionless. Yet the comedy needs some vivid opponents, some characters who are not merely springboards for Woody's own shtick but who have a sharp comic style of their own. Much the same surrounding blandness (where it is even less justifiable thematically) also infects Woody's fellow convicts in *Take the Money and Run,* the revolutionaries in *Bananas,* and the Russian soldiers in *Love and Death.* All these films are underpopulated, Woody himself (with varying assistance from The Girl) carrying the entire comic burden.    Allen seems to surround himself with somnambulists.

Transfixed on himself, and getting his audience hooked on him as well,    Allen continues to make movies about Woody. Enchanted still, we go to his movies because we want to see more of him. But Woody is surely not an inexhaustible reservoir of comic fecundity, and no doubt one of the changes in the design of his future movies will be more generous comic opportunities for his fellow performers. There are already signs that his comic hogging is remediable—in his scenes with Diane Keaton in *Annie Hall* and *Manhattan* and with Zero Mostel in *The Front.*

What does a comedy look like?    Allen has said that some of the old comedies, particularly those of the Marx Brothers and W. C. Fields, looked as though they had been made in an empty lot.    Allen never wanted his own comedies to have that shabby, down-at-heels quality, and of course they never have. But at the same time he realized that comedies can't look beautiful either, and that the visual style he had always admired in the work of favorite directors like Bergman and Fellini was unavailable to him. "In comedy," he has said, "it's very difficult to do *anything* filmically. Everything has to be spare and quick and precise. The match has to be struck and the flare has to go up. None of the things that really good directors like. It's best in comedy to work directly on behavior, not on effects."

The main goal in comedy is to protect the joke, and so the technique of great comic film makers like Chaplin and Keaton is plain, disciplined, tight. The two knowing comedians used only what they needed in order to make their routines look comfortable in front of the camera, and there are few visual flourishes in their work. They knew exactly where to place the camera, when to move it, and where to edit—their lean, no-frills style is simple but shrewd. Silent-movie comedy presents whole figures in real space, and preserving the actors' movements, the grace and wit of their mime—Chaplin's song and dance at the end of *Modern Times,* Keaton maneuvering himself from the roof of a building onto a car in one unbroken arc of motion—takes precedence over every other consideration of visual style. For the best silent comedies the camera served as a neutral recording instrument, the observer rather than the creator of beauty.

The early sound comedies, like the early sound movies of every genre, are static and lumpy. The visually threadbare comedies of the Marx Brothers and W. C. Fields have none of the restrained visual grace of the classic silents—as the great comics talk, deftly plying their trade, the camera for the most part remains in place.

For his own comedies   Allen has tried to rediscover some of the original visual poetry of the silents while avoiding the perfunctory, visually deadpan style of the Marx Brothers' farces. *Everything You Always Wanted to Know About Sex\** (\**but were afraid to ask*) was   Allen's first visually stylish comedy, the first of his films where decor and pictorial style support the jokes. Though there are sight gags in *Take the Money and Run* and *Bananas,* there is no visual wit in either: the film technique, the use of the camera, the style of editing do not *create* comedy as they do in *Sex.* The first two look like straight films and sound like comedies, while *Sex* looks as well as sounds funny. Both *Take the Money and Run* and *Bananas* introduced but did not resolve the problem of how to set comic action in the real world. *Money* takes place in real prisons and banks and rural landscapes; *Bananas* moves from New York to a South American setting in which there are indications of genuine poverty. Neither movie finds a way of filming farce in the real outdoors. The silent clowns could do it because silence acted as a distancing factor, a buffer between real settings and stylized action. But in   Allen's early movies there is a visual clash when he places exaggerated comic routines in realistic backgrounds. By the time of *Sleeper* and *Love and Death,* however, the contrast between movie realism and comic theatricality has been accounted for. The futuristic white sets in *Sleeper* provide a suitable environment for horseplay, although some outdoor shots near the end, where the actors simply look like actors cutting up for the camera on location, are jarring. *Love and Death,* with its burnished colors, its rich creamy lighting, its palatial settings, and stunning landscapes with their echoes of master paintings, looks too good—far too classy—for a comedy, which is exactly the point. Allen by now uses the imbalance between "high" form and "low" content as part of his comic technique; the contrast between the formal, carefully composed visuals—the sheer lushness and beauty of the compositions—and the often knockabout level of the comedy adds to the comic surprise that runs throughout the movie. *Love and Death* is clearly made by a man who both loves aoves and enjoys parodying Beautiful Movies.

Beauty with a capital *B* has surfaced in  Allen's comedies only in ways that, so far, are themselves comic. (When  Allen wanted to indulge himself by being *seriously* beautiful, he made *Interiors,* a high drama that has only its exquisite interior decoration and its elegantly spare color scheme—its parade of pretty pictures—to recommend it.) In *Everything You Always Wanted to Know About Sex,* which is a great-looking movie,  Allen parodies the visual styles of Antonioni (white on white, which he uses again in *Sleeper,* for comic effect, and in *Interiors*), of *Fantastic Voyage,* and of Universal horror movies. The love story between man and sheep looks like a deluxe woman's picture, with the glowing yellow lighting supplying just the right atmosphere for a glossy Hollywood romance. Throughout, the visual richness is never used for its own sake, which would of course undermine the comedy, but is ironic, providing contrast and surprise and commenting as well on its own pretentiousness. All that gooey lighting and those stark semiabstract compositions in white send up their own beauty.

*Annie Hall* and *Manhattan* use visual elegance not for parody or comic contrast but to enhance dramatic values. The new look is in keeping with the more sober comic style of the films. For *Annie Hall,* Allen wanted three different textures: a photo album yellow for the scenes set in the past; a bleached, overexposed look for the scenes in Los Angeles to convey the scorching California sun that he dislikes; and a sharp, clean color for the New York scenes set in the present. Though most of the laughs are verbal rather than visual, the studied design never intrudes on the comedy—no mean feat.

*Manhattan* is Allen's most visually sophisticated film to date. Even more than *Annie Hall* it is a comedy that doesn't look like a comedy. Stately in pace, with long takes, the camera often remaining on a scene for a beat or two after the actors have left the frame, photographed in clean black and white (itself a sign of Allen's burgeoning self-consciousness as a film maker), the movie is a true visual experiment, an attempt to see how elegant a comedy can look and still pass as a comedy.

Two shots (among many possibilities) indicate the deliberateness and formality of Allen's design. Isaac and Tracy run into Yale in a corner at the Museum of Modern Art; after a moment, out from behind a wall, steps Mary Wilke making a delayed entrance: Allen's homage to his favorite co-star Diane Keaton. Allen exploits the sharp white angles of the room for their sleek impersonality, their Mondrian abstractness. In another equally calculated moment, Isaac and Tracy are at his apartment, talking quietly in the dark. Photographed in long shot they occupy only a fragment of the left side of the frame, while to the right the large room is plunged into darkness broken only by light Allen (streaming from an upstairs room) which partially illuminates a spiral staircase. Allen holds this elegantly composed shot for a daringly long time, with no intercutting or camera movement to break the uninterrupted flow of the dialogue, which in contrast to the visual deliberateness sounds casual and improvised.

Throughout the film    Allen offers Wellesian compositions with depth and shadow and stark chiaroscuro lighting that turns the actors into silhouetted figures; he indicates alienation by creating gaping spaces between characters; he suggests psychological entrapment through visual means, boxing his characters into corners or observing them behind objects or through windows and doors. Walls, blinds, and glass become images of exclusion and separation. And behind and surrounding the personal drama is the city, vital, pulsating, dynamic, yet wonderfully soft and delicate too, the lights of skyscrapers dancing in the distance, the lights of the Queensboro Bridge casting a magical glow in the most romantic shot in the film, when Isaac and Mary sit in the early morning fog on a bench overlooking the East River. The rich, flowing Gershwin score and New York in all its majesty and thrusting beauty embrace the characters and help to give the film its special celebratory tone. *Manhattan* is pure poetry in motion, a moving, dark romantic comedy that indicates    Allen's triumphant mastery of his craft and that promises visually dazzling comedies in the future.

# 8

# The Comedian's Progress: The Eighties

T HE FACE looks a little different, this time. In the opening shot of *Stardust Memories* (1980) Allen's gaze is slightly averted as he slumps in an existential stupor. Where *Annie Hall* begins with Allen peering directly into the camera, eager to establish a bond with his audience and sounding peppy as he talks about his usual subjects—anxiety, alienation, and self-loathing—here in contrast his whole face droops. His exhaustion forbids laughter, and audiences in 1980 acknowledged this "new" Woody Allen with obedient silence.

His brooding, de-clowned face, grainy black and white photography, an ominous ticking clock that provides the lone sound effect—each carefully selected detail warned us that Allen had something else in mind besides laughs or romance. *Stardust Memories* represented an opening round in the film maker's war against "Woody Allen." Of course, at least since the time of *Love and Death* there had been signs of Allen's restlessness, his nagging dissatisfaction with the limits of "pure" comedy, but in *Stardust Memories* the burden of being a world-renowned funny man is no longer merely implied; it provides the motor for the entire film. *Stardust Memories* announced that Allen wanted to become someone else, someone both "other" and better—more serious, more probing—that a zany comedian, a professional New York neurotic and cutup.

To underline his seriousness about being serious he places jokes at arm's length. His character, Sandy Bates, is a film director who attends a festival devoted to his work and during question-and-answer sessions distributed throughout the film his rapid-fire gags seem valedictory, as if Allen himself is staging a farewell to stand-up comedy. "Did you study at film school?" "No, they study me." "Your films are psychological, but where do you stand politically?" one fans asks. "I'm for total complete democracy," Sandy snaps back, "and I believe in the American system too." "You studied philosophy in college, didn't you?" "Yes. I got one hundred on the existential philosophy exam by not answering any of the questions." "You've been accused of being narcissistic." "Well, actually, the Greek god I would identify with is not Narcissus but Zeus."

Even the jokes that take place offstage have a nostalgic tinge. When Sandy chases a pigeon out of his apartment, we're reminded of the episode with the live crabs in *Annie Hall.* When he tells his current girlfriend that the only things he's good at are art and masturbation, we recall Woody's comment to Diane Keaton at the end of *Sleeper* that his only beliefs are death and sex, "things which come once in a lifetime." Some of the sharpest comic routines, such as a skit about Sidney Finkelstein's escaped anger (as wonderfully wacky as anything in *Bananas* or *Everything You Always Wanted to Know About*

*Sex*), occur in films within the film, as bits and pieces from Sandy's work in progress or as excerpts from the old movies of his being screened at the festival. Because the sketches are introduced suddenly, disruptively, we often are more concerned with how they fit into the narrative than with their content. Throughout *Stardust Memories,* then, there is an anti-comic impulse—funny business is enclosed in frames within the frame.

Allen doesn't let us forget that he is striking out in new directions, and he tries to silence criticism by anticipating it. Looking at the rushes of Sandy's new film, studio executives denounce it as too "fancy" and accuse him of trying to "fob off private suffering as art." "What does he have to be so upset about?" an exasperated studio boss asks. "Doesn't he realize he has the greatest gift of all, the gift of laughter?" "This is how he makes his living?" an old Jewish man complains at the end of the festival. "I like a melodrama, a musical, a comedy. But this?"

Most of Allen's work of the eighties has been an attempt to fulfill the "promise" expressed in this arty, curmudgeonly, transitional film as, with varying success, he has continued to challenge himself and his audience by making movies that are not merely comic and that both prod and stifle laughter in sometimes audacious counterpoint. Significantly, Allen published his third collection of essays at the same time that *Stardust Memories* was released, during the last week of September, 1980. Written over a five-year period, from 1975 to 1980, *Side Effects* contains more of "Woody" than the film does; for all their intermittent flashes of despair, the essays are jauntier, more gag-filled, and have more of the high-flown antics of the old comic roustabout than the downbeat film. In these pieces written for *The New Yorker,* in which small matters are blown up to epic scale and high-rent themes are struck down from lofty perches, Allen replays familiar strategies.

In his work throughout the last decade the director has mixed and matched the strained seriousness of *Stardust Memories* with the giddy, surreal, high-stepping comic performance of *Side Effects.* Here is a quick overview of Allen's progress in the eighties. In 1980, *The Floating Light Bulb,* a modest family play written rather stiffly in a style of conventional Broadway realism, was produced at the Vivian Beaumont Theatre in New York's Lincoln Center. *A Midsummer Night's Sex Comedy* (1982) is a romantic period comedy, *la ronde* in turn-of-the-century Westchester County. *Zelig* (1983) is a mock-documentary about a man with amazing powers of self-transformation. *Broadway Danny Rose* (1984) is a shaggy-dog story about a talent agent perched on the fringe of a bygone theatre world. In a lighter, more appealing vein than *Stardust Memories, The Purple Rose of Cairo* (1985) continues Allen's exploration of the way movies interact with "real" life. *Hannah and Her Sisters* (1986) is a family romance set in Allen's Manhattan. *Radio Days* (1987), another family romance of sorts, is a nostalgic look at the impact of radio. *September* (1987) is a mercilessly straight drama set in a house in Maine populated by a group of Allen neurotics who don't have a laugh or even a smile among them. *Another Woman* (1988) is another Allen essay in the total repression of the comic spirit, a portrait of the midlife crisis of a female professor of philosophy. The "Oedipus Wrecks" segment from *New York Stories* (1989), a joking treatment of the same subject, has Allen himself playing a character who's fifty and farblonget. *Crimes and Misdemeanors* (1989) is a crime thriller intercut with further, mostly comic variations on Allen's favorite topic, the Manhattan mating dance.

"I don't want to make funny films anymore," Sandy
Bates wails, early on in *Stardust Memories.* "They can't
make me." Fortunately, Allen hasn't followed through on
Sandy's threat, and while over the last decade he has
mixed colors and generally darkened his palette, he hasn't
entirely forsaken his origins. Of his work in the eighties
*Zelig, Broadway Danny Rose,* and "Oedipus Wrecks" are
closest to the "old" Woody Allen, while to varying degrees *A Midsummer Night's Sex Comedy, The Purple Rose
of Cairo,* and *Hannah and Her Sisters* are reflective comedies that joust with philosophical "problems." *September*
and *Another Woman* are the kind of effortfully deep movies Sandy Bates might have made if he was feeling particularly punishing and puritanical, while at the end of the
decade *Crimes and Misdemeanors* is the successful hybrid,
a truly serious dramatic comedy that Allen has been building toward since *Stardust Memories.*

Turning out hits and misses, originals and retreads,
Allen in the last ten years has carved out a singular place
for himself in American movies. At a time when films have
become increasingly corporate-minded, he has completed
a series of small personal works, New York films in sensibility and by and large in subject matter, that ignore West
Coast trends. At a time when movies are inundated with
car chases, explosions, violence, and special effects, Allen
has written screenplays in which characterization and language have priority. While mainstream movies quote from
and imitate the latest hits, *Rambo* or *Indiana Jones* or
*Lethal Weapon* or *Back to the Future,* Allen's movies refer
to each other or to a literary and high cinema pantheon
that includes Renoir, Bergman, Fellini, Antonioni, Chekhov, and Shakespeare. Achieving a degree of control over
his work which approximates that of the foreign masters
he reveres, Allen in the eighties has become a full-fledged

American auteur, a film maker who writes, directs, often acts in, and even supervises the promotion of his own movies.

Addressed to an audience of the already converted, Allen's pictures are not big moneymakers. Duds like *September* and *Another Woman* had only limited distribution, and none of his work has been shown in some rural areas, where his producers fear it might be indecipherable. Yet in an industry in which moviemakers and studios are typically bound by a single project only, Allen's relationship to Orion Pictures endures. In effect, Woody Allen is like the manager of his own stock company; he's the monarch of a small but remarkably stable duchy. He has his own team: producers Jack Rollins and Charles H. Joffe; editor Susan Morse (who has worked on all his films since *Manhattan*); cinematographers Gordon Willis (who shot all the films from *Annie Hall* through *Broadway Danny Rose*), Carlo Di Palma *(Hannah, Radio Days, September),* and Sven Nykvist *(Another Woman,* "Oedipus Wrecks," *Crimes and Misdemeanors);* and a group of actors who return for encores. Like a contract director in the studio era, Allen can count on steady employment, yet he has far more control than even the most prestigious of the studio directors could ever have claimed. More or less free to do what he wants, he can risk failure and yet continue to be funded. And whether his work pleases or puzzles he's able to move on to the next project. In the eighties he made more movies than any other American director.

Fragments ripped from a larger whole, each of his films is in a sense a work in progress, part of an open-ended opus that may remain forever provisional, forever unfinished. As Allen discourses on some of his favorite things—Manhattan, modern neurosis, mating habits, movies, mortality, and the meaning of work—his films talk to each other. One film emerges from, continues or contradicts, another, and as he ricochets from comedy to drama, examining the same subjects from a variety of points of view, his work sets up a vast network of intertextual citation.

To find out what has been on Allen's mind for the last decade a good place to begin is with his own iconography. How has he cast himself? What has happened to his Woody persona? How much has he changed? How much *can* he change? In *Stardust Memories* Allen plays a film maker at a creative and personal crossroads. In *A Midsummer Night's Sex Comedy* he is an inventor, a cerebral sensualist afloat on crackpot schemes and an enflamed desire for a former lover. In *Broadway Danny Rose* he's a small-time talent agent, a loser on the edge of the theatrical jungle. In *Zelig* he's the ultimate nebbish, a chameleon who changes his appearance to blend in wherever he happens to be. In *Hannah and Her Sisters* he's a hot-shot tv producer faced with a (false) prognosis of terminal illness who takes a sabbatical and converts to Catholicism. In *Crimes and Misdemeanors* he's an idealistic documentary film maker. And in "Oedipus Wrecks" he's a fifty-year-old lawyer who has yet to sort out his problems with his mother.

Whether insiders (as in *Stardust Memories* or *Hannah*) or outsiders (as in *Broadway Danny Rose, Zelig,* or *Crimes and Misdemeanors*), Allen's characters are typically beleaguered, nearly upended by anxiety. Restless and ambitious, they seek change: a new job, a new relationship, a new appearance, a new system of belief. Romance, like philosophy, confounds them, and while Allen the film maker has attained a totalitarian control over his work, the characters he plays remain vulnerable, fearful of losing or never gaining mastery over their lives.

As writer and director Allen in the eighties has broken the mold set early in his career; as performer, however, he has not been able to make the same kind of leap. Unlike Zelig, Woody Allen cannot remake himself. With his horn-rimmed glasses, owlish eyes, dishevelled hair, floppy clothes, and thin wiry body, he not only looks the same from role to role, he sounds exactly the same too. His deeply regional accent is glued to him even in period pieces like *A Midsummer Night's Sex Comedy* and *Zelig,* in which his contemporary New York voice, as earlier in *Love and Death* and *Sleeper,* is comically anachronistic. Likewise his whine and his stammer (turned up to full volume in "Oedipus Wrecks" and *Broadway Danny Rose,* muted in *Hannah* and *Crimes*) and the way his sentences unravel remain fixtures of his verbal style.

His persona is capable of only minor modulations: the first shot in *Stardust Memories,* for instance, or the climactic moment in *Broadway Danny Rose* in which his star client fires Danny and, for the first time in the film, Allen's clown mask melts to reveal a Chaplinesque pathos. But for the most part, with a voice scarred with New York inflections and a face flushed with urban dis-ease, Allen is trapped by his Woody persona. Though in the eighties his characters have delivered fewer quips and one-liners, they remain enfolded within a comic framework; humor— irony, jabs, self-mockery—continues to be their mode, the way they relay as well as alleviate their frustrations. When he banishes laughter from his work, as in *September* and *Another Woman,* Woody is nowhere to be seen, and in films of mixed moods like *Hannah and Her Sisters* and *Crimes and Misdemeanors* Allen plays supporting roles. His presence lightens both films.

To expand the scope of his work, and to explore the kind of meditative bittersweet seriocomedy that most interests him, Allen has had to allow other characters besides Woody to confront the issues that continue to engage him. If his films of the last decade are only occasionally a showcase for his own persona they are certainly a tribute to Mia Farrow, who is in every one of them beginning with *A Midsummer Night's Sex Comedy.* Like Griffith working with Lillian Gish, like Von Sternberg fiddling with the iconography of his favorite performer, Marlene Dietrich, like Hitchcock and his icy blondes, like Elia Kazan sparking and being sparked by Marlon Brando, and like Martin Scorsese collaborating with Robert De Niro, Allen and Farrow are made for each other. If Woody began to close in on him, Mia offered fresh possibilities, and indeed her screen presence has charged his creativity throughout the eighties.

Like Diane Keaton, Farrow has a low-key, naturalistic, hesitant style which incites Allen's Pygmalion instincts, his itch to mold and shape, precisely to direct. Farrow, however, has proven more pliable than Keaton. Where *Annie Hall* and *Manhattan* trace Keaton's growing independence, her desire to explore life on screen and off apart from her mentor, Farrow apparently is content to remain an Allen team player. Since she began working (and living) with Allen she hasn't acted for anyone else, while Keaton even in her Woody period appeared in other directors' films. Farrow places a trust in her director that seems absolute. She'll do anything he asks, whether in a showy starring role or a modest supporting one, whether in comedy or drama; and since her track record with Allen is immaculate, a bull's-eye every time, she is right to do so.

Allen has devoted much of his time in the eighties to

exploring Farrow's potential. In *A Midsummer Night's Sex Comedy* she's a dizzy sprite who doesn't know her own mind. In *Zelig* she's an unassuming psychiatrist who cures and then marries the mutable hero. In *Broadway Danny Rose* she's a mobster's widow, an Italian floozie who speaks in a thick New Jersey accent, has a beehive hairdo, and hides out behind dark sunglasses. In *The Purple Rose of Cairo* she is a battered wife who escapes by going to the movies. She's Hannah in *Hannah and Her Sisters,* the most centered member of the family. In *Radio Days* she's a squeaky-voiced cigarette girl who becomes a low-toned gossip reporter, a full-fledged radio star. In *September* her zonked-out character falls in love with an unreceptive man and battles her callous mother. In *Another Woman* she's pregnant, and depressed by the prospect of a future barren of love or achievement. In "Oedipus Wrecks" she's the Gentile fiancée of a Jewish man whose mother disapproves of her (of course). In *Crimes and Misdemeanors* she's an ambitious film producer who seemingly falls for the wrong man.

More malleable than Woody, Farrow can play light comedy, farce, and gloomy drama. In *A Midsummer Night's Sex Comedy* she enacts the enchantingly-named Ariel Weymouth with summery effervescence; she gives Sally White, her idiotic character in *Radio Days,* a wonderfully cartoonlike overstatement while in *September* she stills laughter and charm altogether. In *Hannah and Her Sisters* and *The Purple Rose of Cairo* she performs with an ambivalence that has become Allen's forte; watching her you feel she could turn in a flash from making you laugh to making you cry.

The sheer simplicity of her acting, and the fact that her director is really the star of his own movies whether or not he actually appears in them, prevent her from ever giving an old-fashioned star turn, but occasionally Farrow is rewarded for her loyalty. Her roles in the two *Roses* are acting plums clearly intended to show her off. As Cecilia, the moviegoing waitress in *Purple Rose,* she's wistful, dreamy, fragile—the qualities Farrow has always had but that never before were so beautifully orchestrated. As Tina Vitale in *Broadway Danny Rose,* a tootsie with spiked heels who speaks in a snarl, she's virtually unrecognizable; only toward the end, as her character begins to melt when she discovers to her surprise that she kind of likes the nerdy agent who has come to escort her to her boyfriend's nightclub opening, do traces of the original Mia Farrow emerge.

In the last decade Allen has covered his usual turf like a man with a lot on his mind, and he has sometimes overreached. As the utterly stillborn *September* and *Another Woman* testify, he clutches when he eliminates all traces of comedy from his work. If I have yet to believe him when he gets stern about big subjects like God and death and the fate of the cosmos, as the sardonic lyric poet of the mores of upper-middle-class Manhattan I think he remains unsurpassed. What Allen continues to do best—exploring romantic and familial relationships; the ways movies and other artifacts of popular culture saturate our lives; the limits of meaning to be plucked from professional achievements like writing and moviemaking—is what he has always been good at. "The same only different" is the way I would describe Allen's attempts to deepen his work in the eighties.

He may yearn for higher realms but it is as a chronicler of modern romance that he continues to be most incisive. Who belongs with whom? Which of the characters in his group portraits are right for each other? Over and again these are the questions he asks and knows how to answer. And if his own characters are often adolescent participants in romantic rondelays, as their creator he is astute: the films ultimately confirm that Woody knows best. Blending satire with compassion, Allen has a sharp eye for the follies of people falling in and out of love.

Avoiding predictable pairings is one of the ways he keeps his work fresh, and in the eighties his romantic couplings often surprise. We might expect that in the films in which both Allen and Farrow appear their characters would end up together, but that rarely happens. And when it does it isn't inevitable. Sometimes, as in *Broadway Danny Rose* and *Zelig,* the two of them merge despite major obstacles; in the former romance sneaks up on them across a vast cultural breach, and in the latter the hero has to shed his chameleonism before he is ready for love. In stories where they would seem to be ideally mated they prove not to be. Sex doesn't jell for them in *A Midsummer Night's Sex Comedy.* In *Crimes and Misdemeanors* Farrow's character rejects Allen's for a rival suitor. And in "Oedipus Wrecks," Lisa (Farrow) takes a powder, leaving Sheldon (Allen) free for Treva (Julie Kavner), a soon-to-be carbon copy of his mother. If in Allen's past romances opposites attract, here familiarity breeds balance if not exactly content, and the film suggests that Jewish Treva will prove a more suitable mate than Gentile Lisa. In *Hannah and Her Sisters* Allen's and Farrow's characters used to be married yet no lingering attachment or animosity binds them: they seem quite free of each other. The varying ways the director and his star interact over the decade, then, highlight a key Allen theme, the fragility and uncertainty of romantic attraction.

Typically unhappy with where they are and who they are with, Allen's lovers and would-be lovers are bitten by the lure of change; they're pricked by the notion that the grass is probably greener somewhere else. In generous films like *A Midsummer Night's Sex Comedy* and *Hannah and Her Sisters,* Allen nudges his baffled romancers in the right direction. The charming pattern of *Midsummer,* with echoes of Shakespeare and Bergman's *Smiles of a Summer Night,* is to move initially mismatched couples to their appropriate partners. Over the course of a weekend in the country Allen shuffles his deck so that by the end A loves B loves A, at least for a little while. In this version of *la ronde,* dalliance refreshes and in the pursuit of sexual gratification the revelers are changed for the better. With their author's blessings, the four major figures in *Hannah and Her Sisters* also end up contentedly mated. After a fling with his wife Hannah's nubile sister Lee (Barbara Hershey), Elliot (Michael Caine) returns to his marriage with appreciation—a sexual liaison, which he temporarily mistook for true love, has helped him over the hurdles of middle-aged malaise. And Mickey Sachs (Allen) finds redemption not in the places he has looked for it—work and religion—but through marriage to Holly (Dianne Wiest), Hannah's neurotic sister, with whom he had a disastrous first date.

"Relationships don't last," Alvy Singer says in *Annie Hall,* and as if to underline that belief Allen has made three films since *Hannah* which contradict its spirit of romantic harmony. *September, Another Woman,* and *Crimes and Misdemeanors* are overrun with the consequences of making the wrong romantic choices. Where characters in the earlier films are rewarded in their pursuits, these late eighties' pieces provide variations on love's labors lost. In *September* Elaine (Farrow) not only desires a man who has eyes only for her unhappily married best friend, she is also unable to respond to an older man who wants to take care of her. In *Another Woman* Marion (Gena Rowlands) achieves self-understanding when she confronts the fact that she chose to marry a priggish man (the ever-pompous Ian Holm) who allowed her to remain where she is, stuck in her head, rather than a bearlike lover (Gene Hackman) whose sensuality threatened her.

In *Crimes and Misdemeanors,* Allen's darkest romantic fable to date, love is potentially lethal. In this version of Manhattan mating, the characters look for love in all the wrong places. When his nagging mistress Delores (Anjelica Huston) insists that he divorce his wife in order to marry her, Judah Rosenthal (Martin Landau) arranges to have her killed. Barbara (Caroline Aaron), who places and answers ads in lovelorn columns, dates a seemingly suitable guy who ties her to her bed and then defecates on her. Barbara's brother Clifford Stern (Allen) is romantically stranded: his ice-cold wife (Joanna Gleason) finds a new love, and Hallie Reed (Farrow), the woman he likes, chooses his rival, his brother-in-law Lester (Alan Alda), a man who already has everything anyway. In this film the romantic chase incurs a variety of crimes and misdemeanors, and the stakes are higher than simply a bruised ego. This is Allen's anti-love story for the age of AIDS— Delores' obsession with Judah is one of the fatal attractions that have been filtering into movies since the mid-eighties.

Part of Allen's stretching strategies over the last decade has been to add a moral or philosophical underlining to his characters' perpetual pursuit of the ideal relationship, and so he hooks his recurrent theme of how A does or does not love or belong with B to sometimes hefty thematic bait. Though in a benevolent film like *Hannah and Her Sisters* Allen's characters seem content at least for the moment to be cradled by their relationships, more typical are their efforts to defeat the disappointments of love by *doing* something: by writing or attempting to write serious books, like characters in *A Midsummer Night's Sex Comedy, September,* and *Another Woman;* by becoming famous, like Zelig and his therapist, the radio stars in *Radio Days,* a lounge lizard singer on the tip of the big time in *Broadway Danny Rose.* Like Holly in *Hannah and Her Sisters,* a failed actress who discovers she has talent as a writer, many of Allen's characters seek a creative outlet, and throughout the decade in different moods— here gravely, there satirically—the theme of achievement is sounded insistently, a reflection perhaps of the director's own well-known and self-evident compulsion to keep on working.

What can work give us? How much can it redeem us? are questions the movies continue to ask. "Work" usually means creative endeavor and "good work" is the kind that the director in *Stardust Memories* aims for, the kind in which the creator creates independently, beyond the reach of the tentacles of commerce. But "work" as protection against the abyss can be less exalted, too, as in the end of *September* where the heroine is saved from her demons when she becomes absorbed in the details of selling her house. "There are so many things to do, selling a house," she says, almost gratefully, while her friend attempts to bolster her shaky ego when she says, "Soon you'll leave here, you'll start over again in New York; there will be a million things to keep you busy." Though it is stated artlessly—Allen is mimicking the ending of Chekhov's *Three Sisters*—the sentiment is nonetheless revealing.

While Allen's characters, whether of high or low estate, in comedies or dramas, keep busy creating and relating, they are plagued by self-doubts and intimations of meaninglessness. The ending of *Radio Days,* I think, best expresses Allen's recurrent intuition that our lives are written in sand (the theme of Shelley's "Ozymandias" clearly haunts the film maker's imagination). Gathered on a hotel rooftop to celebrate the arrival of a new year is a group of radio celebrities, two of whom pause to consider whether or not their fame will endure. "Everything passes . . . it doesn't matter how big we are." One by one, as if they are withdrawing ghosts, the "stars" leave the roof, and only the blinking neon lights of a studio-created midtown Manhattan remain as the narrator (Allen himself) regretfully says, "I never forgot those radio stars but I must admit each new year their voices get dimmer and dimmer."

Reaching for ways to express his sense of our insignificance, his lurking fear that "work" and striving may all be sound and fury signifying nothing, Allen is not always so delicate as in *Radio Days,* and in a hard-core drama like *September* his sense of proportion unravels. "It's all random . . . the universe, vanishing forever . . . all time, all space, a temporary convulsion . . . haphazard, morally neutral, and unimaginably violent," a scientist (Jack Warden) stutteringly intones. When he says that he "gets paid to prove it," he doesn't crack a smile, and we aren't supposed to either; we're meant to take his recitation as the real thing. As if answering the scientist's negativity, a rabbi (Sam Waterston) in *Crimes and Misdemeanors* affirms his belief that there *is* in fact "a moral structure to the world" and that he could not go on if he didn't truly believe it.

But the film doesn't agree with him. In Allen's last film of the eighties, his most achieved attempt to date to make a grown-up philosophical comedy in which his usual subjects of relationships and work are embedded in a story driven by moral urgency, good guys finish last. The rabbi is going blind; a truth-seeking philosopher who spends his life pondering ultimate questions of value commits suicide; and centrally, and most troubling of all, the criminals, Judah and his low-life brother who hire a hit man to kill Judah's mistress, remain unpunished. At first paralyzed with anxiety—he is an optometrist who has been brought up to believe that the eyes of God observe his every thought—Judah is gradually, almost magically, unburdened. At the end, two years after his crime, his marriage has been restored and he radiates well-being. Can his self-reclamation be explained away simply by saying that people like Judah (who after all is "one of us") cannot think of themselves as evil and so make self-justifying excuses? Or is it more than that, a perception that God may not be looking, that "morality" is in fact infinitely flexible, merely a prop to defend ourselves against a "random universe"?

A mordant black comedy in which characters do not reap what they have sown, *Crimes and Misdemeanors* is haunted by the existential uncertainties that hover over Allen's work in the eighties. How can higher meanings endure, what does "meaning" mean, in the kind of unstable and morally treacherous world the film coolly depicts? In this one Allen for the moment seems to be throwing up his hands. The surprising resolution of Judah's story is the equivalent of a metaphysical shrug.

Allen is empowered when, as in *Crimes and Misdemeanors,* he designs his moral fable to provoke debate rather than, as in *September* and *Another Woman,* to declaim or to legislate. *Crimes* is intended to make us uneasy, to prod us to consider why and how Judah cures himself. Like Allen's most characteristic work, the film is provisional, constructed so as to set up a dialogue with future work. How will Allen answer himself? Will there follow in the nineties an anti-*Crimes and Misdemeanors* as this film is an anti-*Hannah?*

Another of Allen's devices for deepening his work has been his heightened self-reflexiveness, released at full tilt in *Annie Hall* and then explored in varying ways in the eighties in *Stardust Memories, Zelig, Radio Days, Broadway Danny Rose, The Purple Rose of Cairo,* and *Crimes and Misdemeanors.* Like work, romance, God, and death, "the movies" preoccupy Allen—he's a true cinéaste who makes movies about making movies *(Stardust Memories, Crimes and Misdemeanors);* movies that cite other movies *(Crimes, Zelig, Hannah);* and movies in which going to the movies is an important theme *(Crimes, Hannah, Purple Rose of Cairo).* As reviewers have frequently noted, Allen's work in the eighties is laced with tributes to some of his favorite films: *Stardust Memories* is a reverent take-off on Fellini's *8½; September* is patterned on Ingmar Bergman's chamber dramas; *Another Woman* imitates Bergman's *Wild Strawberries;* and *Singin' in the Rain, Mr. and Mrs. Smith,* Betty Hutton, Edward G. Robinson, Chaplin, and a documentary on Mussolini are among the films and icons quoted in *Crimes and Misdemeanors.*

Throughout the decade Allen celebrates the medium as a kind of white magic—only in the movies can we be released so easily from the laws of space and time. In a memory fragment in *Stardust Memories* and in *The Floating Light Bulb* Allen presents an image of his younger self as a whiz-kid magician, and in a quite tangible sense his movies are an extension of childhood magic acts; except for the earthbound *September,* all the eighties work contains magical motifs. An enchanted wood in *A Midsummer Night's Sex Comedy;* Zelig's surreal capacity to transform himself; a movie character who walks off the screen to enter real life in *The Purple Rose of Cairo;* a larger-than-life-size mother floating in the air above Manhattan in "Oedipus Wrecks"; dream imagery and, in a number of the films, flashbacks in which characters in the present observe scenes from the past that they summon as if by magic—with its unique capacity to baffle physical reality Allen uses film to embody his flights of fancy.

What the movies do to us and for us is the sustained subject of *The Purple Rose of Cairo.* In the Depression a hash-house waitress (Mia Farrow) goes to the movies to escape from her dead-end job and her punishing marriage to a two-timing, pot-bellied male chauvinist (Danny Aiello, who else?). At the local Jewel Theatre, Cecilia can luxuriate in the fake worlds concocted by the Hollywood dream factories. Serenaded one week by Fred Astaire, she is engrossed the next by an improbable adventure story, "The Purple Rose of Cairo," set both in "Africa" and a swank, art deco Manhattan. When the handsome leading man Tom Baxter (Jeff Daniels) steps out of the film to join her in the real world, she lives out a zealous moviegoer's ideal fantasy. She is pursued not only by Tom Baxter, movie adventurer, but also by the actor, Gil Shepard (Jeff Daniels also), who has created Tom and is eager to control him (shades of Woody Allen, master controller, leak into the film's premise). At the end, after having been courted by the star and his flickering alter ego, Cecilia is abandoned: Gil Shepard returns to Hollywood to continue his career, Tom Baxter is enfolded once again within the world on screen. What happens to Cecilia? She goes back to the Jewel, there to lose herself in the sound and light show of this week's feature, an RKO musical. And enveloped by the voice and the image of Fred Astaire, her face gradually loses its lines of tension and her eyes glisten.

Entranced, blissful, jubilantly voyeuristic, Mia Farrow's expression at the end makes the ritual of moviegoing seem cathartic, positively purifying. But at the same time Allen seems to question if this kind of intense watching—scopophilia to the nth degree—is really good for you. "I'm a real person, I have to choose the real world," Cecilia tells Tom Baxter when she has decided that Gil Shepard is the one she will go off with; yet retreating to the movies has helped her to elude the problems of the "real world." Though they provide pleasure movies can be misused—containing the tragic irony of the dream they can be, as they are for Cecilia, delusion and detour.

Like looking in *The Purple Rose of Cairo,* listening in *Radio Days* is a benediction but also a crutch, a way of avoiding life. The family in *Radio Days,* like Cecilia at the the movies, turns on the radio to supply the action missing in their own drab world, and the disembodied voices issuing from a machine variously inform, soothe, stimulate, tickle, and fool them. Radio voices arouse their envy and greed, stir the desire to imitate (listening, Cousin Ruthie "does" Carmen Miranda), and, as the family rabbi intones, induce "bad habits, lazy dreams, bad values." "Why can't you be a genius? You're too busy listening to the radio," the father scolds his son.

But to overstate the warnings built into the films about losing it at the movies or by tuning in to radio is to miss Allen's enormous affection for popular entertainment. Indeed, going to the movies saves Mickey's life in *Hannah and Her Sisters.* Terrified about his health, fed up with his job in the compromise-ridden world of television, on the verge of complete despair, Mickey (Allen) goes to the movies, to see the Marx Brothers in *Duck Soup*—and is restored. Laughing at the wacky Marxes, he's healed. Movies also relieve Allen's equally tense film maker in *Crimes and Misdemeanors;* going to see good old films creates bonds with his niece and with a co-worker he's attracted to. Being a cinephile is a mark of distinction, another way in which Allen's good guy is superior to the television honcho (Alan Alda) who looks only at images of himself and who presumably wouldn't know the difference between John Ford and Henry Ford.

To support his growing didactic habit Allen typically sets up his stories in a schematic comparison/contrast format. In his group portraits characters are included for their opposing colors, and several films construct parallel worlds in which fiction—movies, dreams, and fantasies—intersect with and comment on "real" life. Dualism courses through the work of the eighties—in the bifurcated plots, the thematic doubling, the contrasted characters, in the light-dark alternations within and between films.

Allen's persistent double-strandedness is particularly apparent in *Crimes and Misdemeanors*. As the film unfolds we might well ask, we are indeed encouraged to examine, why the story cuts back and forth between two groups of characters who have only a tenuous connection—Allen's documentary film maker, Clifford Stern, is married to the sister of one of Judah Rosenthal's patients. Judah's story of arranging to have his mistress killed is so riveting (it's Allen's first crime thriller, a contemporary noir which explores the criminal potential in a model upper-middle-class citizen) we might wonder why Allen doesn't simply tell it straight instead of interweaving it with the problems Clifford encounters working half-heartedly on a film about his crass brother-in-law. Judah's dark fable is disrupted by the essentially comic tone of Clifford's story, yet another Allen essay about urban neurotics preoccupied with Making It. Immediately recognizable,

Clifford is a restrained version of the Woody persona—he makes fewer jokes and he's genuinely attracted to the life of the mind: the figure he wants to make a film about is a true intellectual, a philosopher whose epistemological quest Allen does not satirize. Judah, on the other hand, a man of gargantuan bad faith, is an unfamiliar figure in the Allen corpus, and appropriately there isn't a comic vibration in Martin Landau's marvelously tense performance. His face a mass of winces, his clenched voice barely masking his inner coils, and with a distracted look in his eye, Landau plays Judah like a man who suffers from perpetual indigestion.

These two characters, who meet only in the final scene, in which Judah tells his story to Clifford as a story, as potential material for a movie, furnish contrasting examples of Allen's thesis that God can't possibly be looking over us: Clifford, a man with all the right values who tries to live blamelessly, is bereft at the end while Judah has conquered his demons. That Lester the tycoon wins the charming heroine from Clifford provides further proof that in the kind of topsy-turvy world the film constructs virtue does not insure victory.

Allen's spliced narrative, filled with parallels and pitted with scenes from movies that comment on the action, is rigorously academic. His overcalculation is dangerous, and indeed in *Interiors, September,* and *Another Woman* this kind of deliberateness was fatal. But here, in his sturdiest serious work to date, there are pay-offs. Assembling his fragments in order to illustrate his point, Allen seems to stitch Judah into a predetermined pattern, as if, while the character slips further into moral blasphemy, selling his soul to retain his public image, he is enacting a scenario that has already been played out. The movie's cool overcontrolled style tightens the noose around Judah, while the contrasting comic episodes bind him to a familiar world, the world of "our" Manhattan, and thereby heighten the tension of watching one of us become a murderer.

The two-panel form of *Crimes and Misdemeanors* evolved from the parallel motifs of earlier eighties work in which two worlds, two groups of characters, variously collide with or comment on each other. Life as against the movies provides the dual register in *Stardust Memories* and *The Purple Rose of Cairo;* radio stars and their listeners comprise the double set of characters in *Radio Days;* two women separated by a thin wall are the contrasted pair in *Another Woman.*

In *Stardust Memories* "reality" and the movie world become so entangled that we aren't always sure of the boundaries between them, and at the end we discover that in a sense we've been tricked and that everything——from the framing story of the director attending a retrospective of his work to the pieces of his movies we are shown to the fragments of his own free-floating memories which crisscross the present action——has been part of a movie, indeed the movie we have just seen. The director's life and his art have merged into a single indivisible text, *Stardust Memories,* the movie. For both the moviegoer and the movie character in *Purple Rose,* however, real life and the movies are not interchangeable, and unlike Sandy Bates, who can circulate freely among the images created by his own imagination, Cecilia and Tom are, respectively, expelled from the movies and from reality. "Real life is not like the movies" is the lesson both characters must learn.

*Radio Days,* too, separates producers from consumers: those who provide entertainment inhabit a different world from those who desire it. The film interweaves two groups—the narrator's family of avid radio listeners and the radio celebrities—who never meet within the same frame. (With typical ambivalence Allen doesn't automatically favor one group, creators or audience, over another. The fans in *Stardust Memories* look like fodder for Weegee or Diane Arbus, but in *Radio Days* he's affectionate toward the average folks who listen in while he pokes the radio stars for their egos and their perishable accomplishments.)

*Another Woman* introduces a variation on Allen's thematic doubling. In the studio to which she goes each day to write, Marion overhears the confessions of patients visiting an analyst whose office is on the other side of the wall. The tortured words of a pregnant client incite her own recollections, a litany of failed relationships with her father, brother, husbands and lovers.

In Allen's two-world movies, images on a screen or voices on a radio or in the next room have keen transforming powers. His susceptible characters, the ones who watch and listen, are like white tablets waiting to be written on—to be filled—by influences from realms outside their own.

Increasingly, in a pattern first formalized in *Manhattan,* Allen lines up his characters like debaters. They square off, announcing their sexual and philosophical attitudes. Thus, *A Midsummer Night's Sex Comedy,* along with *Crimes and Misdemeanors* Allen's most schematic piece of the eighties, is driven by differences between characters. Leopold (Jose Ferrer) is an academic skeptic who believes only in what he can see ("apart from this world there are no realities"); Andrew (Allen) is a dewy-eyed inventor ("there's more to life than meets the eye") who wants to fly and who builds a magic box through which he communicates with the spirit world. In the height of sexual ecstasy fuddy-duddy Leopold dies and is transformed into a sybarite who intones from beyond ("you're right, there *is* magic in the wood"), while Andrew, who has been stalled sexually as as well as scientifically ("because of my problem in bed with my wife I can't fly") is also "cured." The third male, drawn in contrast to both Leopold and Andrew, is Maxwell (Tony Roberts), a lusty doctor who has written a treatise on natural science (Leopold is the author of a book on conceptual pragmatism) and whose philosophy of "gather ye rosebuds" is challenged when he falls hopelessly in love with Leopold's fiancée.

"She gives off animal vibrations; maybe I should ask for lessons," Andrew's frigid wife Adrian (Mary Steenburgen) says about Dulcy (Julie Hagerty), Maxwell's frolicsome hot-to-trot nurse. The third female, Ariel (Farrow), combines Adrian's seeming demureness with Dulcy's carpe diem spirit; though she was raised in a convent and despite her asexual sprite-like appearance, Ariel is in fact a woman with quite a past, a "frivolous person" by her own estimate who proves the ideal mate for the satyr-like doctor. In conflict with each other and themselves, by the end of Allen's brightest piece of the eighties all the characters are fulfilled. (In this period piece note that only the men have professions; the women are their bodies, present in order to satisfy male desire. While Allen will never be a feminist hero, and while his often-cited misogyny erupts throughout the eighties, admirable women who combine careers with full personal lives have become increasingly evident in his work.)

In *Crimes and Misdemeanors* and *Hannah and Her Sisters,* as earlier in *Interiors,* family groups offer a readymade core of characters from which Allen draws typically steep divisions. The brothers in *Crimes* are in fact so radically different—Ben an other worldly rabbi, Lester a show biz whiz kid—that they don't really seem to be brothers at all but pawns of the scriptwriter. Although again Allen builds the characters on the ways in which they differ from each other, Hannah and her sisters are a more believable family unit. Hannah is a serene peacemaker and a successful actress who nonetheless has blurred vision on the subject of her husband's infidelity. Holly is written as the anti-Hannah, a twitchy New York misfit—a failed actress and a woman without a man—who finds both a man and a career in the course of the film. The third sister, Lee, is the outsider in this creative family, a rudderless, male-attracting woman whose strongest drive is to have relationships with older men.

Emphasizing character observation over what-happens-next Allen's group portraits are an ideal showcase for the kind of naturalistic ensemble acting style he has been developing at least since *Annie Hall* and *Manhattan.* In his work, no matter how fantastic or absurd the action, he directs his performers to be absolutely true-to-life. Dialogue sounds like the real thing—his characters often speak at the same time or cut in on each other so that their words overlap, blur, and collide; and caught up in the excitement of the moment they stumble, pause, backtrack, circle the same few words over and over. Speaking typically in erratic rhythms and in an understated, loose, off-the-cuff style they sound as if they're really talking rather than delivering memorized dialogue. Characters who are related—siblings, married couples, parents and children—actually sound as if they have spent lifetimes talking at and to each other. And listening to them we become privileged eavesdroppers.

Allen is known for breaking a directorial taboo: he gives actors line readings, demonstrating the exact way he would like his words to be spoken. It's no surprise then that we can catch Allen's own inflections in the delivery of most of his performers. He is also tyrant-like in allowing his actors to read only the pages in which their own characters appear. But he does permit actors the freedom to improvise, to discover their own words to complete a scene, and as a result the acting in his films is often wonderfully fresh, filled with "found" moments that seem to have emerged spontaneously rather than from directorial calculation.

Allen has built up his own stock company, and the mutual familiarity between the director and his ensemble is another reason that his performers all seem to be speaking the same language. In addition to Mia Farrow, house favorites include Dianne Wiest, Sam Waterston, Julie Hagerty, Julie Kavner, Tony Roberts—actors Allen uses more than once because he likes the way they handle his dialogue. What he evidently appreciates are voices edged with an ironic undertone and with comic anxiety; voices like Keaton's and Farrow's which can slide from comedy to drama and in which light top notes are supported by at least the promise of inner rumblings. The crack in Sam Waterston's voice, as in Dianne Wiest's, accommodates simultaneous currents of humor and tension.

In the eighties Allen has become a master director of screen acting, with a touch as distinctive as that of Orson Welles. (Like Welles, Allen comes to film from another medium, and just as Welles's apprenticeship in radio influenced the way he orchestrated dialogue in his films, so vestiges of Allen's beginnings in stand-up comedy are echoed in the verbal rhythms he imposes on his performers.)

In straight comedy and in seriocomedy like *Hannah and Her Sisters,* Allen coaxes uniformly deft work from his ensembles; his ear fails him only in the dead-weight entries like *September* and *Another Woman,* in which in leading rolès Elaine Stritch and Gena Rowlands respectively are excruciating. With her boozy, foghorn voice and coarse face, Stritch is not remotely convincing as Mia Farrow's mother—even though they play an estranged mother and daughter, they don't sound as if they have ever been introduced. While Farrow's unforced acting is true even in these strained circumstances—she knows just how much the camera needs—Stritch emotes in a belabored Broadway style that is never at home on the screen; she acts Allen's ersatz domestic drama as if it is classic theatre. In casting Gena Rowlands as a genteel, repressed philosophy professor Allen slips again: with her sloppy speech and hardened face Rowlands is no high-toned academic.

Throughout the eighties Allen has retained a loose story-telling style. Riffs on a basic premise, his screenplays have continued to be anecdotal and episodic—his free-form, pearls-on-a-string pattern recalls his origins as a stand-up comic. Having worked out his own increasingly mannered formula, he tells his stories in his own way; neither well-made in the old-fashioned sense nor compelling as stories, his narratives are designed primarily to give him leeway in which to examine his favorite topics in a variety of moods. Of the work of the last decade it seems to me that only the Judah Rosenthal portion of *Crimes and Misdemeanors* has a fully satisfying plot, a narrative with genuine momentum. *Hannah and Her Sisters, A Midsummer Night's Sex Comedy, September,* and *Another Woman* are group portraits that hold us (or fail to) according to how we respond to the characters, how curious we are about how they will be paired off. *Zelig, Radio Days, The*

*Purple Rose of Cairo,* "Oedipus Wrecks," and even the oddball *Broadway Danny Rose* (a film not quite like any of its neighbors) are sketches, in effect *New Yorker* pieces writ large, and in spite of their considerable charm and Allen's lean and limber syntax (his movies rarely run longer than eight-five minutes), they feel slightly overextended.

His variations-on-a-theme format then gives Allen a fluid frame within which he can conduct his ongoing debates with himself about love, work, higher meaning, faith and doubt. Since singleness of tone or statement seems now to threaten his creative instincts, he requires double vision in order to sustain contrasts within and between films. To continue to make the kind of sobering comedy that has become his specialty, he needs to be released from having to tell a continuous or even consistent story and to be able to undermine his comic world view so that, triumphantly as in *Crimes and Misdemeanors,* laughter catches in our throats. Once he becomes resolved, or God forbid, contented, he may stop making movies altogether. For Allen the readiness is all, a stance abetted by the story form he has developed.

Although his work has grown increasingly assured, Allen has not become blasé, and ways in which film can handle space and time continue to engage him. Even the doomed dramas are made by a director clearly enchanted by the possibilities of *mise en scène.*

From the fragmentation of *Zelig* and *Radio Days* to the deliberate stasis of *September,* virtually all of his eighties films confront formal challenges. *Zelig* and *Radio Days,* in fact, are his most complexly organized films to date, the work of a film maker delighted by his medium's ability to juggle shards of visual and aural information, its almost magical properties of collapsing, shuffling, resewing real time and space. In a series of brief scenes both films provide a montage-like overview of their subjects, the documentary-like "biography" of a chameleon and the impact of radio on a representative New York family. No scene or moment is allowed to linger; the films move along at a non-stop clip as Allen the master assembler imposes order on his thousands of pieces of celluloid. Conversely, *September* (which seems to have been made to give Allen a change of pace, the chance to explore sustained scenes) obeys a strict theatrical unity of time and place. The action never leaves the inside of a house in Maine whose ownership becomes a point of bitter contention between mother and daughter, and the outside world is indicated only through summer sounds like the hum of birds and the rattle of crickets. In this claustrophobic closet drama (Allen on all fours to his hero Ingmar Bergman) time and space are as confined as in the collage-like *Zelig* and *Radio Days* they are open-ended.

To suture his narrative fragments Allen often needs a voice within the text to act as a guide—it's no wonder that he uses voice-over narration more than any other contemporary film maker. In *Radio Days* he himself is the narrator, and his own halting, gentle voice, filled with warmth for the remembrance of things past, gives the film an autobiographical glow. In *Zelig* the narrator speaks with voice-of-God authority in a style that slyly parodies newsreels of the thirties and forties.

Allen's invisible speakers are another way for him to assert his control over his movies and over us: voice-over narration provides summary and helps to anticipate upcoming events as it also allows Allen to cut memory fragments into the present action. He often depends on voice-over as a way of penetrating a character's thoughts——Marion's voice-over in *Another Woman* functions typically as a segue from present to past or from reality to fantasy. The past invades the present in most of the films, but when there is no voiceover to center the image, as in *Stardust Memories,* both the tense and the reliability of what we are seeing remain ambiguous. The past cuts into the present so quickly, and without any voice-over preparation, that we're disoriented: are we witnessing an event that "really" happened, or one that the character, Sandy Bates, has only imagined?

Because voice-overs can be used to insinuate choral comment, they support Allen's teacherly tendencies. He uses speakers to make sure we get the point, and his voice-in-the-text is often the aural equivalent to the stark Brechtian announcements that punctuate *Hannah and Her Sisters.* The titles ("God, she's beautiful . . . ," "The hypochondriac," "The anxiety of the man in the booth," "The big leap," "The audition") introduce scenes and break up the flow of the story into separate episodes, and together with the multiple voice-overs prepare us for what it is we are supposed to glean from each act. The titles, white lettering against an inky black background, and the voice-overs give the film a contemplative caste and an aura of greater depth than I think it really has.

In *Broadway Danny Rose,* Allen's most relaxed movie of the decade, the one with the most modest thematic stakes, he uses voice-over simply as a means of underlining the "story" status of his narrative. A group of comics gathered at New York's Carnegie Deli commemorate Danny Rose by telling what turns out to be the saga of how a perennial loser ends up a romantic winner. That Danny's unexpected romantic conquest is narrated as a story and one moreover which is embedded within a frame within the film gives it stature, though without making a fuss about it. Perhaps the fact that this time Allen's character is the subject of the story rather than the storyteller accounts for the film's low blood pressure; at any rate, alone among his eighties work, *Broadway Danny Rose* is just for fun.

As Allen has become a more sober director, one who flaunts his auteur credentials, he has continued to make "beautiful" movies. Whether they are intended primarily for delight or revelation all of his work in the last decade looks like serious business.

In the color-saturated eighties, Allen's choice to shoot *Stardust Memories, Zelig, Broadway Danny Rose* and the film within the film in *Purple Rose of Cairo* in black and white is experimental, a sign that he's his own boss. Black and white today has much the same value that filming in color did in the Golden Age; it's a declaration that the project is special and (reversing historical precedent) that it is stylized, less "real" than the standard-make color movie. The intense chiaroscuro of *Stardust Memories* recalls the art house foreign films of the fifties and sixties; the black and white in *Zelig,* on the other hand, recreates the look of old documentaries. The grainy stock together with the speeded-up movements and "flickering" voices gives the film a remarkably creased surface. Its expert mimicry falls short only when Allen attempts to imitate a Warner Brothers biopic of the thirties based on the life of Zelig—the film stock and the actors who impersonate Zelig and his savior look too smooth and modern. Similarly the thirties movie set within *Purple Rose* looks too crisp, just as the actors in this inner movie look more now than then. Although it is more straightforward than it is for virtuoso pieces like *Zelig* and *Stardust Memories,* the black-and-white photography in *Broadway Danny*

*Rose* appropriately places the action in a time that was, somewhere in an indefinite past.

Allen's use of color in the eighties has been similarly distinctive. *Purple Rose, Radio Days,* and *A Midsummer Night's Sex Comedy* are richly detailed period films; *Hannah and Her Sisters* and *Crimes and Misdemeanors* have much the same visual signature as his two straight-arrow dramas, *September* and *Another Woman*—all four are designed to assert their moral earnestness.

*A Midsummer Night's Sex Comedy* has an uncharacteristic country setting, and for once Allen does not get the vapors in the outdoors. Alive with summer greens and teeming with sunlight that splashes the characters, this is a joyous *plein air* comedy that looks like an Impressionist canvas stirred to life. This time light and fresh air and the unspoiled lush rural landscape of an earlier era are routes to enchantment; in this bright green world romance blooms and prigs and sensualists alike are happily transformed.

*Midsummer* is set at the turn of the century; *Purple Rose* takes place in the Depression, while *Radio Days* is set in the forties, and in all three films the color seems steeped in time past, washed in reminiscence. While greens dominate *Midsummer,* earth tones, browns, russets, and maroons saturate the other two, suggesting sepia-tinted photographs in old family albums. Outlines of people and objects are often blurred, to create a hazy burnish that betokens a longing for the past; with their softened edges the films depict the past as a gauzy, floating world which can easily absorb the fantasies—the movie magic—that punctuate the action.

*Stardust Memories* introduced elements of visual style that Allen has continued to draw on particularly for the heavyweight entries like *September, Another Woman,* and the Judah Rosenthal section of *Crimes and Mis-demeanors.* A *mise en scène* of alienation appears throughout these films: characters stand uncomfortably against stark white walls, stare moodily into off-screen space, are placed in off-center one-shots that confine them to their own frames, talk to characters hidden behind doors or cabinets. Allen sometimes allows the camera to remain for a few beats after characters have exited the frame. Reverberating with echoes of Antonioni, this visual vocabulary of angst is pretentious and often old-hat. In *September,* filmed entirely with a red filter, and *Another Woman,* drenched in yellows and burnt oranges, and filled with characters placed in the frame to indicate how alone they are, Allen's attraction to high class goyish suffering is killing. Both movies have a glazed, airless, slow-motion quality, as if everything were taking place underwater.

While the threat of "no more comedies" announced in *Stardust Memories* has happily not been fulfilled, Allen in the eighties has made comedies which very much want to have something to say. And in Europe especially the Allen of the last decade has been hailed as a provocative thinker, a film maker as pundit and guru. Two perceptive recent studies, Graham McCann's *Woody Allen,* published in England in 1990, and French critic Robert Benayoun's 1988 *The Films of Woody Allen,* have enshrined him as a deeper artist than I think he yet is, treating him as a director whose comedies, seriocomedies, and dramas alike are achieved pieces of philosophical reflection. The Woody Allen I still like best is the one who doesn't push for big statements or feel that simply to invoke subjects like God and death in a popular movie is the same as dramatizing them, or who doesn't confuse kvetching with "philosophy." But even if Allen approaches intense themes like a fired-up undergraduate exposed for the first time to the world of Great Ideas, he does confront issues that most film makers avoid, and his work throughout the eighties has a genuinely thoughtful coating. His best movies, nonetheless (except for the dark passages of the breakthrough *Crimes and Misdemeanors*), remain his lighter ones—he continues to be a shrewd observer of the world he knows best, that of the agitated Manhattan overachiever. He's sturdiest when planted firmly on native ground.

Clearly he wants to go on finding ways of darkening his comedy, to bend his original comic style to accommodate a wider range of moods and themes, and to do this successfully he may have to continue to focus less on himself. In the coming years the comedian surely will be pushed even further into the wings so that the film maker can take center stage. But even if Woody never tells another joke, his contribution to American comedy is secure, his comic films, essays, and albums assured of a high and lasting place in our popular culture. It may indeed be because he felt he had nothing further to prove or to explore in virgin comedy that he has been so eager during the last decade to move ahead to mixed genres. But even if he miscalculates from time to time, even if he borrows voices from the literature and films he loves, and even if he reaches for a dramatic form that he has yet to claim as his own, his ambition, his technical command, and his ability to make his actors inhabit the frame as if they truly belong there are entirely admirable.

The comedian's progress: 2000 will almost surely indicate a record of experiment and achievement that bears only the faintest traces of the original Allen schlemiel but that will continue to surprise and delight and occasionally to infuriate us.

# 9

## The Comedian's Progress: The Nineties

A T a glance, the nineties were not a good time for Woody Allen on screen or off. His movies from Manhattan played to declining attendance, at least in America, and received some tepid reviews from critics who had been ardent supporters for decades. Backstage shakeups—Allen several times changed his studio affiliation and dismissed some longtime employees—also tarnished his image. And, of course, dominating the period was his real-life role in the tabloidlike narrative of his relationship with Soon-Yi Previn, the adopted daughter of Mia Farrow.

And yet Allen endured. From 1990 to 2000 he wrote and directed eleven films, starred in three films for other directors, returned to television for two projects, and wrote *Central Park West*, a one-act play produced off Broadway in 1995. He continued his regular Monday evening performances with his jazz band, and his 1997 European tour with the band was the subject of a documentary. The professional scorecard is rosier than the film maker's receding grosses might suggest. No single film of the nineties achieved the kind of breakthrough that *Annie Hall* represented in the seventies or *Crimes and Misdemeanors* in the eighties, but there also wasn't a clinker on the order of *Interiors* or *September* or *Another Woman*. The films range in merit, with the commanding, visceral *Husbands and Wives* (1992) at the top, and the soft-focus *Sweet and Lowdown* (1999) at the bottom. But in a way it is a mistake to evaluate each film on its own; rather, the canon, as always, should be looked at as chapters in an unfinished, and probably unfinishable, supertext. As in the past, the movies are linked by two kinds of dialogue: the one that buzzes from film to film; and the one that connects each work to the film maker's biography.

"The same, only different," might describe Allen's corpus of the nineties, in which he returns obsessively to themes that have preoccupied him for decades. In the face of critical and popular disfavor, Allen, an unreconstructed auteur, has persisted in making movies his way. At the risk of being out of step with the times, Allen has remained in step with himself. Faithful to his fabled neuroses, he is a "Method" film maker who continues to draw on his entangled inner life, a web of cravings, phobias, and anxieties. Affairs of the heart remain his beat, and in the land of Allen, sex is the unstoppable Force, the unavoidable First Cause. In his Manhattan mating dances, the questing, often treacherous, always unpredictable heart, as ever in his work, is subject to fits. Impulsive, easily wounded, in love with love, often confusing sex with love and misreading their desire, the players in *la ronde* according to Woody Allen change partners frequently. In the film maker's cosmos, romance is fragile; desire fades; temptation is always on a tear; couples form, split, and sometimes re-form. Cheating hearts and wandering eyes infect both genders. Sometimes A loves B loves C; often A and B love each other, but not necessarily at the same time or in the same way. The poet laureate of the hunt for the sexual Holy Grail, Woody Allen is Priapus on the Hudson, in life as in art a man pricked by eros.

Throughout the nineties, Allen in a range of moods continued to explore his enduring theme, the deep and bewitching mysteries of sexual attraction. Sometimes the enigma is pursued in the form of sprawling metropolitan epics, sometimes it is examined within intimate chamber dramas. His films continue to display a distinctive visual sheen, from the ravishing black and white cinematography of *Shadows and Fog* (1992) and *Celebrity* (1998) to the jittery, hand-held camera and the Godardian jump cuts in *Husbands and Wives* and *Manhattan Murder Mystery* (1993) to the elegant long takes that signal the maverick film maker's defiance of the contemporary vogue for fractured editing. And even in the not-fully-achieved projects, the Allen portfolio is studded with immaculate performances. Although there are conflicting reports about how much (or how little) direction Allen gives his actors, the unassailable proof of his instincts for movie acting is on screen. His dossier of the nineties solidifies Allen's place as the foremost director of actors now at work in American films.

Detractors might quip that the best Woody Allen movie of the decade took place off screen. And indeed, the scenario of the film maker's breakup with Mia Farrow, his longtime partner and leading lady, reads like an Allen screenplay for a particularly nasty comedy of bad manners. A middle-aged man, heeding his heart's desire, falls in love with his mistress's alarmingly young, adopted Asian daughter, for whom he must have represented some kind of father figure or father surrogate. The saga resounds with such familiar Allen subjects as infidelity, the lure of forbidden fruit, the pleasure and perils of a May-December romance. In January 1992, Farrow discovered nude photos of Soon-Yi lying on a mantelpiece in Allen's apartment. According to Allen, his affair with Soon-Yi, which had taken them both by surprise, had begun only a month earlier. Although relations between Allen and Farrow had cooled, the actress was understandably enraged. Nonetheless, the estranged couple seemed about to reach an agreement when, after Allen's visit to Farrow's Connecticut home on August 4, 1992, Farrow accused Allen of having molested their adopted daughter Dylan. After a prolonged investigation, the charges against Allen were dismissed, but Farrow won custody of Dylan (now renamed Eliza) and of Satchel (now Seamus), the couple's natural-born son.

In one sense, Allen's private life is none of our business; but in another, because of his fame and because for so long he has insinuated himself into his work, he can't quite claim the same right to privacy as an ordinary citizen. Despite his disingenuous disclaimers over the years that he is not the character he plays in his movies, Woody watchers have concluded otherwise. His films have taught us that relationships are messy and that the rules of attraction are rooted in deception as well as delight. Still, the inescapable news that the artist was no wiser than many of his characters was, if not exactly a surprise, then certainly a disappointment. The circumstances of the scandal rudely contradicted any presumption that Allen's keen observations of sexual politics had protected him from making the same mistakes as his often foolish or misguided characters.

When Allen betrayed Farrow, their son and adopted daughter, and Farrow's other children, on a different scale he also let down his fans, who had regarded him as a moralist of sorts—an artist with superior insights about sexual and romantic conduct. Allen's public disgrace has been followed by partial rehabilitation: in Venice on December 22, 1997, Allen married Soon-Yi; in 1999 the couple had a baby girl, and in 2000 they adopted a newborn girl. His apparently stable marriage has earned him a pardon from some fans, but the impact of the revelations of 1992–93 will continue to haunt him for years to come.

At the least, the scandal has provided a grid against which to read Allen's recent work. How could it be otherwise, for a director whose his life and art always had an incestuous convergence? How could America's most rapturously personal film maker possibly avoid incorporating the aftershocks of his offstage trial-by-fire? Indeed, the films address viewers who are presumed to be veterans of the Allen-Farrow wars. Aspects of the scandal narrative, treated varyingly in anger, sorrow, defiance, apology, or affirmation, supply an unavoidable subtext to the work of the nineties.

The post-scandal Woody Allen is most fully revealed in a film Allen himself did not direct. *Wild Man Blues* (1997), by the esteemed documentary film maker Barbara Kopple, is ostensibly a concert film of Allen's European tour with his New Orleans jazz band, but the real focus is how much of his off screen self Woody Allen, consciously or unconsciously, allows to be revealed. He's cagey, and it would be naïve to assume that he allowed Kopple unrestricted access, or that the film's portrait of Woody Allen has been unmediated by the director himself. The film maker who has attained virtually unprecedented control over his work is going to expose only as much of the person behind the persona as he feels his audience has any right to see. If not for the scandal, he doubtless would never have consented to appear "as himself"—indeed, the events of 1992–93 forced him to claim a connection between himself and his persona that he had previously denied. Rather than the punishing, controlling, cold-hearted, self-absorbed figure depicted in Mia Farrow's scorching 1997 memoir, *What Falls Away*, the star of Kopple's documentary is remarkably similar to the movie icon beloved by millions. As in his own films, the comedian excels in playing "Woody Allen," a finicky, twitchy, whiny wisecracker subject to depression who is by turns irritating and lovable. "I would rather be bitten by the dog than licked by it," he cringes, and remains unpersuaded even after his sister, Letty Aronson, explains that "dogs' mouths are cleaner than people's." When Soon-Yi, obviously having learned to cater to Allen's obsessiveness, comments that "the shower was excellent, wasn't it?" he concurs, but raises an important caveat. "The drain was in the center." (As reported by Mia Farrow in her memoir, the placement of a shower drain provoked a major domestic contretemps.) "I always have to have my own bathroom because I'm crazy," Allen confides in an aside to the camera, playing "Woody."

Throughout, seemingly on the spur of the moment, Allen delivers one-liners packed with his distinctive brand of ironic, self-deprecating wit. Dipping into a pool in his incredibly deluxe suite in a Milan hotel, he observes wryly, "I never swam in my own apartment before, except in a plumbing emergency." Anxious about how his performance will go over in London, he speculates, "If I'm not good these people will hate me in my own language." When his father suggests that his famous son would have been better off as a pharmacist, Allen quips, "I'd get more business than the people who come to see my films." In a delightful interchange with an exuberant Italian fan who showers him with admiration, Woody pleads, "Don't stop!"—a moment that even an obdurate Allen foe could not help but be charmed by.

From time to time, Allen displays a darker side. "When I'm here in Europe, I miss New York," he confesses in a sober tone. "I don't want to be where I am at any given moment." "I'm depressed, it happens every day," he says, depleted, his Woody mask momentarily removed. The obligations of being a celebrity clearly puzzle and at times overwhelm him;

mobbed by crowds, he seems a tiny, frightened figure. But the film shows him struggling to be "Woody
Allen." "Wave to the people, they've been waiting
here to see you," his sister instructs him. "I will
speak because they expect to be spoken to, but I'd
rather not," Allen says, promising, in effect, that he
will perform Woody at least briefly for the fans.

The portrait of the artist that is constructed
in *Wild Man Blues*—witty, accommodating, soft-
spoken, polite but distant—is a product of damage
control. As such, however, it is inevitably hampered
by Allen's evident reluctance at being observed, his
moodiness, and his generally ambivalent, self-
absorbed personality. The documentary also functions as a kind of propaganda for Soon-Yi. Under the
circumstances, she is remarkably poised, and though
she has a limited repertoire she performs as naturally
as Allen does for Kopple's snooping camera. Like
Letty Aronson, she is attentive to Allen's neuroses
and his needs; when he's depressed, she's quick to pat
his knee. But she also calls him on his foibles. "You
see every place as a closing when you play only
once," she observes. "That makes no sense: It's an
opening." "You tend to latch onto only one person
[and ignore all the others] in the band; you look like
a crazy [when you do that]," she reprimands. "You
should tell the band how good they were." "I think
I did tell them they were good, I hope I did," he
answers meekly.

An independent, stolid young woman with a
hard edge (she, too, after all, betrayed Farrow),
Soon-Yi is clearly not intimidated by Allen's fame.
She admits she has never read anything of Allen's

and has seen only a few of his films. "My favorite is *Manhattan*," she says, with no apparent awareness that she is playing the Mariel Hemingway role for real. When an interviewer asks her what she thought of *Interiors*, she cleverly answers, "I'd rather not say." "I look like a goof," Allen comments, perusing a batch of photographs. "Nerd comes to mind," Soon-Yi responds, her timing as deft as Allen's. But the film can't disguise the fact that Allen and Soon-Yi are indeed an odd couple who apparently have very little to say to each other.

A careless tone that sometimes creeps into Allen's generally playful, teasing, affectionate treatment of Soon-Yi contains portents of trouble in paradise. "Go with one of your twitty teenage friends," he tells Soon-Yi, urging her to see *Annie Hall* ("it's a picture I think you'd enjoy"). "[Imagine] two scuzzballs like us in this big apartment," he says, commenting on their imperial suite in Milan. "They're used to dignitaries and politicians; this kid was eating out of garbage pails in Korea."

In the potent and notorious last scene—what Allen in an aside calls "the luncheon from hell"—the director, Soon-Yi, and Letty, returned from abroad, visit Martin and Nettie Konigsberg, Allen's aged parents. (Martin died at 100 in January 2001.) "Were you the wrong parents for me?" Allen chides, savoring the chance to bait his parents, toward whom he evidently harbors ancient resentments. "You beat me; I could have been a drug addict or a criminal," he hisses at Nettie. Stung, Nettie snaps back. "You were brought up in a household that knew right from wrong. Don't think you [became what you are] on your own. You had plenty of help," she says, seemingly unaware of the ironic double meaning of her claim. Trying to tilt the battle in his favor, Allen asks how Nettie feels about his dating an Asian woman. (The question is a double whammy, a way of insulting his mother and his girlfriend.) "I don't think it's right," Nettie says, as Allen surely knew she would. "I'd prefer you fall in love with a Jewish girl. Someday Jews will be extinct."

Thrust back into the kind of argument he likely has been waging with his parents his entire life, Allen is unguarded; the "Woody" mask slips, and beneath the wisecracks and asides he becomes a son locked in a primal struggle with a clobbering mother and disapproving father. (Allen may feel he has been a victim of parental abuse, as this luncheon battle indicates, but the judge who denied him custody of Satchel and Dylan in his court battle with Farrow wrote a blistering assessment of the film maker's own parenting.) "All right, sir, you can go home now," Nettie tells an off screen interviewer; as the last line of the film, it recalls the KEEP OUT sign that concludes *Citizen Kane*. Yet for all Allen's attempts in the film to control his iconography, *Wild Man Blues* remains a fascinating text for Woody-watchers that contains the core themes that Allen explores in his own work of the nineties and reveals more of the comedian's private self than he may have intended it to.

The first two entries of the decade, both pre-scandal, are fantasies of escape and transformation that contain hints of the director's coming break with his leading lady. In *Alice* (1990), the title character (enchantingly performed by Mia Farrow in her final starring role for Allen) is released from a loveless marriage to a wealthy, distracted, philandering businessman (a stand-in for the director himself?). In *Shadows and Fog*, a nerd named Kleinman (=small man, and played, of course, by Allen) is rescued from a paranoid nightmare. Alice's lament, "I'm at a crossroads, I'm lost," is equally applicable to Kleinman. Trapped by dead-end lives, both characters urgently require altered states. It is tempting to read the two works as murmurs from the film maker about his estrangement from Farrow. In this light, *Alice* is a generous farewell to his longtime partner. Alice is not only freed from her husband Doug (played by the ever-icy William Hurt, surely the coldest actor in Christendom), she also has an affair with an attractive jazz musician (Joe Mantegna) before leaving Manhattan for Calcutta, where she goes to help the sick and the poor. "They have 10,000 unlisted diseases in Calcutta," Doug sneers.

A pampered Upper East Side matron who wants more—or rather, in a material sense, less—from her life, Alice Tate is a lady who lunches and shops. Back pains send her to the Chinatown office of Dr. Yang (Hollywood veteran Keye Luke, majestic in his final role), who shrewdly diagnoses her condition. "Problem is not back," he states in a terse, oracular style, pointing to Alice's head and heart. With the help of this preternaturally wise Asian (an in-house reference to Allen's own Asian liberator?), Alice, like Ibsen's Nora in *A Doll's House*, learns how to slam the door in her husband's face.

Each time Alice is driven in her limousine to Chinatown, the music slides from jazz, associated with the Upper East Side, to Asian motifs, connoting a downtown world bubbling with Eastern mysticism. Painted in red, Dr. Yang's office, unlike Alice's baronial apartment uptown, looks like a place where magic can happen. (Framing "Orientalism" in this way, Allen collides with political correctness, a familiar strategy in his work.) On each of Alice's visits, Dr. Yang dispenses herbs with wondrous properties. The first herb untangles her sexual inhibitions, and she is able to flirt outrageously with Joe, the jazz musician she meets at her children's private school. "I love the sax," she tells him, her inflection lined with double entendre. The second herb makes Alice disappear. Invisible, she observes Joe seduce his ex-wife and Doug make love with a co-worker in his office. The magic herbs and the ghost of a sexy, deceased lover (Alec Baldwin) nudge Alice, a repressed, guilt-prone Catholic, toward infidelity and carnal pleasure.

Alice and Joe become lovers in a charming scene in which rain patters on the skylight in Joe's apartment. "Was I terrible?" Alice asks. "You were the best," Joe assures her. *Alice* celebrates adultery: Who wouldn't wish the title character to enjoy herself with the doe-eyed saxophonist rather than continue to be shackled to her frostbitten husband? But as Dr. Yang warns, "Love is most complex emotion. No logic to emotion. Where there is no rational thought, much suffering." Predictably unpredictable, like most of Allen's screen lovers, Joe decides he belongs with his ex-wife, but he ends the affair with a gentleness and tact that Allen will not be able to manage in the real world. Yielding to and enjoying sex, Alice also transcends it. Her affair frees her to leave for Calcutta to realize a long deferred goal. Like her idol, Mother Teresa, Alice wants "to help sick old people." At the end, voice-overs of Upper East Side gossips relate that Alice has returned from Calcutta and is working on the Lower East Side. In the final shot, we see Alice swinging her kids in a ramshackle playground and smiling beatifically.

The film's Upper East Side—Woody Allen turf— is richly rendered: An early scene is a virtuoso long take in which the camera moves deftly around the Tates' elegant, burnished-yellow Manhattan lair. As a maid, a nanny, a masseuse, and a pretentious dec- orator enter on cue, the film both satirizes the kind of rarefied enclave that Allen himself lives in, while at the same time positioning the spectator in an admiring relation to it. But the leap of spirit that Alice undergoes, from idle wife consumed by materi- alism to a life of service to the disadvantaged, is one that Allen is unable to negotiate. Suggesting spiritual transcendence, or its afterglow, is beyond his capaci- ties, and in the face of "Calcutta," he is mute. He neither shows Alice in Calcutta, nor does he attempt, other than the shot at the end, to present her after her experience there has changed her. Alice's will to serve and her adherence to a Catholic worldview that both cripples and ultimately helps to save her, are issues that Allen, a Jewish cynic, can treat only in passing. But despite its gaps his film is a moving embrace of self-transformation. As the wise Dr. Yang assures Alice, "Mrs. Tate has better idea of who she is, what are her innermost feelings."

244 The Comedian's Progress: The Nineties

"I'm unemployed, a lynch mob is after me, I'm wanted by the police": Summing up his plight, Kleinman, the terminally hapless antihero of *Shadows and Fog*, concludes, "I'm an ink-stained wretch." Like Alice, Kleinman needs a way out of his existential quicksand. The original bad luck schlemiel, Kleinman is awakened in the middle of the night by a group of vigilantes on the trail of a mysterious killer. "Do you know my assignment? No one's told me what I'm supposed to be doing," he whines, frustrated at being forced to take part in a Plan that has not been explained to him. "Running around all night in a fog," he is rebuffed by neighbors, his former and present fiancées, his boss, and coworkers. A psychic identifies him as the killer. And so ill-starred is he that, in bed with a prostitute, he is impotent.

But, as with Alice, there is a way out. An amateur magician, Kleinman is asked to join a traveling circus. At first he resists: "I have to return to real life." When he recognizes how important illusions are ("[people] need them, like the air," the magician tells him), Kleinman accepts the job. Released from bondage to a "real" world where failure and humiliation have been his destiny, Kleinman enters the idealized realm of an itinerant artist where he is free to spin illusions.

In *Alice*, Allen bestows a fulfilling independence on Farrow; in this fable, he blesses his own flight. For the second time in a row, however, he also takes good care of Farrow who, in her winsome waif mode, plays Irmy, a sword-swallower (calling Dr. Freud!) in the circus passing through town. Irmy (like Farrow herself) is involved with a clown (John Malkovich) who wants to avoid emotional entanglements. "A family is death to the artist," he proclaims, echoing Allen's own reluctance to make a full commitment to Farrow and her large family. When Irmy discovers the clown having sex with Maria (Madonna), another circus performer, she runs away. Taking shelter in a brothel, Irmy, a virginal-looking sensualist, succumbs to a hot-to-trot student's $700 offer to spend the night with him. But Allen decrees a happy end for the character. Reunited with the chastened clown and becoming the mother of an orphan she finds in her wanderings through the shadows and fog, she gets the family she craves.

*Shadows and Fog*, like *Alice*, is an appealing oddity in the Allen canon in which, once again, the film maker's thematic ambitions exceed his grasp. Allen's favorite themes are tied to a feeble, unfocused allegory that doesn't fully support them. As a metaphor for Kleinman's existential quandary, "the Plan" lacks resonance. In recurring scenes in a brothel, prostitutes and their clients sound like undergraduates putting on philosophical airs as they talk casually about God, the nature of reality, the lure of suicide. The magician's last-minute paean to art and Kleinman's embrace of illusion over reality are also sketchy—ideas from the Woody Allen trunk. The spurious glaze of Higher Meaning is most apparent in the film's treatment of the killer, or is it the Killer? In *Death*, the not-well-wrought early one-act play that the film is expanded from, the killer on a rampage is likened to the figure of Death in a medieval morality drama. But in the film Allen cheats. When he shows "Death" in action, strangling a doctor eager to investigate "the nature of evil," the figure is demoted to a serial killer in a horror movie. In the finale, Allen tries, unconvincingly, to re-hoist the strangler to an allegorical level by making him disappear. But the film's cavalier, contradictory treatment of death (or Death) and its pseudophilosophical patina are secondary to its double benediction: a family for Irmy-Mia, the world of creative "magic" for Kleinman-Allen.

Taking a break from Manhattan, Allen sets his would-be allegory, *Shadows and Fog*, with its echoes of Kafka's *Trial* and Bergman's *Seventh Seal*, in a claustrophobic, studio-created, medieval-looking European village thick with chiaroscuro and *Stimmung*. Allen's mise-en-scène, steeped in minatory shadows and with narrow, winding streets that enfold the nighttime wanderers in mazelike spaces, recalls such German Expressionist silent films as *Nosferatu* and *The Cabinet of Dr. Caligari*. Music from Kurt Weill and Bertolt Brecht's *Threepenny Opera* and *Mahagonny* reinforces the Germanic aura, against which the actors' flat American accents, and Allen's New York–accented verbal twitches in particular, ripple comically. Allen's eye and his characteristically astute casting (playing prostitutes, the tough-looking Jodie Foster and Lily Tomlin introduce a potent resistance to the ravenous heterosexual clients their characters are expected to service) compensate for his thematic uncertainty.

The slight, quirky *Alice* and *Shadows and Fog* could be regarded as warm-ups for Allen's three major ensemble pieces of the decade, *Husbands and Wives*, *Deconstructing Harry* (1997), and *Celebrity*, in which the film maker returns to more familiar territory, the psychology of sexual pursuit. Egoists driven by their compulsions, the male protagonists in these panoramic Manhattan tales of genital jousting are variations on the core Allen type; trolling, whether for ripe students, nubile celebrities, or available sisters-in-law, the characters crave variety and freedom. Gabe Roth (Woody Allen) in *Husbands and Wives* is a college professor and a published novelist of modest renown. Harry Block (Allen), the object of deconstruction, is a successful novelist about to be honored by the college from which he was expelled. Lee Simon (Kenneth Branagh) in *Celebrity* is a literary bottom feeder, a failed novelist peddling a screenplay who earns his living as a journalist. Far from having exhausted his favorite topic, Allen, perhaps because of the pressures in his life at the time, perhaps because of his own aging—a powerful, insistent libido in advancing middle age is a force to be reckoned with!—attacks it with a heightened, almost at times demonic, intensity. Thorny, scabrous, and as scandalous in their way as the disintegration of the director's affair with Farrow, the films are decidedly "unpleasant" comedies in the Shavian sense in which Allen speaks to and sometimes assaults his audience in new ways. With increasing confidence he merges light with dark tones within the same work—the three movies are unsettled hybrids of comedy and drama, as if *Annie Hall* has mated with *Another Woman*.

Profanity ("I think of fucking every woman I meet," Harry confesses to his therapist) reflects the

fury of the characters (and of the film maker?). And
Allen's film language too—the roving, jittery, hand-
held camera in *Husbands and Wives*; the sweeping
tracking shots in *Celebrity*; the jump cuts and the
fractured crosscutting in *Deconstructing Harry*—
sizzles with a newfound abrasive energy. The films
themselves seem to reflect, even to participate in, the
sexual heat that seizes their protagonists. In these
mordant demi-comedies, the camera is as subject to
fits and flux as the middle-aged characters behaving
like randy adolescents.

*Husbands and Wives* opens with the sharpest
scene in Allen's work of the nineties. Sally (Judy
Davis, sublime) and Jack (Sydney Pollack), the best
friends of Gabe and Judy (Mia Farrow), jauntily
announce their decision to divorce just as the two
couples are about to go out for dinner. The weaving camera and the jump cuts enfold the characters
in a mise-en-scène simmering with tensions. Working
in the naturalistic, quicksilver style that has become
Allen's signature, the four performers play with—
and against—each other like finely tuned instru-
ments. Pollack oozes the kind of self-satisfaction
that's ripe for a fall. Judy Davis, the Allen performer of the decade, creates an archetypal urban
neurotic, a character pulsing with emanations
from a turbulent and at this point unexamined
inner life. And performing together for the last
time Allen and Farrow thrust and parry with an
intimacy born of their long association. Allowing
his actors to im-provise, Allen instructed the cinematographer, Carlo Di Palma, to follow their
movements—visually and aurally, the result is a furi-

ous vitality, Allenesque comedy of manners ratcheted up to fever pitch.

"Do you ever keep things from me? Am I cold in bed?" Judy, disturbed by the unexpected announcement of the divorce, asks Gabe after their friends have departed. Before sex, Gabe, who doesn't want a child, orders Judy, who does, to put in her diaphragm. "You really trust no one," she snaps. "No wonder people accuse you of cynicism."

"Released" by their friends' divorce, Gabe and Judy yield to temptation. To an off screen interviewer each of the characters checks in with from time to time, Gabe claims never to have cheated on Judy. But it's clear that sex consumes him—practically his first words in the film are his reference to a student thesis on "Oral Sex in the Age of Deconstruction." To the interviewer he recalls Harriet Harmon, a "sexually carnivorous" early lover. "Highly libidinous," "she made love with other women and wound up in an institution. She was great but nuts." Reveling in the *jouissance* of recollected, unbridled lust, Gabe admits to a passion for "kamikaze women" who "crash their plane into you."

When Rain (Juliette Lewis), a nymphet-named student who specializes in "the midlife crisis set," flashes her eyes, he tumbles. Gabe shows her a novel he is writing about males preoccupied with sex. Her critical response—"the leading characters are shallow, wasting time on a sexual woman who is psychotic"—only deepens his attraction. "My heart does not know from logic," Gabe reports, recycling a familiar Woody Allen line (one that the film maker himself used offstage in defense of his affair with

Soon-Yi). "There was something in my marriage I was not getting, and Rain was exciting." During Rain's birthday party, thunder and lightning, behaving with Shakespearean force, echo Gabe's sexual commotion. "Don't do this to me," he says weakly, as Rain asks for a serious kiss. "Why do I hear $50,000 worth of therapy?"

Judy meanwhile introduces Sally to a coworker, Michael (Liam Neeson, almost illegally attractive in the role), before she realizes her own interest in him. Showing Michael her poems, which she has withheld from Gabe because he is "so critical," Judy begins to confront the failure of her marriage. In an ironic reversal of the way the scene will be played off screen, it is Farrow who announces to Allen the end of their relationship. "You use sex to express every emotion except love," she tells him, then says with quiet, irrefutable conviction, "It's over, and we both know it."

Jack and Sally launch their own egg hunts. Like Gabe, Jack is a victim of his lust. When a lubricious colleague at work gives him the number of an expensive call girl, he hesitates, then picks up the phone. After he and Sally split, Jack takes up with Sam (Lysette Anthony), a young yoga instructor who believes in astrology, then turns against her violently because, though it takes him time to realize it, she isn't Sally. Single and mistakenly convincing herself that she likes it, Sally is a sexual nervous wreck, boiling with anger and repressed desire. Her conflicts make her death on a date. When she meets a male friend to go to the opera, she momentarily excuses herself to make a fierce phone call to Jack. "I'm fine," she assures her date afterwards, her every gesture and membrane signaling otherwise. "They should have cut his fucking dick off," she explodes when she realizes she is about to see *Don Giovanni*, a story about a compulsive fornicator. When Michael puts the make on her, she backs off. "I can't go so fast, metabolically it's not my rhythm." As she confesses to the interviewer, in bed with Michael she became distracted trying to decide if the males she knows are foxes or hedgehogs.

One and a half years after Jack and Sally made their fateful announcement, Gabe, who has broken off with Rain because of the difference in their ages, is the only solo act in the quartet. Judy has married Michael, Jack and Sally are back together. "I don't mind being alone now," Gabe tells the interviewer. "My new novel is more political, less personal." "Is it over? Can I go now?" he asks. It's the last line of the film.

Off screen, obeying the illogic of emotion, Allen abandoned Farrow, but on screen he once again made sure that her character was provided for. This time, however, Judy's "happy" ending is less certain. Judy has a handsome new husband, but the film raises doubts about whether she will be able to keep him. "She was passive/aggressive, she gets what she wants," her first husband reports unflatteringly; and as Gabe tells her, "You're not really stable." "I hope I didn't push [Michael]," Judy states in her final interview; but we have seen that she has forced herself on a man who seems to prefer Sally. Judy evokes a divided, ambivalent response not only from Michael but also likely from the viewer and seemingly from the film maker as well. Knowledge of the unfolding offstage drama—it was during the filming of *Husbands and Wives* that Farrow found the photographs of Soon-Yi—adds disquieting subtextual ripples to the film's portrait of Gabe and Judy's dissolving marriage.

*Deconstructing Harry* continues where *Husbands and Wives* left off. Gabe, alone, working with renewed concentration on his writing as he teases stories out of his calamitous private life, has been transmuted into Harry. Another compulsive, whining womanizer who seems destined for erotic disappointment, Harry is a pill-popping hypochondriac facing a creative and existential impasse. "I still can't get my love life in order: I still love whores, I have not grown up," he confesses to his therapist. Crazed by sex, he seduces one of his wife's patients; in an elevator on the way to a tryst with his sister-in-law, he meets and seduces Fay (Elisabeth Shue), a fan of his writing. "Promise me you won't fall in love with me, I have too many phobias," he warns her.

"You take everybody's suffering and turn it into literary gold. How could you write that book?" screeches his irate sister-in-law, Lucy (the great Judy Davis creating another vivid depiction of psychic disarray). Beside herself with fury and mortification—in his just-published novel Harry has exposed their affair—she has come to shoot him. But Harry saves his life by telling his overwrought ex-mistress a story drawn from his novel-in-progress about his literary alter ego, Harvey, who wants sex with every woman except his wife. Harvey, who conducts his liaisons in the apartment of a friend, Mendl Birnbaum, awaits his "Oriental passport to paradise," an Asian pin-up who is a walking wet dream (a gesture toward the public's perception of why Allen fell for Soon-Yi?). Lust is intercepted by the arrival of Death, come to claim Mendl. A surreal sex farce, the Marx Brothers crossed with Ingmar Bergman, the story cracks Lucy up; laughing, she puts down her gun. Harry's talent saves his skin.

The episode establishes the film's unorthodox, open-ended form: Scenes from Harry's work regularly intersect a story set in "real" space and time, in which Harry travels upstate to receive a tribute from his alma mater. (The film's basic narrative premise recalls that of Bergman's *Wild Strawberries*.) Allen travels with Cookie, a black hooker (Hazelle Goodman) [another example of the auteur's refusal to appease the captains of political correctness]; his son, whom he has kidnapped from his enraged ex-wife, a therapist (a revved-up Kirstie Alley, who brings down the house); and a buddy (Bob Balaban) who drops dead en route. As Harry quips, "I show up [for my tribute] with a hooker and a dead body." His ex-wife interrupts the ceremony; Harry is charged with kidnapping, arrested, and jailed. This skeletal frame is bombarded with flashbacks from Harry's life and (played by a different set of actors) with parallel scenes from his novel that creatively rework the author's biographical reminiscences. Reality and illusion collide in intricate Pirandellian pirouettes.

A road movie pitted with detours, *Deconstructing Harry* is Allen's most complexly structured work to date. To keep up, viewers must devise their own map. This whirling dervish dark comedy is a caustic, foul-mouthed, embittered dissection of a creative artist hooked on work and sex—in other words, it is Allen's sly response to critics of his personal life.

"I write stories and stop," Harry complains in one of his sessions with his analyst. Distributed throughout Harry's pilgrimage are a few of these narrative fragments, the flotsam of the writer's turbulent inner life. One short story is about an actor who is suddenly out of focus. "You expect the world to adjust to the distortion you've become," Harry's therapist suggests as a possible interpretation. In another story, Epstein (another surrogate for Harry) marries his third analyst (played by the unlikely and usually coarse-grained Demi Moore, here, under Allen's watch, a deft comedienne). For her neurotic Jewish patient, the gentile who knows "all [his] perversions" converts. She performs prayers before every meal and every round of oral sex, and then runs off with an Israeli patient. When Harry stops en route to visit his sister Doris (the wonderfully wry Caroline Aaron), she accuses him of being a self-hating Jew. "Look at how he talks about them in his stories," she observes to her orthodox husband, echoing a familiar complaint of some of Allen's Jewish viewers. Her comment is the cue for the most wickedly entertaining inner story in the film, in which Max, a Jewish paterfamilias, murders and then eats his first wife, his mistress, and his child. "Max is a version of Daddy whom you hated," is the way Doris, probably correctly, decodes the ghoulish fable.

At the tribute, when a fuddy duddy academic asks Harry what he has been working on, the film flips into a garish recreation of hell. On a lower level, Harry meets his late, unlamented father, and a rival writer (Billy Crystal), who stole one of Harry's girlfriends. The two authors compare their sins. "I had two blond Wasp sisters at once," Harry confesses. A visual departure from the rest of the film, the sequence is ugly looking and Allen and Billy Crystal, surprisingly, are dull together. Momentarily, the auteur seems to lose his footing.

"I'm depressed, I'm spiritually bankrupt, the universe is coming apart," Harry, sounding off like an exaggerated version of Woody Allen in *Wild Man Blues*, announces to Cookie. "I'm the worst person in the world," Harry wails. "Who's worse?"

"Hitler," Cookie responds, putting a stop to his orgy of self-loathing.

A student at the tribute eagerly tells him that she likes deconstructing his stories because "they are happy underneath, only you don't know it." "You give people pleasure in your work," one of Harry's literary creations assures him. "I love you all," Harry tells his characters in a last-act conclave that recalls the one between the director and his creations at the end of Fellini's *8½*. Restored, Harry returns to his typewriter, and in a finale that rhymes with the opening, writing saves Harry's life. He begins working on a story, a facsimile of the one we have just seen, about "a guy who can't function except through his writing."

What other possible conclusion is the audience expected to come to except that Harry, a guilt-ridden, self-lacerating Jew who uses his life as the inspiration for his stories, is Woody (notice the echoing

names) thinly disguised? The film is Allen's answer
to the chorus of condemnation that greeted news of
his "extramarital" affair as well as to the critics
who had been nudging him to change his tune, to
find other fixations besides nubile women young
enough to be his granddaughter. In caricaturing the
public perception of him as a sex-addicted worka-
holic—an image that Allen himself has fostered—he
seeks to defuse the prosecution. In giving so much
apparent ammunition to his denouncers—see what
a prick I am, how I use people for my work, how
untrustworthy I am in affairs of the loins and the
heart—he enforces a countermove. "Oh, you're not
*that* bad," as Cookie assures him (and us): Hitler,
after all, was far worse. It's as if Allen decided to
paint a portrait so extreme that his detractors might
be coaxed into reevaluating their estimate of him.
Allen's achievement in this bitter, coruscating comedy
of literary and sexual bad manners is to have constructed a self-defense in the form of an apparent
self-critique. Beneath the film's top layer of self-
incrimination is an act of quite daunting hubris.
Harry, after all, is an artist who, in fact, "give[s]
people pleasure in [his] work," and an apparent
schlemiel who continues to attract a bevy of attractive Christians. Having passed through his
Walpurgisnacht, he emerges creatively refreshed,
back at work drawing more stories—a potentially
never-ending series—from his closely examined life.
Deconstructing Woody, a decades-long project for
dedicated Allen watchers, is an invitation the auteur
continues to extend, and this film assures us that,
as the guy with the gifts (for telling stories and for

captivating shiksas), he's the one who sets the rules of the game.

Hovering over the phallic towers lining Central Park West in the opening of *Celebrity* is a skywritten plea: "HELP!" The image, it is revealed through slow disclosure, comes from *The Liquidator*, a film in the making. Lee (Kenneth Branagh), the antihero of *Celebrity*, the "real" film, is visiting the set in order to interview the film's star, Nicole Oliver (Melanie Griffith). "HELP!" appears again in the final shot of Allen's urban odyssey, as Lee attends the premiere of *The Liquidator*; and by this time it's clear that the sign expresses Lee's existential crisis. Having published two "self-indulgent, sophomoric, solipsistic" novels that were "critically dismissed," Lee is a hack journalist trying to sell a screenplay about an armored car robbery and struggling with an outsized literary novel in which celebrity-worship is a metaphor for a bankrupt society. Without the literary acclaim that sustained Gabe or Harry, Lee is the most bereft of Allen's metropolitan voyagers of the nineties. Tellingly, Allen chose not to play the role.

Like the other Allen antiheroes, however, Lee moment by moment is sustained by the stratagems of a modern day Lothario. If scrawny, cartoon-cute Woody Allen remains a screen lover with a quizzical, controversial sex appeal, Kenneth Branagh invests his character and the film with an unassailable erotic charge. The luscious women he encounters on the job are apparently his for the taking. "My body belongs to my husband, but what I do from the neck up is my own business," movie star Nicole Oliver croons, as, post-interview, she begins to unzip Lee's pants. "Do I know you?" Lee asks Nola (played by Winona Ryder, an uneven, sometimes callow performer, here operating at perfect pitch), a ravishing extra on the set of *The Liquidator*. His trite come-on apparently hits its target. Covering a fashion story, he hooks up with a superstar model (Charlize Theron, radiating an aura of entitlement) who asks to drive his car. Mere proximity to her causes Lee to hyperventilate. "You are the most beautiful creature I've ever seen," he whispers in a voice choked with longing. "Every curve fulfills its promise. If the universe has any meaning at all, you are it." When she announces that she is "orgasmic," "polymorphously perverse," and that "every part [of her body] gets erotic pleasure," Lee's desire is aroused to a toxic level. When he touches her hand, she melts. "*It's only her hand*," he sighs, facing the camera, the character's pleasure and pain exquisitely coalescing in a moment that surely ranks among the most potent expressions of heterosexual male desire in American movies. Written and played for comedy, the scene nonetheless resonates with a sexual heat that is no laughing matter.

For Lee, sex is inescapable. When he tries to interest a sybaritic movie star (Leonardo DiCaprio) in his armored car robbery script, the actor invites him to an orgy with two nymphets. When Lee runs into Nola at Elaine's (the real life Upper East Side bistro that is unaccountably Allen's favorite Manhattan watering hole), she sets a time and place for an assignation. "Can I make you a more European offer [than meeting me at] a kiosk at midnight?" she asks.

"I created you twice in fiction before I met you; you were the obscure object of desire in my two books," he assures her. (Allen's revelers court each other in beautifully shaped sentences; language itself seems saturated with the free-floating desire that courses through the film.)

A scarred veteran of the relationship wars, Lee is a sexual winner who can't help losing. Ending his marriage to Robin, a repressed Catholic (played, with ferocious intensity, by Judy Davis, who else?), Lee is about to have a new roommate, Bonnie, a statuesque editor at a publishing house (Famke Janssen) who loyally promotes his work. When, on moving day, thinking he is in love with Nola, Lee informs Bonnie that he has met someone else, she swipes his novel-in-progress and hurls it into the Hudson. But Lee has leaped before he looked, failing to heed Nola's warning that she cannot be faithful. Feeling crowded by his attention, she wants to date a director. Lee is so hapless that even the one sure thing, sleeping with the supermodel, is squelched when she scurries away after he smashes his car into a plate glass window.

At the end Lee is alone at the premiere of *The Liquidator*, dazed by his misfortune. His ex-wife and his paramours, who are all at the premiere, have landed comfortably for the time being. "I hope something breaks for you," Robin tells him patronizingly, hammering the final nail into his existential coffin. As Lee, the apparent winner, has fallen, Robin, the apparent loser, has risen. The film charts her rehabilitation from a dumpy, enraged, jilted spouse to a poised, happily married, now pregnant television interviewer. To be sure, in this light-and-shadow comedy, Robin's "ascension" is touched with irony—as the hostess of an interview show on which she chats up celebrities du jour, whose fame is as fleeting as Lee's flings, she is complicit with the circuit of celebrity worship that the film disdains.

The most underrated Allen film of the nineties, a kaleidoscope of urban malaise shot in shimmering black-and-white, *Celebrity* has a symphonic texture. Although he was widely criticized for imitating his director's familiar stammering delivery, the British Branagh, mastering a nearly flawless American accent, delivers far more than a virtuoso impersonation. Giving the character a roiling inner life and darkening the sexual comedy with a melancholy undertone, he adds fresh accents to the Woody Allen part.

Where the film slips is in exploring the subject announced in the title. Allen's swipes at the celebrity-worshipping worlds of movies, art, fashion, television, and publishing that Lee passes through are lazily conceived. As both portrait and analysis of the celebrity virus, *Wild Man Blues* is far more penetrating.

Allen throughout the decade continued to revisit crime, his favorite subject next to sex. As he handles them, however, the two subjects are entwined; criminals and crime scenes have terrific sex appeal for the film maker, and in a number of his movies crime is equivalent to sexual release. Like his absorption with sex, his attitudes about crime carry a transgressive charge. "What goes through someone's mind when you pull the trigger?" a rich young woman, a writer, asks a hit man in *Sweet and Lowdown*. "It always came kind of natural to me, ever since I was fifteen and picked up a gun." "I'm scared," the woman, who is fascinated by this rattler, says. "Because I kill for a living?" "No, because I find you attractive." Allen, too, is clearly titillated by characters who defy the law.

In *Crimes and Misdemeanors* Allen approached criminal behavior with a psychological and philosophical depth that he chose to bypass in his work in the nineties. His nineties crime trio, *Manhattan Murder Mystery*, *Small Time Crooks* (2000), and *Bullets over Broadway* (1994), is just for fun, movies made to reassure the fans that the "old" Woody Allen is still on tap.

Larry and Carol Lipton (played by Allen and Diane Keaton), the middle-aged couple in *Manhattan Murder Mystery*, suffer from the usual marital woes. "Do you still find me attractive?" Carol asks, worried that the two of them may be "turning into a pair of old shoes." Larry, an editor at a publishing house, enjoys old movies and sports, just like Woody Allen himself; Carol relishes opera and the finer things. Life suddenly improves for the restless, dissatisfied Carol when she suspects that an elderly neighbor, Mr. House (Jerry Adler), might have done away with his wife. "We're on the threshold of a mystery," she exclaims. To Larry, however, the possibility of uncovering a crime next door—the film's premise is an homage to Hitchcock's *Rear Window*—doesn't carry the same charge as it does for Carol, to whom, rather worryingly, it is "the most exciting thing that's happened in our whole marriage." Carol enlists Ted (Alan Alda), a recent divorcé, as a fellow sleuth who, as Carol taunts Larry, has "a million theories" about the crime. "Did you ever sleep with Ted?" Larry wants to know. When Marcia Fox (Anjelica Huston), a take-charge mystery novelist ("I have great sex appeal") edited by Larry, joins the investigation, Carol becomes jealous.

Allen tries to link his recurrent subject, the ebb and flow of romantic couplings, to a mystery plot, but neither the endangered marriage nor the crime narrative is well developed. Unlike Hitchcock, Allen seems to have little interest here in being an anatomist of criminal psychology. Nor does he seem engaged by exploring the Hitchcockian motif of the transference of guilt—in a Hitchcock suspense story, everyone, including the audience, would be implicated in the crime scenario. The narrative tidiness that a mystery demands is not Allen's forté, and his crime plot gets so entangled that his only way out is for mystery maven Marcia Fox to reconstruct the events leading up to and following Mr. House's killing of his wife.

In the showdown, in which his jealous secretary shoots House behind the screen of the repertory film theatre that he owns, suspense is not the director's primary concern. Rather, with terrific ingenuity, Allen's mise-en-scène duplicates the celebrated funhouse climax in Orson Welles's *Lady from Shanghai* that is playing on screen. "I will never say that life doesn't imitate art again," Larry quips. The clever visual and narrative parallels are designed for movie as opposed to mystery aficionados.

Allen's examination of a marriage in trouble doesn't compensate for his ragged storytelling.

Reunited, Allen and his erstwhile Annie Hall (here playing a role that was to have been Mia Farrow's before the scandal erupted) strike no sparks. They seem too familiar with each other's verbal tics, and their timing is peculiarly flaccid. Pitted with fractured syntax and a full battalion of whines, wheezes, and chortles, their improvisations grow wearisome. Her delivery edged with ironic detachment, Keaton doesn't quite seem to believe in the plot. She seems to be along for the ride, doing a favor for her old mentor and former lover.

Technically, too, the film lacks the verve of Allen's most committed work of the nineties. The occasionally wobbly, hand-held camera, peering into the corners of House's apartment and meant to reflect Carol's increasing excitement, seems merely mannered here. With Bobby Short's blazing rendition of "I Happen to Like New York" on the soundtrack, *Manhattan Murder Mystery* opens with an overhead shot of the city at night, sparkling with a million lights. Nothing that follows has the same exhilarating energy.

Even more than his half-hearted suspense comedy, *Small Time Crooks* is Woody Allen lite, a frolic that attempts to recapture the spirit of early work like *Take the Money and Run*. A number of the jokes are downright feeble, and once again Allen's crime plotting is slipshod. Act I depicts a bank robbery supervised by the terminally incompetent Ray (Allen), a former con itching to return to the game. He and his wife Frenchy (Tracy Ullman) hook up with a gaggle of goons to open a cookie store next to a bank. Trying to get into the vault by digging a hole through a basement wall, the bunglers strike a water main—a hoary joke that Allen does nothing to refresh. The heist fizzles—it turns out that they were drilling in the wrong direction because Ray was reading the map upside down—but the cookie boutique thrives.

In Act II, a comedy of manners about the nouveau riche vulgarity of Ray and Frenchy, crime is banished. The couple's East Side apartment, with a harp in the living room and rococo tchotschkes in every corner, is a display of bad taste run riot. "What's bothering me is that we got no class," Frenchy declares before deciding to hire an elegant, high-toned Brit, David (Hugh Grant), to give her some. As Frenchy becomes a willing pupil ("You can see the difference between this Tintoretto and earlier Byzantine work; it characterizes the leap from the ancient to the modern world," David pronounces in sylvan tones corded with seduction), Ray goes for pizza with Frenchy's dumb-as-a-post cousin May (Elaine May), attends baseball games, and watches old movies. "Are you a stroke victim? I should go to operas and churches in Europe?" Ray whines when Frenchy proposes a grand tour. As in *Manhattan Murder Mystery*, a marriage is on the rocks—"if I grow and you stay as stupid as you are we're gonna have big problems," Frenchy warns—and once again crime is the solvent.

In Act III, after accountants bankrupt the cookie empire, Ray happily devises a new crime caper, stealing a necklace locked in a safe in the house of a New York socialite. "I was back in action again: I felt alive," Ray boasts, handing Frenchy the necklace he finally managed to steal after a series of mishaps conceived on the same dopey, low-farce level as the water main gag. But Frenchy bursts his bubble when she points out that the necklace is a fake. "I came away with the wrong thing?" Ray shudders. "That sounds like your m.o.," Frenchy snaps. The lovable, small time crooks are not bereft, however, because Frenchy has retrieved a silver cigarette case she had given David in flush times. Lamely, the film ends with an embrace. "Oh, sweetheart, you're the greatest," Ray cries as the camera lingers for a beat too long on the back of Frenchy's head.

Unlike any other film of the period, *Small Time Crooks* has no thematic or stylistic pretensions. It wants to do nothing other than entertain. Nonetheless, there are vestiges of a skewed moral calculus. On the one hand, the film satirizes nouveau riche taste in furnishings and apparel; on the other, it favors Ray and Frenchy's proletarian crudeness, energy, and warm-heartedness over the well-spoken Englishman, who's a fake, and the icy rich people Frenchy tries to cultivate. As in *Manhattan Murder Mystery*, Allen may treat crime lightly, but the film seems to be saying that, as long as you don't succeed, crime can be good for the spirit. Robbing banks and breaking into safes can do more to save a marriage than putting on airs through upgrading your diction and décor.

Allen's shaggy dog narrative serves as a frame for four splendid performers. As Ray, dressed in hideous bright colors and adopting a shuffling, sloppy gait, Allen pours on the Brooklynese. In this role, Allen recalls the pre–*Annie Hall* Woody, master of slapstick. As Frenchy, tearing into the insults that are her character's stock-in-trade ("You don't have to sell me!" she snaps after Ray announces that he's no genius), Tracy Ullman is a comic tornado operating at full force. Hugh Grant's cad is devastatingly charming, and as sweet May, "dumb like a horse or a dog," Elaine May is endearing.

Crime has a more secure thematic footing in *Bullets over Broadway*, a lushly performed and produced satire of the theatre set in the twenties. To get his play produced, David (John Cusack) and his agent (Jack Weston) make a pact with a gangster, Nick Valenti (Joe Viterelli), who demands a role for his bird-brained, squeaky-voiced girlfriend, Olive (Jennifer Tilly). David squirms—"I sold out! I'm a whore!"—but proceeds because, as an artist, it's his "duty to transform men's souls." "I won't change a word," he warns his agent. But during rehearsals, Olive's bodyguard, a lug named Cheech (Chazz Palminteri), who learned how to read and write "before [he] burned down the school," recognizes what all the theatre professionals involved in the show fail to: David's dialogue is stilted, his playwriting cerebral and academic. "You don't write like people talk," Cheech protests, and, scene by scene, he rewrites the play. The show's august star, Helen Sinclair (Dianne Wiest), observes about the revised script that it "reeks of human sexuality," and maintains that she would "give [her] body freely to the man who wrote those words."

Neither on the stage nor in his life does David, the self-proclaimed artist, succeed with words. When he should speak up, admitting to his girlfriend Ellen

(Mary-Louise Parker) that he is having an affair with Helen Sinclair, for instance, or giving credit to Cheech, he remains silent. When fewer words would be preferable, as in his play, he is prolix. "Don't speak!" Helen, in the throes of one of her numerous offstage arias, repeatedly commands David. She has the right idea. David finds the apt words only at the end, when he confesses to Ellen that there are "two things of which I am certain: one is that I love you; two is that I'm not an artist." The true artist is a hit man for the mob, another Woody Allen criminal with sex appeal and, this time, talent. By his intuitive feeling for what works in the theatre, Cheech is the antithesis of intellectual frauds like David and Sheldon Flender (Rob Reiner), a blowhard fatso who boasts that he is an artist because "[his] plays are written to be unproduced" and who has a clandestine affair with Ellen. "An artist creates his own moral universe," Sheldon pontificates, echoing Allen's own defense of his affair with Soon-Yi.

Sheldon is no artist, but his sentiments aptly describe Cheech, the only artist in sight, a guilt-free, trigger-happy hit man who lives by his own code. "What does it feel like when you kill a guy?" David asks Cheech, fascinated like other Allen characters by a criminal's psychopathology. "It feels OK," Cheech answers. Because Olive is ruining "his" play, he decides to kill her. David, for whom life is more precious than art, is horrified, but to the hit man, the play's the thing. According to Cheech, Olive got just what she deserved. Allen punishes his errant artist— Cheech, a man who lives by the gun, is shot by Valenti's goons. Far more than in *Small Time Crooks*, however, there's a disturbing subtext. Beneath the safe, familiar subjects—the send-up of egocentric theatrical types; gangsters whose raw energy entices the bourgeois characters—is there a wish to absolve artists who follow their own rules? Does the film ask us to exonerate Cheech, despite his violence, because he is a genuine writer? Does his gift excuse, or at least soften, his antisocial behavior? Can the film maker, like his criminal-artist, do what he wants, even if he is guilty of an action, such as seducing his "daughter," that might be unforgivable in the untalented? Keep in mind: David, the non-artist, in the end behaves ethically; Cheech, the bona fide artist, is an unredeemed sociopath.

Although it is only marginally a Woody Allen "crime" movie, *Sweet and Lowdown* is another apology for a socially deviant creator. Like Cheech, Emmet Ray (Sean Penn), a brilliant jazz guitarist and part-time pimp, is the real thing. His music, like Cheech's dialogue "reek[ing] of human sexuality," contains an erotic jolt. But like the clown in *Shadows and Fog* Ray is true only to his art. As he warns his new girlfriend, Hattie (Samantha Morton), "a goddam mute orphan half-wit," "I gotta be free. I like women, but I don't need 'em. That's the way it is with an artist. I let my feelings out with my music." (To Allen's many unregenerate feminist critics, Hattie's muteness provided further evidence of the film maker's misogyny, his wish to control and to silence women. Does Hattie represent Allen's desire to silence a particular woman with a similar name, his overbearing mother Nettie? Or is Hattie Allen's ironic response to the widespread public perception of Soon-Yi as a learning disabled orphan?)

"He's like a cat, feline with a guitar. . . . He can only feel pain for his music. Such is the ego of genius," observes Blanche (Uma Thurman), a writer who falls in love with Ray and succeeds in marrying a man who is not the marrying kind. Blanche is turned on not only by Ray's music, but also by his antisocial behavior and his crypto-criminal aura. She's a goner when she catches him stealing. "You have genuine crudeness," she sighs. As in *Bullets over Broadway*, the director links art to crime.

Allen's affection for jazz, and his skillful, museum-quality recreation of the thirties are exemplary, but Emmet doesn't fill the heroic mold that the film constructs for him. *Sweet and Lowdown* is a mock-documentary in which a number of expert witnesses speak glowingly of the guitarist; the aura of hero worship, in which men look up to other men, is enhanced by Emmet's fetishistic admiration for the historical jazz guitarist Django Reinhardt. Because it isn't nearly as entertaining as the swift and wicked *Deconstructing Harry* or the laff-riot *Bullets*, the film exposes the essentially adolescent nature of Allen's attempt to redeem a quasi-outlaw who uses his guitar as a phallic weapon.

In *Mighty Aphrodite* (1995) and *Everyone Says I Love You* (1996), as in *Sweet and Lowdown*, Allen experiments with new ways of framing familiar topics. A Greek chorus oversees *Aphrodite*; musical numbers punctuate *Everyone*. Like the eyewitnesses and critics interviewed in *Sweet and Lowdown*, these "narrators" are variations on the writerly voice-over technique that Allen has frequently used.

Filmed on location in a rugged, Greek-looking landscape, *Mighty Aphrodite* opens with a chorus intoning in formal diction and moving in ritualized patterns; for a few fleeting moments an alarmed viewer might think the movie is going to be a transcription of a real Greek tragedy. Such fears are immediately pierced when, after invoking fate and desire and Antigone, the chorus mentions Lenny Weinrib, a New York sportswriter with a problem: We're safe on Woody Allen terra firma, after all. And when Jocasta, the mother of Oedipus, remarks to the camera, "I hate to say what they call my son in Harlem," the verbal deflation recalls Allen's early short stories and stand-up routines. Despite its language, however, the chorus functions in a traditional way as the voice of communal reason and moderation. Its goal is to restrain Lenny, determined to locate the birth mother of Moses, the boy he and his wife adopted. "He's playing God; it's hubris," they cluck, echoing complaints of Allen's off screen misconduct. But Lenny, like his creator, ignores community standards. Once he finds Linda (Mira Sorvino), a porno star who has taken the name of Judy Cum, he attempts to mold her. He becomes the young woman's teacher, matchmaker, makeover maven, and, for one time only, bed partner.

In the final scene, in a chance meeting at FAO Schwartz, Lenny introduces Linda to his son, who happens also to be her son, and Linda introduces Lenny to *her* son, who is also Lenny's. Neither parent is aware of their relationship to the other's child.

Does this "virgin" parenthood reflect the film maker's desire to be relieved of parental obligations? In light of our knowledge of the scandal, the incestuous motifs that hover over the scenario cannot be overlooked. Temporarily estranged from his wife, Lenny becomes, in effect, a surrogate father to Linda before he becomes her one-time lover. Family feeling and familial connections that have no formal labels—as the birth mother and the adoptive father of Moses, Linda and Lenny are related in a symbolic sense—are translated into sex.

Pursuing a tricky agenda, *Mighty Aphrodite* is a kind of propaganda comedy in which Lenny's persistent rule-breaking produces a happy ending for everyone. Lenny is reunited with his wife, a career woman who has also been unfaithful. (The repaired marriage is none too convincing, however, since the icy Helena Bonham Carter plays the role.) Linda, who has become a beautician, is happily married to a handsome helicopter pilot who has descended from the sky (Allen's whimsical interpretation of the *deus ex machina*). Kevin (Michael Rapaport), a dopey boxer Lenny had introduced to Linda and who turned against her once he discovered her profession, is married to the right woman, a farm girl from upstate. Even the chorus, having loosened up since the prologue, is happy, singing and dancing in a celebratory mode. "Life is, yes, ironic and strange and beautiful," speaks the chorus leader (F. Murray Abraham), conferring a blessing on Lenny's project and leaving the audience in a rosy mood.

Allen's ace-in-the-hole for his self-endorsement is Mira Sorvino's irresistible Linda. Dressed in garish outfits, Linda lives surrounded by icons of her trade (there's a dildo in the fish tank and a figurine of copulating pigs on the wall) and speaks in a lingo of unguarded sexual candor. "You look like it's been a long time since you had a great blow job," she tells Lenny when she first meets him. Although the character represents another instance of Allen sticking out his tongue at those who have long decried his sexual politics, Sorvino outwits stereotype, creating from a cartoon conception a sweet-natured, vulnerable character who is much wiser than her bimbo packaging would suggest. Notice how she carries herself, and her serene smile, when she walks with Kevin after Lenny has introduced them. Indeed, picking up on Kevin's response to her, the chorus appears in the band shell behind them to sing, "You Do Something to Me."

Allen's treatment of the chorus in this scene, as throughout, suggests that he was itching to make a musical. In his next film, he did. Like *Mighty Aphrodite*, *Everyone Says I Love You* is Woody Allen in an upbeat mode. This is another ensemble comedy, but one from which the bitterness and fury of *Husbands and Wives*, *Deconstructing Harry*, and *Celebrity* have been exorcised. The large, wealthy Manhattan family at the center is afflicted, but ever so lightly this time, with the usual Allen tics. A daughter, D. J. (Natasha Lyonne, hard as nails), who narrates, changes boyfriends with lightning speed. Her mother Frieda (Goldie Hawn) is a parlor liberal with an interest in prison reform. She advocates open prisons and "better cuisine; let the prisoners decorate their cells with their own personal decorators." Like many other Allen characters, she is attracted to criminals, but when an ex-con, Charles Ferry (Tim Roth), one of her pet projects, seduces her daughter, Skylar (Drew Barrymore), charity evaporates. But Skylar, engaged to the proper Holden (Edward Norton), a junior partner in the law firm of her father (Alan Alda), falls for the sexy outlaw only temporarily: She loses interest when he takes her on a date to rob a bank. Frieda's ex, Joe (Woody Allen), a writer who lives in Paris, makes a career of falling in and out of love. He is becalmed for a time when he successfully seduces Von (Julia Roberts), an American he meets in Venice and whom he courts, plied with secret knowledge that D. J. has gleaned from overhearing Von's sessions with her analyst (the invasion-of-privacy motif Allen used before in *Another Woman*). That Julia Roberts, America's reigning sweetheart, plays Von might well prompt viewers who don't get Allen's sex appeal to accuse him of wishful thinking on an Olympian scale.

In this best of all possible worlds, all the characters end up where Allen thinks they belong. Skylar returns to Holden. D. J. has a new beau. Von returns to her husband. Joe dances on the banks of the Seine with his ex-wife, who assures him that he is her favorite and that, isn't it wonderful?, they are better friends divorced than when they were married. Even an errant son who had turned Republican recovers, his dereliction explained by the fact that oxygen hadn't been going to his brain. The mating games are set in the film maker's three favorite cities, Manhattan, Paris, and Venice, lovingly photographed as ideal stages on which to conduct airy rites of courtship accompanied by song and dance routines. Shots of Manhattan in winter, fall, spring, and summer enshrine it as a town for all seasons, an urban fairy-land, delicate and enchanted.

Allen's musical ideas—the way songs intersect the narrative—are clever and varied. At the beginning, a song, "Just You, Just Me," is shared by many characters, principals as well as passersby from different social classes. Music is installed as the language of love, a Romance language everyone can speak. When "Making Whoopee" is sung by patients in a hospital, the film flips into an engaging musical surrealism, as it does again when Grandpa and a chorus of corpses rise up from their coffins to sing "Enjoy Yourself." "My Baby Just Cares For Me" becomes a big production number in the Fifth Avenue jewelry shop of Harry Winston. Songs also have a more personal connection to the singer. "If I Had You," the ex-con warbles to Skylar on the family's expansive verandah overlooking Central Park. "All My Life," Von sings to Joe, thinking for the nonce that he is the man of her dreams. "I'm Through with Love," a momentarily dejected Joe croons, overlooking a Venetian canal. The finale, set at a Marx Brothers tribute at the Paris Ritz, is a rousing production number in which the entire company, in French and wearing Groucho masks, performs "Hooray for Captain Spaulding," Groucho Marx's number from *Animal Crackers*.

The loopy charm of Allen's musical concepts, however, is seriously compromised by his cast of delightful performers who happen to be tone-deaf singers. Tim Roth, Drew Barrymore, Edward Norton, Julia Roberts, along with Woody Allen himself, are painful to listen to, even for a few bars. "We're not the usual family in musical comedy," D. J. explains at the start. "We've got dough." And to account for the universal happy endings, she suggests that the story "had to be a musical because otherwise nobody would believe it." But this is authorial subterfuge: What distinguishes the characters from those in regulation musical comedy is the fact that they are so patently unmusical. And the result is a desecration of the kind of popular American music of the past that Allen venerates. Would the film maker cast a comedy with performers who either don't get the jokes or don't know how to deliver them?

Allen's résumé of the nineties is punctuated by work for hire: the unwatchable *Scenes from a Mall* (1990), directed by Paul Mazursky; an uninspired cartoon, *Antz* (1998), in which Allen supplies the voice of a neurotic worker ant; a dead-in-the-water television adaptation of Neil Simon's irredeemably mediocre *Sunshine Boys* (1996); the mystifyingly awful *Picking up the Pieces* (2000), directed by Alfonso Arau, a straight-to-video oddity in which Allen plays a magician who hacks his wife to bits. The dreary catalogue of assignments confirms that when writing, directing, and performing his own intensely personal material, the comedian's gifts survive. Despite occasional disappointments, he remains America's foremost independent auteur. The tumultuous events of his private life, however, which supplied a fertile creative ground for this most self-referential of film makers, have also left lingering scars on his reputation. Do you like the artist or the man? is a question that a number of the post-scandal movies pose. I still like the artist.

# Selected
# Bibliography

Adamson, Joe. *Groucho, Harpo, Chico, and Sometimes Zeppo: A Celebration of The Marx Brothers.* New York: Simon and Schuster, 1973.

Adler, Bill, and Jeffrey Feinman. *Woody Allen: Clown Prince of American Humor.* New York: Pinnacle Books, 1975.

Agee, James. "Comedy's Greatest Era," in *Agee on Film.* Boston: Beacon Press, 1964.

Allen, Woody. *Death.* New York: Samuel French, Inc., 1975.

———. *Don't Drink the Water.* New York: Samuel French, Inc., 1967.

———. *Four Films. Annie Hall. Interiors. Manhattan. Stardust Memories.* New York: Random House, 1982.

———. *Getting Even.* New York: Random House, 1971.

———. *God.* New York: Samuel French, Inc., 1975.

———. *Hannah and Her Sisters.* New York: Vintage, 1987.

———. *Play It Again, Sam.* New York: Samuel French, Inc., 1969.

———. *Side Effects.* New York: Random House, 1980.

———. *Three Films. Zelig, Broadway Danny Rose. The Purple Rose of Cairo.* New York: Vintage, 1987.

———. *Without Feathers.* New York: Random House, 1975.

Alley, Robert. *The Front*. New York: Pocket Books, 1976.

Baxter, John. *Woody Allen: A Biography*. New York: Carroll & Graf, 1999.

Bellow, Saul. *The Adventures of Augie March*. New York: Avon, 1977.

———. *Herzog*. New York: Avon, 1976.

Benayoun, Robert. *The Films of Woody Allen*. Translated by Alexander Walker. New York: Harmony Books, 1986.

Benchley, Robert. *Benchley Lost and Found*. New York: Dover Publications, Inc., 1970.

Bergson, Henri. "Laughter," in *Comedy*, ed. Wylie Sypher. Garden City, New York: Doubleday Anchor, 1956.

Björkman, Stig. *Woody Allen on Woody Allen*. New York: Grove Press, 1993.

Byron, Stuart, and Elizabeth Weis, eds. *The National Society of Film Critics on Movie Comedy*. New York: Grossman Publishers, 1977.

Charney, Maurice. *Comedy High and Low*. New York: Oxford University Press, 1978.

de Navacelle, Thierry. *Woody Allen On Location*. New York: William Morrow and Company, Inc., 1987.

Durgnat, Raymond. *The Crazy Mirror: Hollywood Comedy and the American Image*. New York: Horizon Press, 1970.

Eyles, Allen. *The Marx Brothers: Their World of Comedy*. New York: A. S. Barnes, 1966.

Farrow, Mia. *What Falls Away*. New York: Doubleday, 1997.

Fox, Julian. Woody. *Movies from Manhattan*. Woodstock: The Overlook Press, 1996.

Gilliatt, Penelope. "Guilty, With an Explanation." *The New Yorker*, February 4, 1974, pp. 39–44.

Girgus, Sam B. *The Films of Woody Allen*. New York: Cambridge University Press, 1993.

Gittelson, Natalie. "The Maturing of Woody Allen." *The New York Times Magazine*. April 22, 1979, pp. 30–32, 102–7.

Goldman, Albert. *Ladies and Gentlemen, Lenny Bruce*. New York: Random House, 1974.

Gornick, Vivian. "Face It, Woody Allen, You're Not a Schlep Anymore." *The Village Voice*, January 5, 1976, pp. 9–11.

Greenfield, Robert. "Seven Interviews with Woody Allen." *Rolling Stone*, September 30, 1971, p. 16.

Groteke, Kristi and Marjorie Rosen. *Mia and Woody. Love and Betrayal*. New York: Carroll & Graf, 1994.

Guthrie, Lee. *Woody Allen: A Biography*. New York: Drake Publishers, 1978.

Heller, Joseph. *Catch–22*. New York: Dell, 1979.

Holtzman, William. *Seesaw: A Dual Biography of Anne Bancroft and Mel Brooks*. New York: Doubleday, 1979.

Howe, Irving. *World of Our Fathers*. New York: Simon and Schuster, 1976.

Kerr, Walter. *The Silent Clowns*. New York: Alfred A. Knopf, 1975.

Lax, Eric. *On Being Funny: Woody Allen and Comedy*. New York: Charterhouse Press, 1975.

———. *Woody Allen. A Biography*. New York: Da Capo Press, 2000.

Lee, Sander H. *Woody Allen's Angst: Philosophical Commentaries on His Serious Films*. Jefferson, North Carolina: McFarland & Company, 1997.

Lerman, Leo. "Woody the Great." *Vogue*, December 1972, pp. 144–51.

Lloyd, Harold. *An American Comedy*. New York: Benjamin Blom, 1971.

Malamud, Bernard. *The Magic Barrel*. New York: Avon, 1980.

———. *Pictures of Fidelman*. New York: Pocket Books, 1975.

———. *Rembrandt's Hat*. New York: Pocket Books, 1974.

Mamber, Stephen. "Woody Allen." *Cinema* (Beverly Hills), Winter 1972–73, pp. 10–12.

Marx, Groucho. *Memoirs of a Mangy Lover*. New York: Da Capo Press, 1997.

Mast, Gerald. *The Comic Mind: Comedy and the Movies*. Second edition. Chicago: The University of Chicago Press, 1979.

McCaffrey, Donald W. *The Golden Age of Sound Comedy*. South Brunswick, New Jersey and London: A. S. Barnes, 1973.

McCann, Graham. *Woody Allen*. Cambridge, England: Polity Press, 1990.

Meade, Marion. *The Unruly Life of Woody Allen*. New York: Scribner, 2000.

Moews, Daniel. *Keaton: The Silent Features Close Up*. Berkeley: The University of California Press, 1977.

Mundy, Robert. "Woody Allen." *Cinema* (Beverly Hills), Winter 1972–73, pp. 6–8.

———. and Stephen Mamber. "Woody Allen: An Interview." *Cinema* (Beverly Hills), Winter 1972–73, pp. 14–21.

Perelman, S. J. *The Most of S. J. Perelman*. New York: Simon and Schuster, n.d.

Rosenblum, Ralph, and Robert Karen. *When the Shooting Stops ... the Cutting Begins*. New York: The Viking Press, 1979.

Roth, Philip. *Goodbye Columbus*. Boston: Houghton Mifflin, 1959.

———. *Portnoy's Complaint*. New York: Random House, 1969.

Schickel, Richard. "The Basic Woody Allen Joke." *The New York Times Magazine*. January 7, 1973, pp. 10, 33–37.

Sennett, Mack. *King of Comedy*. Garden City, New York: Doubleday, 1954.

Tyler, Parker. *Chaplin. The Last of the Clowns*. New York: Horizon, 1972.

Wernblad, Annette. *Brooklyn Is Not Expanding. Woody Allen's Comic Universe*. Cranbury, New Jersey: Associated University Presses, 1992.

Wisse, Ruth R. *The Schlemiel as Modern Hero*. Chicago: University of Chicago Press, 1971.

Yacowar, Maurice. *Loser Take All: The Comic Art of Woody Allen*. New York, 1979.

# Filmography

*What's New, Pussycat?* (1965). Director: Clive Donner, Producer: Charles K. Feldman. Screenplay: Woody Allen. Photography: Jean Badal. Music: Burt Bacharach. Editor: Fergus McDonell. Cast: Peter Sellers, Peter O'Toole, Romy Schneider, Capucine, Paul Prentiss, Woody Allen, Ursula Andress. United Artists. 120 minutes.

*What's Up, Tiger Lily?* (1966). Original version: Kagi No Kagi ("Key of keys") (Japan, 1964). Script and dubbing: Woody Allen, Frank Buxton, Louise Lasser, Len Maxwell, Mickey Rose. Music: The Lovin' Spoonful. American International. 79 minutes.

*Casino Royale* (1967). Directors: John Huston, Kenneth Hughes, Val Guest, Robert Parrish, Joseph McGrath. Producers: Charles K. Feldman and Jerry Bresler. Screenplay: Wolf Mankowitz, John Law, Michael Sayers, suggested by the novel by Ian Fleming. Photography: Jack Hildyard. Editor: Bill Lenny. Cast: Peter Sellers, Ursula Andress, David Niven, Orson Welles, Joanna Pettet, Deborah Kerr, Daliah Lavi, Charles Boyer, John Huston, Kurt Kaznar, George Raft, Jean-Paul Belmondo, Woody Allen, William Holden, Angela Scoular. Columbia. 131 minutes.

*Don't Drink the Water* (1969). Director: Howard Morris. Producer: Charles Joffe. Screenplay: R. S. Allen and Harvey

Bullock, based upon the play by Woody Allen. Editor: Ralph Rosenblum. Cast: Jackie Gleason, Estelle Parsons, Ted Bessell, Joan Delaney, Avery Schreiber. Avco Embassy. 98 minutes.

*Take the Money and Run* (1969). Director: Woody Allen. Screenplay: Woody Allen and Mickey Rose. Photography: Lester Shorr. Editors: Paul Jordan and Ron Kalish. Music: Marvin Hamlisch. Cast: Woody Allen, Janet Margolin, Jacqueline Hyde, Marcel Hillaire, Lonnie Chapman, Louise Lasser, Jackson Beck. Produced by Charles H. Joffe for Cinerama Releasing Corporation. 85 minutes.

*Bananas* (1971). Director: Woody Allen. Screenplay: Woody Allen and Mickey Rose. Photography: Andrew M. Costikyan. Music: Marvin Hamlisch. Editor: Ron Kalish. Cast: Woody Allen, Louise Lasser, Carlos Montalban, Natividad Abascal, Jacobo Morales, Roger Grimsby, Howard Cosell, Allen Garfield, Princess Fatosh. United Artists. 82 minutes.

*Play it Again, Sam* (1972). Director: Herbert Ross. Screenplay: Woody Allen, based on his play. Photography: Owen Roizman. Music: Billy Goldenberg. Editor: Marion Rothman. Cast: Woody Allen, Diane Keaton, Tony Roberts, Jerry Lacy, Susan Anspach, Jennifer Salt, Joy Bang, Viva, Diana Davila. Paramount. 84 minutes.

*Everything You Always Wanted To Know About Sex\* (\*but were afraid to ask)* (1972). Director: Woody Allen. Screenplay: Woody Allen. Photography: David M. Walsh. Editor: Eric Albertson. Cast: Woody Allen, John Carradine, Lou Jacobi, Louise Lasser, Anthony Quayle, Tony Randall, Lynn Redgrave, Burt Reynolds, Gene Wilder, Jack Barry, Robert Q. Lewis, Pamela Mason, Regis Philbin, Geoffrey Holder, Jay Robinson. United Artists. 87 minutes.

*Sleeper* (1973). Director: Woody Allen. Screenplay: Woody Allen and Marshall Brickman. Photography: David M. Walsh. Editor: Ralph Rosenblum. Music by Woody Allen with the Preservation Hall Jazz Band and the New Orleans Funeral Ragtime Orchestra. Cast: Woody Allen, Diane Keaton, John Beck, Mary Gregory, Don Keefer. United Artists. 88 minutes.

*Love and Death* (1975). Director: Woody Allen. Screenplay: Woody Allen. Photography: Ghislain Cloquet. Editor: Ralph Rosenblum, Ron Kalish. Music: S. Prokofiev. Cast: Woody Allen,

Diane Keaton, Georges Adet, Frank Adu, Lloyd Battista, Jack Berard. United Artists. 85 minutes.
*The Front* (1976). Director: Martin Ritt. Screenplay: Walter Bernstein. Cast: Woody Allen, Zero Mostel, Herschel Bernardi, Michael Murphy, Andrea Marcovicci. Columbia. 94 minutes.
*Annie Hall* (1977). Director: Woody Allen. Screenplay: Woody Allen, Marshall Brickman. Photography: Gordon Willis. Editor: Ralph Rosenblum. Cast: Woody Allen, Diane Keaton, Tony Roberts, Carol Kane, Paul Simon, Shelley Duvall, Janet Margolin, Colleen Dewhurst, Christopher Walken. United Artists. 93 minutes.
*Interiors* (1978). Director: Woody Allen. Screenplay: Woody Allen. Photography: Gordon Willis. Editor: Ralph Rosenblum. Cast: Kristen Griffith, Marybeth Hurt, Richard Jordan, Diane Keaton, E. G. Marshall, Geraldine Page, Maureen Stapleton, Sam Waterston. United Artists. 93 minutes.
*Manhattan* (1979). Director: Woody Allen. Screenplay: Woody Allen, Marshall Brickman. Photography: Gordon Willis. Editor: Susan Morse. Music: George Gershwin. Cast: Woody Allen, Diane Keaton, Michael Murphy, Mariel Hemingway, Meryl Streep, Anne Byrne. United Artists. 96 minutes.
*Stardust Memories* (1980). Director: Woody Allen. Screenplay: Woody Allen. Photography: Gordon Willis. Editor: Susan Morse. Cast: Woody Allen, Marie-Christine Barrault, Jessica Harper, Louise Lasser, Charlotte Rampling, Tony Roberts, Helen Hanft, Anne DeSalvo, Joan Neuman, Eli Mintz. 91 minutes.
*A Midsummer Night's Sex Comedy* (1982). Written and directed by Woody Allen. Photography: Gordon Willis. Production designer: Mel Bourne. Editor: Susan E. Morse. Cast: Woody Allen, Mia Farrow, Julie Hagerty, Tony Roberts, Jose Ferrer, Mary Steenburgen. Produced by Robert Greenhut for Rollins-Joffe Productions. Distributed by Orion Pictures. 87 minutes.
*Zelig* (1983). Written and directed by Woody Allen. Photography: Gordon Willis. Production designer: Mel Bourne. Editor: Susan E. Morse. Cast: Woody Allen, Mia Farrow, Susan Sontag, Irving Howe, Saul Bellow, Bricktop, Dr. Bruno Bettelheim, Professor John Morton Blum. Produced by Robert Greenhut for Rollins-Joffe Productions. Distributed by Orion Pictures. 80 minutes.

*Broadway Danny Rose* (1984). Written and directed by Woody Allen. Photography: Gordon Willis. Production designer: Mel Bourne. Editor: Susan E. Morse. Cast: Woody Allen, Mia Farrow, Nick Apollo Forte, Sandy Baron, Corbett Monica, Jackie Gayle, Morty Gunty, Gerald Schoenfeld. Produced by Robert Greenhut for Rollins-Joffe Productions. Distributed by Orion Pictures. 85 minutes.

*The Purple Rose of Cairo* (1985). Written and directed by Woody Allen. Photography: Gordon Willis. Production designer: Stuart Wurtzel. Editor: Susan E. Morse. Cast: Mia Farrow, Jeff Daniels, Danny Aiello, Dianne Wiest, Van Johnson, Milo O'Shea, Zoe Caldwell, John Wood, Deborah Rush, Alexander H. Cohen, Karen Akers, Camille Saviola. Produced by Robert Greenhut for Rollins-Joffe Productions. Distributed by Orion Pictures. 84 minutes.

*Hannah and Her Sisters* (1986). Written and directed by Woody Allen. Photography: Carlo Di Palma. Production designer: Stuart Wurtzel. Editor: Susan E. Morse. Cast: Michael Caine, Mia Farrow, Dianne Wiest, Woody Allen, Barbara Hershey, Max von Sydow, Lloyd Nolan, Maureen O'Sullivan. Produced by Robert Greenhut for Rollins-Joffe Productions. Distributed by Orion Pictures. 107 minutes.

*Radio Days* (1987). Written and directed by Woody Allen. Photography: Carlo Di Palma. Production designer: Santo Loquasto. Editor: Susan E. Morse. Cast: Mia Farrow, Julie Kavner, Wallace Shawn, Josh Mostel, Dianne Wiest, Jeff Daniels, Tony Roberts, Danny Aiello, Kitty Carlisle Hart, Diane Keaton. Produced by Robert Greenhut for Rollins-Joffe Productions. Distributed by Orion Pictures. 89 minutes.

*September* (1987). Written and directed by Woody Allen. Photography: Carlo Di Palma. Production designer: Santo Loquasto. Editor: Susan E. Morse. Cast: Mia Farrow, Dianne Wiest, Sam Waterston, Denholm Elliott, Elaine Stritch, Jack Warden. Produced by Robert Greenhut for Rollins-Joffe Productions. Distributed by Orion Pictures. 82 minutes.

*Another Woman* (1988). Written and directed by Woody Allen. Photography: Sven Nykvist. Production designer: Santo Loquasto. Editor: Susan E. Morse. Cast: Gena Rowlands, Ian Holm, Gene Hackman, Philip Bosco, Sandy Dennis, Betty Buckley, Blythe Danner, Mia Farrow. 84 minutes.

*New York Stories* (1989). "Life Lessons" directed by Martin Scorsese. "Life Without Zoe" directed by Francis Coppola. "Oedipus Wrecks" written and directed by Woody Allen. Photography: Sven Nykvist. Editor: Susan E. Morse. Cast: Mae Questel, Woody Allen, Julie Kavner, Mia Farrow. Produced by Robert Greenhut for Rollins-Joffe Productions. Distributed by Touchstone Pictures. 126 minutes.

*Crimes and Misdemeanors* (1989). Written and directed by Woody Allen. Photography: Sven Nykvist. Production designer: Santo Loquasto. Editor: Susan E. Morse. Cast: Caroline Aaron, Alan Alda, Claire Bloom, Woody Allen, Martin Landau, Sam Waterston, Joanna Gleason, Mia Farrow. Produced by Robert Greenhut for Rollins-Joffe Productions. Distributed by Orion Pictures. 104 minutes.

*Alice* (1990). Written and directed by Woody Allen. Photography: Carlo Di Palma. Production designer: Santo Loquasto. Editor: Susan E. Morse. Cast: Mia Farrow, Joe Mantegna, Keye Luke, William Hurt, Caroline Aaron, Julie Kavner. 106 minutes.

*Shadows and Fog* (1992). Written and directed by Woody Allen. Photography: Carlo Di Palma. Production designer: Santo Loquasto. Editor: Susan E. Morse. Cast: Woody Allen, Mia Farrow, John Malkovich, Madonna, Donald Pleasence, Lily Tomlin, Kathy Bates, John Cusack, Julie Kavner, Kenneth Mars, Jodie Foster, Fred Gwynne, Kate Nelligan. 86 minutes.

*Husbands and Wives* (1992). Written and directed by Woody Allen. Photography: Carlo Di Palma. Production designer: Santo Loquato. Editor: Susan E. Morse. Cast: Woody Allen, Mia Farow, Sydney Pollack, Judy Davis, Juliette Lewis, Lysette Anthony, Liam Neeson, Blythe Danner. 107 minutes.

*Manhattan Murder Mystery* (1993). Directed by Woody Allen. Written by Woody Allen and Marshall Brickman. Photography: Carlo Di Palma. Production designer: Santo Loquasto. Editor: Susan E. Morse. Cast: Woody Allen, Diane Keaton, Alan Alda, Anjelica Huston, Jerry Adler. 104 minutes.

*Bullets over Broadway* (1994). Directed by Woody Allen. Written by Woody Allen and Douglas McGrath. Photography: Carlo Di Palma. Production designer: Santo Loquasto. Editor: Susan E. Morse. Cast: John Cusack, Jack Warden, Dianne Wiest, Joe

Viterelli, Jennifer Tilly, Chazz Palminteri, Mary-Louise Parker, Tracy Ullman. 98 minutes.

*Mighty Aphrodite* (1995). Written and directed by Woody Allen. Photography: Carlo Di Palma. Production designer: Santo Loquasto. Editor: Susan E. Morse. Cast: Woody Allen, Mira Sorvino, Helena Bonham Carter, F. Murray Abraham, Claire Bloom, Michael Rapaport, Jack Warden. 95 minutes.

*Everyone Says I Love You* (1996). Written and directed by Woody Allen. Photography: Carlo Di Palma. Production designer: Santo Loquasto. Editor: Susan E. Morse. Cast: Woody Allen, Goldie Hawn, Alan Alda, Tim Roth, Julia Roberts, Drew Barrymore, Edward Norton, Natalie Portman. 101 minutes.

*Deconstructing Harry* (1997). Written and directed by Woody Allen. Photography: Carlo Di Palma. Production designer: Santo Loquasto. Editor: Susan E. Morse. Cast: Woody Allen, Caroline Aaron, Kirstie Alley, Richard Benjamin, Billy Crystal, Bob Balaban, Hazelle Goodman, Mariel Hemingway, Judy Davis, Amy Irving, Julie Kavner, Tobey Maguire, Demi Moore, Elisabeth Shue, Stanley Tucci, Philip Bosco, Robin Williams. 95 minutes.

*Celebrity* (1998). Written and directed by Woody Allen. Photography: Sven Nykvist. Production designer: Santo Loquasto. Editor: Susan E. Morse. Cast: Kenneth Branagh, Judy Davis, Leonardo DiCaprio, Joe Mantegna, Bebe Neuwirth, Melanie Griffith, Winona Ryder, Charlize Theron, Gretchen Mol. 113 minutes.

*Sweet and Lowdown* (1999). Written and directed by Woody Allen. Photography: Fei Zhao. Production designer: Santo Loquasto. Editor: Alisa Lepselter. Cast: Woody Allen, Sean Penn, Samantha Morton, Uma Thurman. 95 minutes.

*Small Time Crooks* (2000). Written and directed by Woody Allen. Photography: Fei Zhao. Editor: Alisa Lepselter. Cast: Woody Allen, Tracy Ullman, Elaine May, Hugh Grant, Michael Rapaport, Jon Lovitz, Tony Darrow. 94 minutes.

# Index